Kraftwerk

Kraftwerk

Music Non-Stop

edited by
Sean Albiez
and
David Pattie

continuum

NEW YORK • LONDON

2011

The Continuum International Publishing Group
80 Maiden Lane, New York, NY 10038
The Tower Building, 11 York Road, London SE1 7NX

www.continuumbooks.com

Library of Congress Cataloging-in-Publication Data
Kraftwerk : music non-stop / edited by Sean Albiez and David Pattie.
    p. cm.
  Includes bibliographical references and index.
  ISBN-13: 978-1-4411-6507-7 (hardcover : alk. paper)
  ISBN-10: 1-4411-6507-X (hardcover : alk. paper)
  ISBN-13: 978-1-4411-9136-6 (pbk. : alk. paper)
  ISBN-10: 1-4411-9136-4 (pbk. : alk. paper) 1. Kraftwerk (Musical
group) 2. Kraftwerk (Musical group)—Influence. 3. Synthpop
(Music)—Germany—History and criticism. I. Albiez, Sean. II. Pattie,
David, 1963- III. Title.
  ML421.K73K73 2010
  782.42166092'2—dc22   2010019842

ISBN: HB: 978-1-4411-6507-7
         PB: 978-1-4411-9136-6

Typeset by Pindar NZ, Auckland, New Zealand
Printed and bound in the United States of America
by Sheridan Books, Inc

For Celie, Joe, Jacqui and Cameron
(who can sing 'Trans-Europe Express')

Contents

Contributors

Sean Albiez is senior lecturer in popular music at Southampton Solent University. His research and publications include work on German, British and French electronic popular music; Detroit techno; John Lydon and post-punk; electronica, glitch and idm; Madonna; and British punk. He was a member of the industrial-electro-EBM band WMTID in the 1980s, and currently produces electronic music as *obe:lus*. Further information can be found at www.seanalbiez.com.

Carsten Brocker studied Jazz-Piano and Music Education at the Hochschule für Musik 'Carl Maria von Weber' in Dresden and Music Science and Art History at the Technische Universität Dresden, Humboldt Universität zu Berlin and Universität der Künste Berlin. He is working on a doctoral thesis about the interdependence between popular electronic music and electronic instruments. He has performed as a pianist and keyboardist all over Europe; he also works as a music scientist and sound designer. He lives in Berlin.

David Cunningham is principal lecturer in cultural and critical studies at the University of Westminster and Deputy Director of the Institute for Modern and Contemporary Culture. He is an editor of the journal *Radical Philosophy* and has published widely on modernism, aesthetics and the avant-garde, including the co-edited collections *Adorno and Literature* (2006) and *Photography and Literature in the Twentieth Century* (2005).

Mark Duffett teaches in popular music at the University of Chester. With a research background in Elvis fandom, he has written articles for various journals including *Popular Music and Society*, *Convergence* and *Popular Music*. He has also contributed a chapter on Bill Grundy's interview with the Sex Pistols to a forthcoming book on British television, edited by Ian Inglis.

Pertti Grönholm is adjunct professor (docent) in the Department of General History in the University of Turku, Finland. His research is into the politics of history and cultural memory; the political use of historical representations; and historiography, especially in the former Soviet Union, Russia and the Baltic States in the twentieth century. He has written popular articles on Kraftwerk, Krautrock and electronic dance music for music magazines and newspapers, and has lectured on the history of electronic music.

Kyrre Tromm Lindvig is a trained musician, musicologist and journalist based in Oslo, Norway. He completed his PhD, entitled 'Wir fahren auf der Autobahn – Kraftwerk and constructions of Germanness', at the University of Oslo in 2008. He also holds undergraduate degrees in rhetoric, classical percussion, philosophy and harmony. He has released two records as a drummer with the acclaimed Norwegian jazz band Quarter Past and is the co-founder of the synthesizer band Agregat.

David Pattie is professor of drama at the University of Chester. He is the author of *The Complete Critical Guide to Samuel Beckett* (2001) and *Rock Music in Performance* (2007), and has published widely on a number of topics: Popular music, Scottish theatre, contemporary writing for the stage, and performance in popular culture.

Simon Piasecki has worked as a painter, performance artist and academic; he is currently senior lecturer and award leader for the Art, Event, Performance degree at Leeds Metropolitan University. He first met Robert Wilsmore in 1994 as an academic and then as a collaborator in the BET4 Artists collective, showing work in France, Germany and the UK. He has since performed widely throughout Europe and Russia. He has previously published numerous conference papers, articles and chapters. Simon is married and has four children who have heard quite enough of Kraftwerk.

Hillegonda Rietveld is reader in Cultural Studies at London South Bank University, UK, where she teaches topics related to sonic culture. Her publications address the development and experience of electronic dance music cultures and she is the author of *This Is Our House: House Music, Cultural Spaces and Technologies* (Ashgate, 1998). She has been involved professionally in club and DJ culture since 1982, when she released her first electronic recording for Factory Records, as part of Quando Quango. Kraftwerk's *Trans-Europe Express* (1977) has been an important source of musical inspiration.

Joseph Toltz is a professional singer based in Sydney. He has written articles on a diverse range of subjects including the Australian composer Peter Sculthorpe (1994), the Czech children's opera *Brundibár* (2004) and the Jewish approach to visiting the sick (2007). He is in the final stages of his PhD, 'A hidden testimony: musical experience and memory in Holocaust survivors', where he has interviewed 85 survivors living in Australia, the UK, the US and Israel. He is currently teaching courses on popular music and musicology at the University of Sydney and Conservatorium of Music, and has a keen interest in the development of dance music culture in Australia from the early 1980s.

Robert Wilsmore is head of Creative Practice in the Faculty of Arts at York St John University. His practice and research engage with performance, composition, musicology, collaboration and pedagogy. He has collaborated with Simon Piasecki for over a decade; in 2009 Simon pulled him down 199 stone steps in Whitby, Yorkshire, and later that year Robert had Simon kidnapped as part of the latter's Twice Rendered project. Robert has one sibling, an elder brother Stuart, who runs the business set up by their father in their hometown of Chipping Sodbury.

Richard Witts lectures in music at the University of Edinburgh. His latest book is *The Velvet Underground – a Study* (Equinox/University of Indiana Press, 2008), and he is the biographer of the German chanteuse Nico (Virgin Books, 1994). Richard was active as a musician in Manchester, where he co-founded the Manchester Musicians' Collective and played in the post-punk band the Passage (http://www.thepassage.co.uk).

Introduction: The (Ger)man Machines

David Pattie

In July 2006, the *Observer*'s monthly music magazine ran a list of the 50 most influential albums in the history of popular music; at #3, wedged securely between the Beatles' *Sergeant Pepper's Lonely Hearts Club Band* and NWA's *Straight Outta Compton*, was Kraftwerk's 1977 release, *Trans-Europe Express*.

> [This] paean to the beauty of mechanised movement and European civilisation was a moving and exquisite album in itself. And, through a sample on Afrika Bambaataa's seminal 'Planet Rock', the German eggheads joined the dots with black American electro, giving rise to entire new genres. (Anon., 2006)

At the end of the first decade of the twenty-first century, Kraftwerk's position as electronic pioneers is as lofty and as secure as these comments suggest. (If further confirmation were needed, when *Q* magazine the following year celebrated its twenty-first anniversary with an edition that rounded up the 21 most important artists of the Rock era, Kraftwerk, entirely predictably, were there.) However, such high esteem would have come as something of a surprise to at least some of those writing about the band in the 1970s. A throwaway comment in 1977's *Illustrated New Musical Express Encyclopedia of Rock* refers to 'the precise clean beat of the electronic pads [which] simulates [the] gadget-ridden advanced technological environment that their fans presumably live in' (Logan and Woffinden, 1977, p. 134). Lester Bangs, in a deeply ambivalent interview with the band for *Creem* in 1975 (an interview cited frequently in the chapters that follow), explained the band's initial success in the States by invoking two pernicious German stereotypes: the rapacious conqueror and the ruthlessly efficient Teuton (Bangs, 1975).

1

For a band whose status (at least in the English-speaking world) could so easily have been that of novelty one-hit wonders, and whose *modus operandi* was greeted with great suspicion by influential sections of the popular music press, to have reached the secure position that Kraftwerk have suggests that a number of factors, musical, technological and social, have coalesced to the band's undoubted advantage. Moreover, these factors seem to have worked to create what might be termed a 'Kraftwerk mythology', almost without the help of the musicians themselves; after a peak period of creativity in the mid to late 1970s, the group's rate of release slowed markedly, drying up completely for much of the 1990s. The group's two founder members – Ralf Hütter and Florian Schneider – were notoriously hard to contact apart from the flurry of interviews that inevitably accompanied each release and tour; even Schneider's departure in November 2008 was not accompanied by the usual round of press conferences, statements and interviews (the band did not announce that he had left until early January the following year). And yet Kraftwerk have proved enduringly influential: as the above quotes suggest, they are a touchstone in popular music history – and that position is as much to do with the context in which their music was produced as it is the music itself.

This collection draws together a number of essays on the music, its context and its influence; the contributors address the components of the Kraftwerk sound and the creation of the Kraftwerk image, and the influence the band have had on succeeding generations of musicians, especially in Britain and the States. In other words, it looks both at the band itself, and also at the 'Kraftwerk-Effekt' (a term usefully coined by Alex Seago in 2004). These two areas are, of course, profoundly interrelated. Kraftwerk have managed to create a remarkably unified artistic project from a disparate variety of sources. As David Toop put it in 2003, the group's output

> reflects . . . their absorption of Andy Warhol, Gilbert and George, Fluxus, German electronic music, filmmakers such as Fassbinder and Fritz Lang, visionary architects such as Herman Finsterlin and Bruno Taut and the minimalist machine of the Bauhaus – all fused into a technologically fetishised gesamptkunstwerk, [*sic*], the pop equivalent of Bauhaus Totaltheatre [*sic*]. (Toop, 2003, p. 115)

The group's work, in turn, has become an integral part of the aural landscape of late twentieth- and early twenty-first-century popular music. As Seago argues, Kraftwerk are an early example of a by now general shift away from Anglo-American popular music forms as the sole template for the global development of popular music, and a shift towards a 'glocal . . . pop aesthetic with technological, economic and cultural roots distinctly different from those of the traditional Anglo-American pop axis' (Seago, 2004, p. 90).

However, in Kraftwerk's case, this argument can be taken further. As a number of commentators (Reynolds, 1998, 1999, 2005; Toop, 1999, 2001, 2003) have pointed out, and as the quote at the beginning of this introduction suggests, Kraftwerk have managed to exert a profound and lasting influence on the Anglo-American pop axis itself. Derrick May famously described early Detroit techno as sounding 'like George Clinton and Kraftwerk stuck in an elevator with only a sequencer to keep them company' (Reynolds, 1999, p. 14).[1] The synthpop and electro sound of the 1980s bears Kraftwerk's unmistakeable stamp; something of their influence is clearly audible in late 1970s British post-punk, and reappears, like a particularly assertive strand of musical DNA, in the post-punk revival of the early years of this century; and in 2010 when Dr Dre was asked what he was listening to for musical inspiration he replied, 'Right now it's Kraftwerk' (Tardio, 2010). The sheer range and scope of the band's influence seems to suggest something more than the refining of a new musical style; it suggests that there is something endlessly generative in both the band's music and its image. In the next section of this introduction I will argue that this derives from the peculiar, and peculiarly difficult, cultural conditions in which the band formed. Kraftwerk, in other words, are unimaginable outside of the immediate context of German society in the late 1960s and early 1970s; not simply because they reflected the ethos of the time directly in their work, but because their relation to German culture was intrinsically complex – certainly, far more complex and nuanced than the other German experimental groups of the time.

Locating Kraftwerk

As noted in Applegate and Potter (2002), music has held a special place in German culture, as an essential expression of the German psyche. However, as with so much else, this assumption was profoundly shaken by the events of the Nazi period; post-1945, previous assumptions about music's special status were called into question. For example, Thomas Mann's 1947 novel *Dr Faustus* allegorized the country's descent into Nazism through the life of a modernist composer whose career followed two incommensurate trajectories (a commitment to an abstracted, intellectualized compositional style, based on Schoenberg's twelve-note system; a life lived mostly in a traditional German rural setting – an idyll so exaggerated as to be almost absurd). However, it could not be said that, musically, the late forties and fifties saw a full-scale turning away from the past. Some musicians and composers might have sought a new musical language untainted by Nazism (perhaps the best example of this is the growth of interest in atonal, experimental and electronic music – see below), but, according to Fred Ritzel (1998), the popular songs of the period seemed to be governed by a willed blindness to the Nazi period.

In these songs the Germans are portrayed, somewhat awkwardly, as innocent and naïve primitives, who nevertheless possess many sought-after cultural assets. We are led to believe that it is these cultural traditions and not the barbarisms of the immediate past which should determine our vision of the German future . . . In short, a study of post-war German popular music shows us in what vague, ambivalent and contradictory forms the 'Ghosts of the Past' were brought back to life. The key – troubling – message was 'We are still the same old bunch!' (Ritzel, 1998, pp. 307–8)

For musicians who grew to maturity in West Germany in the late 1960s and early 1970s, the idea of 'Germanness in music' was tainted, either by its past associations, or by the use that was made of it in the culture of the time. As Wolfgang Flür put it in a 2007 Radio 4 documentary (Wright, 2007), all that was available to aspiring musicians, certainly as far as indigenous popular music was concerned, were on the one hand the *Schlager* (see Albiez and Lindvig in this collection), and on the other reworked copies of American and British popular songs. That the reality was rather more complex (for example, British musicians especially found Germany a better environment for performance than their own country; and that the apparently opposing forms of rock and roll and *Schlager* intermingled more than Flür suggests [Larkey, 2002]) was beside the point; for a significant number of young musicians, neither the country's musical past nor its musical present were untainted.

Given this, it is unsurprising that those musicians should turn to a variety of musical models which seemed to suggest a way out of this apparent impasse; musical forms which managed to ally themselves with all that was politically and artistically progressive in Western culture at the time, and which were sufficiently distanced from other forms of German music and the heritage those forms implied. And it is ironic that, when this music began to receive attention from the English-speaking music press, that it should receive the dismissive (and rather bigoted) label of 'Krautrock'[2] – as though, once again, the music produced by a generation of young German musicians in the late sixties and early seventies was, first of all, an expression of their national character.

The term Krautrock is not only rather derogatory but it is also (as genre labels tend to be) rather vague – and open to *ex post facto* simplification. For example, the current definition of the genre on the website allmusic.com reads as follows:

Kraut Rock refers to the legions of German bands of the early '70s that expanded the sonic possibilities of art and progressive rock. Instead of following in the direction of their British and American counterparts, who were moving toward jazz and classical-based compositions and concept albums, the German bands became more mechanical and electronic. (Anon., n.d.)

This is a rather good summary of the elements of Krautrock that have proved to be lastingly influential; the commitment to experimentation, the use of emergent electronic technology, the emphasis on rhythmic repetition (expressed most clearly in Can's extended improvisations, and in the *motorik* style of Kraftwerk, Neu! and Harmonia). However, it does not capture the sheer complexity of the musical activity of the time. The bands and musicians who have emerged as the standard-bearers of the form – Tangerine Dream, Can, Faust, the two incarnations of Amon Düül, Neu!, Popol Vuh, Klaus Schulze, *et al.* – were part of an extremely diverse musical culture, which embraced the jazz- and soul-influenced progressive rock of bands such as Guru Guru and Xhol Caravan, the proto-Heavy Metal of the Scorpions and the Pink Floyd-tinged space rock of Eloy.

Common to all the musicians under this general heading, though, was a greater or lesser commitment to what Edward Macan (1997) describes as a progressive ideology; a commitment to expanding the scope of popular music, both by pushing at the boundaries of composition and available technology, but also by creating a synthesis of previously (more or less) distinct musical categories – jazz, classical, electronic/experimental, and so on. There were, as one might expect, some nationally specific inflexions in the German adoption of the progressive model. Unsurprisingly, given the federal organization of West Germany (and the absence of a strong, culturally dominant capital city), the German music scene was geographically quite diverse; Berlin, the old capital, had a thriving musical culture, but the scenes in Cologne, Munich and Düsseldorf were equally healthy. Secondly, the political turmoil of the late 1960s was, as one might expect, filtered through the particular circumstances in which the country found itself. As Michael Rother put it in 1998:

In Europe it was the time of huge social disturbances, political demonstrations (Berlin, Paris, Prague), the reflection upon overcoming of existing structures in general and the desire for a new beginning ... This Zeitgeist is reflected in our music. (Gross, 1998)

In practice, this meant that progressive German bands tended to eschew musical influences which were important constituent elements of progressive rock in Britain. British groups like ELP (Emerson Lake & Palmer) drew directly from the Western classical tradition; Jethro Tull harked back to folk; Yes, Genesis and Renaissance referenced the pastoral tradition in British composition. However, German bands favoured the non-indigenous

(Frank Zappa, Deep Purple, the Moody Blues, *et al.*), or the overtly experimental (Karlheinz Stockhausen, for example, with whom Holger Czukay studied before he joined Can, or the Pink Floyd of *A Saucerful of Secrets* and *Ummagumma*). The national, and entirely understandable, 'desire for a new beginning' in other words was manifest in the musical choices that the German rock groups of the period made; musical forms that linked the bands to a discredited past were replaced by forms which seemed to provide the musical raw material for such a rebirth.

German musicians were also well placed to take advantage of other attempts to create new music – attempts that had begun the moment that World War II ended. In 1946, Wolfgang Steinecke founded a series of study courses at Darmstadt, in Hesse (the Ferienkurse für Internationale Neue Musik Darmstadt, or Vacation Courses for International New Music in Darmstadt; the name underwent two changes, before settling on the almost identical Internationale Ferienkurse für Neue Musik Darmstadt in 1964); the twin aims of the course were, helpfully, clearly reflected in all the versions of the title. The courses aimed to reconnect German musicians and composers with musical trends and ideas that had been banned for most of the past 12 years; and they set out to be international – a crucial factor to emphasize, given the Nazi preoccupation with all things German. At Darmstadt, serialism soon became the musical language of choice; in other parts of the country, and, it is fair to say, for a younger generation of musicians, the drive was towards more extreme forms of atonality. In Cologne, a studio sponsored by the WDR (Westdeutscher Rundfunk) and devoted to experimental music opened in 1952. The organization had close links to Darmstadt (lectures in support of the initiative had been delivered there before the studio opened), and the most famous composer to be associated with the WDR studio, Karlheinz Stockhausen, also lectured at Darmstadt in 1953.

The work at Cologne, though, came quickly to focus on electronic music; those who worked at the studio borrowed from serialism and explored the idea that music was, at base, manipulated, structured sound. They employed various techniques – tape manipulation, the use of sine-wave generators, and so on – to control not only the arrangement of notes in sequence, but also their pitch, timbre, duration and type of attack. Stockhausen, writing in 1956 about the first major work to emerge from the Cologne studio (*Gesang der Junglinge*), described the composition as an '[attempt] to form the direction and movement of sound in space, and to make them accessible as a new direction for musical experience' (Chadabe, 1997, p. 40). A description of music as sound which was echoed, decades later, by Edgar Froese of Tangerine Dream (Stieg, 1994), and Can's founder member Holger Czukay (Czukay, 1997). Why, though, this interest in the expressive power of electronically manipulated sound? Partly the answer comes, once again, from the immediate past; the idea of a musical language which relied on conventional notions of melodic and (especially) harmonic structure was tainted by its association with the cultural policies of the Nazi regime. Also, and paradoxically, a commitment to the atonal-linked post-war German music to the spirit of cultural experimentation of the Weimar years; it simultaneously denied one version of German history, and reaffirmed another.

There was, though, another factor that contributed to the growing interest in experimental and electronic music; one that was, for the early Kraftwerk, far closer to home. By the 1960s, the German economy was booming: in particular, the industrial heartland of the Ruhr had become one of the most economically successful regions in Europe. For bands and musicians who grew up in the region, technology was entirely quotidian. In an interview with *Triad* magazine in 1975, Hütter and Schneider were asked where they stood in relation to the musical label 'space rock' – a term applied to a number of other German bands of the time. Their answer is instructive:

Hütter: We have aspects in our music that refer to space, like 'Kometenmelodie', but we also have some very earthly aspects that are very direct and not from outer space but from inner space like from the human being and the body, and very close to everyday life.

(Smaisys, 1975)

The experience of growing up in a location where new technologies were applied directly, of being part of the 'industrial generation', gave Kraftwerk's music a subtly different orientation to that of other German bands of the period. Tangerine Dream, for example, would give their music titles which emphasized the aura of otherworldliness, which was very much part of the image of the band ('Fly and Return to Comas Sola', from *Alpha Centurai*, 'Birth of Liquid Pleiades', from *Zeit*). In contrast, the titles of some early Kraftwerk tracks seem like labels from a maintenance manual ('Megaherz', from *Kraftwerk 2*, for example). Characteristically, Tangerine Dream's early music (before the band's discovery of sequencers on the title track of the album *Phaedra*) is based on musical elements that drift (the title track of *Alpha Centauri*) and drone (all four tracks on *Zeit*). Kraftwerk's early music, on the other hand, seems closer to the working through of a mechanical system. For example, 'Ruckzuck' (*Kraftwerk 1*) is structured around the relation between the flute and the other instruments; as the flute speeds up, the other instruments chase it, until the system abruptly breaks down.

In other words, the immediate musical and cultural context within which the band found themselves was one that placed its greatest emphasis on newness of all kinds: a new approach to composition, to technology and to music's place in German culture. What is interesting (and what is explored in a number of the chapters that follow) is the use the band made of this context. In 1976, interviewed for *Synapse* magazine, Hütter and Schneider showed themselves aware of the possible pitfalls of a year zero approach to music.

> Ralf Hütter: Most electronic musicians are afraid of tonality. When you see the world of frequencies there is tonality, you cannot deny it. The dictatorship of tonality or the dictatorship of non-tonality is the same.
>
> Florian Schneider: The outer musical world.
>
> Ralf Hütter: So when we feel harmony we play harmony, when we feel disharmony, or free tonality or openness we play open. It makes no difference, it's the range of frequencies.
>
> (Lynner and Robbley, 1976)

From the band's third album (*Ralf and Florian*), Kraftwerk's music has swung between the two poles outlined above: whether alternating the ascending block chords of 'Trans-Europe Express' with the rhythmic metal soundscapes of 'Metal on Metal', or running the sampled sounds of laboured patterned breathing alongside the more conventionally harmonic 'Tour de France Soundtracks'. However, the mixture is more complex than the simple alternation of harmony and disharmony; there is, in the band's music, a strong echo of the classical German tradition (note, for example, the keyboard solo in 'The Model', or the flurries of neo-classical note clusters in 'Franz Schubert') alongside odd echoes of American pop and rock (the *eins, zwei, drei, vier* which introduces 'Showroom Dummies', taken, as Hütter admitted, from the Ramones; the often-remarked-upon echo of the Beach Boys in 'Autobahn') and an increasing interest in dance music of various kinds (see Toltz, Duffett and Rietveld in this collection).

Similarly, the band's relation to technology is interestingly nuanced. Whereas other bands used new instruments and recording methods to map out a route to the future, Kraftwerk's approach was far more down to earth. This approach, it could be said, lies behind one of the most notable phrases associated with the group.

> Ralf Hütter: . . . we call ourselves 'the man machine', which means the machines are not subservient to us and we are not the sounds of the machine, but it's some kind of equal relationship, or you might even say friendship between man and machine, and not opposed.
>
> (Hütter, 1978)

Statements like this led directly to the kind of judgements made by the *NME* and by Lester Bangs: judgements in which the stereotype of the ruthlessly efficient German was conflated with that of the emotionless, robotic scientist. However, there is another way of reading this term and it is, simply, to take the statement at face value. There is, in Hütter's comment, the strong suggestion that an engagement with technology is not in fact a mark of the artist's dehumanization, but rather a mark of the assimilation of artist and instrument – and, as such, no different to the relation between guitarist and guitar (see Brocker and Pattie in this collection). More than this, it could be said that Kraftwerk's relationship to technology is bound up in their relation to their immediate environment; rather than using technology to map out an escape route towards the further reaches of the cosmos, it is used to recreate the mechanized soundscapes of the modern, industrialized city. In this, they demonstrate an intrinsically modernist approach to the relation between music, technology and the urban environment (see Cunningham in this collection for an exploration of the band's relation to modernism). As Barbara Barthelme notes:

> The city as a living environment is marked by soundscapes as well as by masses of houses. It is also a sign of the myth of the city that it is regarded as the technical extension of the human being. It is a giant tool, a prosthesis replacing the senses of locomotion through which man creates his world. (Barthelme, 2000, p. 104)

In other words, the technologized city itself is an unfinishable musical experiment – a soundscape endlessly recreated from the interaction between the individual and the urban environment. In 'Trans-Europe Express', the imagined journey across the continent ends in Düsseldorf – an appropriate terminus, given the fact that, sonically, Kraftwerk's music was profoundly shaped by their home city. When the band first opened Kling Klang (their home studio, and the base of the band's operations for more than three and a half decades) in 1970, it was oddly fitting that they should choose a location in a Düsseldorf industrial estate. Fitting because, in the midst of the soundscapes of the most technologically advanced area in Germany, the band created music which reflected, not the role of technology in the as-yet-unrealized future, but the integration of technology and human life in the present.

By allowing the various competing elements of the German musical tradition equal access to their music, alongside the overtly, atonally experimental; by using technology not as an escape route, but as an inescapable part of contemporary urban life; and by blending those approaches with elements taken from Anglo-American rock, the band showed themselves very adept at identifying and utilizing the various musical vocabularies that were available to them. What is striking, though, is that they did so entirely unapologetically. Without denying the musical rupture imposed by Nazism (as is evinced by Hütter's frequently quoted remark about reconnecting the band's music with the traditions of the Weimar republic) the band were willing to make use both of the avant-garde musical culture that surrounded them, and the German musical culture they had inherited. Given this, it is perhaps unsurprising that Kraftwerk were able to influence such a large swathe of musicians in the years to come – after all, their own music had itself evolved as a complex response to a very complex culture.

The chapters

The chapters below reflect the complexity of Kraftwerk's image and output in various ways: divided into two sections, they explore Kraftwerk's music, the band's use of technology and their relation to the development of popular music, from the 1970s to the present. Part 1, Music, Technology and Culture, focuses on the band itself, its music, and its relation to its immediate context. Sean Albiez and Kyrre Lindvig explore Kraftwerk's relation to German culture through the lens of their first international successes, 'Autobahn' the track and *Autobahn* the album. David Cunningham addresses the question of Kraftwerk's relation to modernism; Pertti Grönholm, their relation to the processes of popular music stardom. In a co-written chapter, Simon Piasecki and Rob Wilsmore reflect on the band's position on the cusp of an evolution in the development of musical genres. Carsten Brocker provides a detailed discussion, based on first-hand accounts, of Kraftwerk's use of technology. Finally, David Pattie examines the image of the band in performance – an increasingly important part of their work. In Part 2, Influences and Legacies, Kraftwerk's impact on other musicians and musical genres is discussed. Sean Albiez and Richard Witts, in two complementary chapters, deal with the influence Kraftwerk exerted (or seemed to exert) on a generation of British musicians in the late 1970s and early 1980s: both chapters argue that this relation was rather more complex than is usually thought to be the case. Similarly, Joseph Toltz's and Mark Duffett's chapters deal with the influence the band had on the development of electro, hip-hop, techno and house in the US – and, once again, argue that this influence is based as much on misunderstanding and creative reinterpretation (especially, as Duffett points out, when the racial politics of this interaction are taken into account). Finally, Hillegonda Rietveld's chapter ties both sections of the book together, using 'Trans-Europe Express' as a means through which both Kraftwerk's relation to European and American culture, and the relation of those cultures to the band, can usefully be understood.

Notes

1. However, it is worth noting that the assumed opposition in this statement misrepresents the inherently hybrid musical/racial identity of Kraftwerk's music, as several essays in this collection point out (see Toltz and Duffett in this collection).

2. The precise derivation of this term is unclear: it is sometimes ascribed to a 1972 article by Ian MacDonald for the *NME* (*New Musical Express*), but the term seems to have been in use before then. However, the term passed into wider usage by the early 1970s (Faust, famously, titled a track 'Krautrock' on their fourth album); and it is still useful – both because it covers the period, and because it draws one's attention inexorably to an underlying cultural stereotype that coloured (and still colours) the media's response to Kraftwerk (see Wright 2007, for a very recent example of this).

References

Anon. (2006), 'The 50 albums that changed music'. *Observer*, 16 July. http://www.guardian.co.uk/music/2006/jul/16/popandrock.shopping (last accessed 22 April 2006).

—— (n.d.), 'Kraut rock'. *allmusic*. http://www.allmusic.com/cg/amg.dll?p=amg&sql=77:2677 (last accessed 22 April 2010).

Applegate, C. and Potter P. (2002), 'Germans as the 'people of music', in C. Applegate and P. Potter (eds), *Music and German National Identity*. Chicago: Chicago University Press, pp. 1–35.

Bangs, L. (1975/1996), 'Kraftwerkfeature or how I learned to stop worrying and love the balm', in *Psychotic Reactions and Carburetor Dung*. London: Serpent's Tail, pp. 154–64.

Barthelme, B. (2000), 'Music and the city', in H. J. Braun (ed.), *Music and Technology in the Twentieth Century*. Baltimore: Johns Hopkins University Press, pp. 97–105.

Chadabe, J. (1997), *Electronic Sound: The Past and Promise of Electronic Music*. London: Prentice Hall.

Czukay, H. (1997), 'A short history of the Can – discography. *Perfect Sound Forever*. May. http://www.furious.com/PERFECT/hysterie2.html (last accessed 22 April 2010).

Gross, J. (1998), 'Michael Rother interview'. *Perfect Sound Forever*, March. http://www.furious.com/Perfect/michaelrother.html (last accessed 22 April 2010).

Hütter, R. (1978), 'Interview'. *WSKU* (*Kent – Ohio*), first broadcast 19 June. http://kraftwerk.technopop.com.br/interview_108.php (last accessed 22 April 2010).

Larkey, E. (2002), 'Postwar German popular music: Americanization, the cold war, and the post-Nazi Heimat', in C. Applegate and P. Potter (eds), *Music and German National Identity*. Chicago: Chicago University Press, pp. 234–50.

Logan, N. and Woffinden, B. (eds) (1977), *The Illustrated New Musical Express Encyclopedia of Rock*. London: Salamander.

Lynner, D. and Robbley, B. (1976), 'A conversation with Ralf Hutter and Florian Schneider of Kraftwerk'. *Synapse*, September/October, 10–11. http://www.cyndustries.com/synapse/synapse.cfm?pc=35&folder=sept1976&pic=11 (last accessed 22 April 2010).

Macan, E. (1997), *Rocking the Classics*. Oxford: Oxford University Press.

Mann, T. (1968), *Dr Faustus*. London: Penguin.

Reynolds, S. (1998), *Energy Flash: A Journey through Rave Music and Dance Culture*. London: Picador.

—— (1999), *Generation Ecstasy*. London: Routledge.

—— (2005), *Rip It Up and Start Again*. London: Faber & Faber.

Ritzel, F. (1998), 'Was is aus uns geworden? Ein Haufchen Sand un Meer: emotions of post-war Germany as extracted from examples of popular music'. *Popular Music*, 17, (3), 293–309.

Seago, A. (2004), 'The "Kraftwerk-Effekt": transatlantic circulation, global networks and contemporary pop music', in *Atlantic Studies*, Vol 1, No 1, London: Routledge, pp. 85–106.

Smaisys, P. (1975), 'Interview: Ralf Hütter & Florian Schneider'. *Triad*, June. http://pages. ripco.net/~saxmania/kraft.html (last accessed 22 April 2010).

Stieg, E. (Presenter) (1994), 'Edgar Froese radio interview'. *Radio Ffn Grenzwellen*, first broadcast April 1994. http://www.arm.ac.uk/~ath/music/td/interviews/interview. froese.200394.html (last accessed 22 April 2010).

Tardio, A. (2010), 'Dr. Dre says he's listening to Kraftwerk, Parliament Funkadelic'. *Hip-Hop DX*, 9 April. http://www.hiphopdx.com/index/news/id.11005/title.dr-dre-says-hes-listening-to-kraftwerk-parliament-funkadelic (last accessed 22 April 2010).

Toop, D. (1999), *Exotica: Fabricated Soundscapes in the Real World*. London: Serpent's Tail.

—— (2001), *Ocean of Sound*. London: Serpent's Tail.

—— (2003), 'Kraftwerk: sound in straight lines', in *Dazed and Confused*, Vol 2, No 6, p. 115.

Wright, C. (Prod.) (2007), *Kraftwerk: We are the Robots*. BBC Radio 4 [Documentary], Broadcast 22 November, 11.30 a.m.–12 p.m.

I

Music, Technology and Culture

1

Autobahn and Heimatklänge:[1] Soundtracking the FRG

Sean Albiez and Kyrre Tromm Lindvig

Autobahn *was about finding our artistic situation: where are we?*
What is the sound of the German Bundesrepublik?

(Ralf Hütter qtd. in Dalton, 2009, p. 70)

The year 1975 saw an unusual entry into the pop charts in several countries on both sides of the Atlantic. In the bestseller lists usually dominated by Anglo-American popular music a new kind of hit arrived. It was a song about driving along the autobahn, Germany's extended motorway system, with an intro consisting of slamming car doors, an engine starting and heavily vocoded voices. Then a slow synth bass line entered with a sixteenth-note half-time shuffle feel before the vocal began – in German. Though perhaps viewed initially as a novelty or simple aberration, Kraftwerk and 'Autobahn' came to be understood as a signpost indicating the direction popular music would take in the ensuing decades on the international stage. This chapter will analyse how Kraftwerk as West German trespassers positioned themselves in the Anglo-American-dominated idiom of pop music at the time. It will place special emphasis on the manner in which they engaged with issues of (West) German identity within the 1974 *Autobahn* album, and in encounters with the music press outside the Federal Republic of Germany (FRG) in the aftermath of their international success. It will also suggest it is important to view Kraftwerk's allusions to essentialist Germanic stereotypes in the mid 1970s and since as self-aware, satirical and ironic critiques of socially constructed markers of Germanness.

German national identity and the FRG

In general terms, research on nationalism has identified that essentialist and fixed portrayals of German or any other national identity are flawed constructions, whether developed by national insiders or outsiders. As Özkırımlı (2000) has outlined, discourses around nationalism have generally developed within three umbrella categories: *primordialist, modernist* and *ethno-symbolist. Primordialist* accounts of nationality and the rise of nations suggest that 'ethnic and national identities [can] lay dormant for centuries . . . [b]ut the national 'essence', unchanging and persistent, is always there to be reawakened' (p. 216). This formulation is central to the notion of a German *Volk* (people) and a related Germanic cultural identity that fuelled the development of Germany into a modern nation in 1871. The assumed *Volk* roots of this identity persisted in an amplified form through the Nazi era as a chauvinistic notion of a collective soul or spirit that underpinned the identity of the German-speaking people of Europe.

However, *modernist* theorists of nationalism have portrayed such accounts as flawed. Gellner (1983) discussed national identities as necessary myths that were cultivated in nation-building projects during nineteenth-century industrialization. Hobsbawm (1990) suggested Germany and other modern nations were founded on invented traditions that attempted to bind together disparate peoples so they felt a sense of common national purpose. Anderson (1983) described nations as imagined communities that create a national sense of collectivity. Although the level of falsity within these myths, inventions and imaginings are debated, there is agreement that national identities are not in any way 'natural'. Though *ethno-symbolists* argue *modernist* theorists overlook evidence of persistent national 'myths, symbols, values and memories' (Özkırımlı, 2000, p. 167), Anthony D. Smith, despite holding to this view, 'admits that the traditions, customs and institutions of the past are "reconstructed" and "reinterpreted"' (qtd. in Özkırımlı, 2000, p. 221). Therefore, national identities are never fixed or finished.

During nineteenth-century German nation building, James (2000) indicates the German-speaking peoples of Europe often had little other than their language in common, and that there was a surprising cosmopolitan drive at work in the formation of a German identity, stating:

> In the absence of institutions which might determine appropriate behaviour, Germans had to manufacture their own concept of nationality . . . they needed self-consciously to formulate an imagined national past and idealised future . . . Partly they relied on the rejection of some types of 'alien': defining Germans in opposition to other peoples . . . But the German quest for identity also required the absorption of foreign models into German life. (p. 11)

These foreign (and ancient) models are identified by James as 'France, England, America, Russia, Italy, Poland, Switzerland, and the Netherlands; as well as . . . the vanished worlds of Greece or Rome' (p. 15).

In summary, German identity by the twentieth century was founded on an imagined and romanticized *Volk* past, combined with cosmopolitan national borrowings and the positing of national and racial stereotypes against which Germany chauvinistically defined itself. Although there may have been some primordial vestiges of continuity between earlier notions of German identity and the German nation, the version of the Germanic presented by the mid twentieth century emerged from the specific hyper-nationalistic political climate of that period. However, it is important to acknowledge that stereotypes and clichés are convenient shorthand commonly used to mark out the boundaries of national identity. As Zelko (2006) indicates,

> Germans, like the people of most nations, have a shared view of their past which owes much to mythology as history . . . this view is distilled into a series of clichés which explain the national character in a way that resonates with both natives and foreigners. (p. 1)

Whether fantasy and fakery are involved in assembling national markers of identity, they remain potent and convenient clichés that are widely disseminated, and are necessary tools for forging a sense of national purpose. In the post-1945 period, like previous periods in German history, attempts were made to create anew a sense of German identity suitable for the prevailing post-Nazi situation. Due to the corrosive effect of Nazi ideology and the destruction and horror wrought by Hitler, the two new Germanies, the FRG and the eastern German Democratic Republic (GDR), struggled to develop a new sense of collective identity. This was further complicated by the vested interests of the allies (the US, UK and France) who managed and underwrote the transformation of the FRG into a unified political system in opposition to the Soviet-backed GDR during the Cold War. This renewal attempted to bypass the calamitous implications of the recent past that now defined German identity for the rest of the world.

In the FRG, this past was largely subjugated in an attempt to rebuild the nation on a new democratic and consumerist model. As Le Gloannec (1994) suggests,

> [West Germany] forged a counterpoint to Auschwitz, offering a modern and flawless present, a democratic and cosmopolitan social and political body, removed from the national past. The new Germany – the Federal Republic – was devoid of asperity and national celebrations; it was smooth, odorless, colorless. In the 1950s, 1960s and 1970s, many of the young claimed to be European.

Underpinning this was an intense emphasis on economic and industrial renewal. The West German chancellor Konrad Adenauer stated in 1953 that 'the most important goal of our policy in economics [is to] modernize industrial plants' and '[r]enewal and modernization, rationalization, education of highly qualified skilled workers [is] urgent' (Welsch, 1996, p. 109). This initially successful policy resulted in the *Wirtschaftswunder* (economic miracle) that brought prosperity to a West Germany that embraced Western capitalist consumer culture under the tutelage of the United States.

However, political tensions developed after the rise in the late 1960s of a critical countercultural younger generation who wanted to open discussions about Germany and its recent violent past, and questioned the capitalist and consumerist basis of the FRG. However, despite the rise in the 1970s of an alternative culture and later an environmental political movement, the FRG state effectively neutralized internal political opposition (Dirke, 1997). This resulted in the rise of extremist terrorist groups and disaffection with mainstream politics. By the mid 1970s, Norbert Elias stated in an assessment of the FRG that 'one of the most astonishing and frightening discoveries is the enormous bitterness and enmity parts of the population feel with regard to other parts' (1997, p. 405). Writing in 1977, he suggested that,

> [r]ight up to the present, the relatively high economic efficiency of the FRG serves to suppress from the public consciousness of the nation the need to look the severe non-economic problems of the West German people straight in the eye. (p. 407)

As a result of such conflict and the separation of the west and east, West Germans were unable to imagine themselves as a complete national community. There appeared to be endemic amnesia where 15 years of Nazi history had been wiped from the collective memory, while the post-1871 German nation was viewed by some with nostalgia and by others with blame. They were also only too aware that the other half of the fractured old German nation was building a society in direct opposition to the liberal democratic aims of the FRG.

It is within this milieu that Kraftwerk worked in relative isolation in Düsseldorf after the late 1960s. Keenly aware of the FRG's inherent problems, they began to address some of the internal conflicts between past and present, technology and nature, the rational FRG and irrational Nazi and Romantic past, folk and mass culture, conservatism and progress, between old and new and between 'man' and machine in their music and art. With the release of 'Autobahn' in 1974, they managed to create a state of the nation address that launched them onto the international stage.

Kraftwerk and 'Autobahn'

Kraftwerk's international success with the 'Autobahn' single and album was initially accidental. A major factor in its popularity was the creation of a 3:27 promotional version of the 22:43 track from the album of the same name. This truncated version when released as a single became a hit in the US, and eventually in many other countries. This single edit was not instigated or originally envisaged by Kraftwerk, and fortuitously came about through the head of Phonogram's Chicago office asking his staff to produce a single version of the album track that had already gained radio play. This promo version received further play, so a single version was released that eventually reached #25 on the Billboard Singles charts. The album attained similar success and reached #5 on the album charts (Barr, 1998, p. 86).

There was a long process of performance and studio experimentation before Ralf Hütter and Florian Schneider achieved international success. Though their earlier albums, *Kraftwerk* (1970), *Kraftwerk 2* (1971) and *Ralf and Florian* (1973) had found their way to audiences outside West Germany, *Autobahn* marked a substantial and unexpected breakthrough into the international music market. It has come to be viewed by Kraftwerk as their *Stunde Null* (Year Zero). The album indicated the future trajectory that Kraftwerk would take in forging a *Gesamtkunstwerk* or complete artistic package that homologously combined the groundbreaking use of electronic music technologies, deadpan half-spoken/half-sung performances of minimalist lyrics, references to technological themes and modes of travel, and refined and conceptual artwork.

An important feature of *Autobahn* was that it explicitly addressed aspects of German identity loaded with references to the Nazi era and beyond. Although Kraftwerk would later eschew national themes in their music, preferring transnational, cosmopolitan and international references, 'Autobahn' in particular represented a confused and contentious emerging post-war FRG identity. Kraftwerk were not the first musicians to create music around the theme of the autobahn. Two decades earlier, in 1954, US jazz musicians Woody Herman and Ralph Burns wrote and released 'Autobahn Blues' soon after a European tour. However, it is Kraftwerk's song that is most widely associated with the autobahns that remain a key signifier of twentieth-century German modernity. As Zeller (2007) has indicated,

> Kraftwerk made a major contribution to the ambivalent assessment of this technological artifact stretching over thousands of kilometers with its 1974 song 'Autobahn'; by using the most modern musical techniques to portray a fast-paced road trip, it surrounded the autobahnen with the aura of a modern sheen and cool technoromanticism. (p. 1)

While by 1974 the autobahns, after 30 years of operation and expansion, perhaps had begun to transcend Nazi associations, they were a highly problematic theme to tackle in the context of a pop song as they retained direct historical links to the Nazi era. The 'sheen' and 'cool' Kraftwerk brought to the autobahn in the context of an international pop hit was potentially why Kraftwerk's success was commercially celebrated (Flür, 2000, p. 64) but ultimately viewed ambivalently in cultural terms (Bussy, 2005, p. 58) inside a divided FRG that was struggling to create a dehistoricized progressive modern identity for itself.

Kraftwerk and German national identity

Music journalists quite early on appeared to have decided that the two most (obvious) productive points of discussion concerning Kraftwerk were that they were West German and they created and performed electronic music. They picked up on and often amplified the links between the band's national status – or associated Germanic or Teutonic historical stereotypes – and their use of electronic technologies such as electronic drum kits and rhythm machines, synthesizers and vocoders. In discussing 'Autobahn', Lester Bangs (1975, p. 154) argued:

> 'Autobahn' is more than just the latest evidence in support of the case for Teutonic raillery, more than just a record, it is an *indictment*. An indictment of all those who would resist the bloodless iron will and order of the ineluctable dawn of the Machine Age.

This tongue-in-cheek portrayal, though clearly humorous, is telling in several ways. It indicates that music journalists on encountering Kraftwerk bought into and constructed a clearly defined 'Kraftwerk *qua* German' identity, positioning them as *essentially* German. In Kraftwerk's *Creem* magazine interview with Bangs in 1975, Hütter and Schneider fielded questions and intimations about their German identity in a seemingly controversial manner. Barr (1998) suggests that they 'deliberately [played] up to the deadly-serious, straight-laced stereotypical image of Germans that many Americans still retained from Hollywood war movies' (p. 90).

Hütter and Schneider seemed to play upon clichéd German stereotypes by referring to how they manipulated and controlled people through technology, to the mechanical nature of the German language and by mentioning the German mentality as being 'more advanced' (Bangs, 1975, pp. 157–9). In a September 1975 interview with Geoff Barton in the British music paper *Sounds*, Hütter and Schneider took these controversial themes even further:

When you are aware that music is a process of brainwashing and manipulation, you realise it can go also in the direction of damage. We have the
power to push the knobs on our machines this way or that and cause
damage . . . It can be like doctors with patients. (p. 22)

Clearly Hütter and Schneider were toying with widely held Nazi-related
German stereotypes concerning technological control and mastery that were
ever present in representations of Germans in popular media culture outside
the FRG (see Witts in this collection). However, these stereotypes had a
historical grounding that still resonated inside and outside both Germanys.
Taken literally, these remarks are disturbing reading. However, based on
subsequent statements the band made concerning German identity and
their relationship to Germany's past, it would appear the band were simply
countering in an ironic or satirical manner the attitudes they encountered
during their US and UK tours. Whether irony or satire, Bangs's interview and
the comments made to Barton in *Sounds* perceptibly shaped the narratives
through which Kraftwerk were initially encountered by audiences in the US,
UK and elsewhere. Misunderstanding and mistaking the satirical element
within Kraftwerk's public announcements became common in media coverage. For example, Goldstein (1977) caustically traded on Nazi-era clichés
concerning Kraftwerk's so-called 'masterplan' for 'world domination'.

However, a further examination of a number of press interviews in the
1975–81 period suggests Hütter and Schneider were keen to challenge the
simplistic assumptions made by interviewers outside the FRG. Although they
played along with stereotypical lines of questioning, they were also willing to
give journalists a geography and history lesson that problematized the naïve
imposition of national stereotypes. For example, Hütter has continually pointed
out in interviews over the past four decades that being based in Düsseldorf
and the Ruhr region meant Kraftwerk experienced a cosmopolitan upbring-
ing. In 1975, Hütter stated that Kraftwerk 'grew up in a sort of crossroads
between France and Germany, so we were exposed to the musique [concrète]
of Paris and the electronic music of Cologne' (Dallas, 1975, p. 16). Elsewhere,
he indicated, outside of the specific field of electronic music Kraftwerk and
Germany had a complex European ethnic heritage, indicating that

[y]ou travel for one hour then you come into a completely different
country. We live a half hour from Holland and Belgium. If you travel
another hour, you go into France. So it's a mixing of different cultures on
the Rhineland . . . My passport says I'm German but in reality, the Rhine
where we live has been German, has been Rumanian [*sic*], French, has
been Dutch, even Russian. The country has been taken over and over
again by different cultures so we are really like a cultural supermarket.
(qtd. in Lynner and Robbley, 1976)

By addressing this issue, Hütter implicitly references the mixing of *musical* cultures that marks German musical identity as a whole. Potter (1998, p. 201), in outlining how German musicologists for two centuries have failed in their attempts to convincingly pinpoint Germanness in music, states that this is due to

> Germany's central location and its long history as a cultural crossroads [which has] made it one of the most cosmopolitan musical landscapes on the continent. This phenomenon probably accounted for Germany's musical strengths over the centuries, but it was also an obstacle to anyone hoping to isolate specifically German elements in the works of German composers.

This historical, cultural and musical cosmopolitanism clearly problematizes simplistic claims concerning German national identity, as well as essentialist claims that Kraftwerk's (or any other German musician's) music is intrinsically German.

Crucial to Kraftwerk's positioning as a Ruhr/Rhineland/Düsseldorf band is the implied notion that, for them, their *Heimat* (homeland) is a highly modernized industrial region of the FRG – not an archaic Alpine idyll or the kind of primordial German forest that formed widely held conservative versions of *Heimat* in German *Volk* culture. Kraftwerk appear to simultaneously allude to the long tradition of German provinciality in German-speaking contexts (Blickle, 2002, p. 158) while potentially and self-consciously forging a new kind of industrial *Heimat*. As Blickle has indicated,

> [t]he idea of *Heimat* – deeply embedded in language, deeply involved in German self-identity and regional self-understanding beyond the political domain – is one of the main elements in contemporary German renegotiations of what it means to be German and to live in a German-speaking environment. (p. 154)

Kraftwerk's subversive renegotiation of *Heimat* into a modern industrial context is sometimes countered by a self-conscious and knowing adoption of German cultural stereotypes. For example, Hütter (qtd. in Bohn, 1981) was willing to explicitly discuss the band's work ethic in terms of a fatalistic Germanic quest to 'do it all the way, imposing the process as a discipline on ourselves, really taking it all the way'. He has also acknowledged an anti-American strain in their work that was a response to post-war cultural Americanization, but views this as 'nothing to do with nationalist feelings, it's more a cultural thing – it has to do with more spiritual feelings, continental feelings' (p. 32).

Hütter has also indicated that an earlier West German gaze that celebrated

Anglo-American musicians and iconography was intentionally subverted by Kraftwerk in the mid 1970s, and has suggested their artistic and visual strategy was a self-reflexive response to this outward gaze.

> [In Germany] people have always taken pictures of English and Americans, and we had to turn the camera and take a picture of ourselves, to expose ourselves to the media, because the post-war German generation remained in the shadow: those who are older than us had Elvis or The Beatles for idols . . . those are not bad options, but if we completely forget our identity, it becomes quickly 'empty' and not consistent. There's a whole generation in Germany, between 30 and 50, who has lost its own identity, and who never even had any. (Alessandrini, 1976)

Another area where Hütter indicates an alternate sense of musical identity is in the embrace of a term that has wider significance than perhaps was realized by non-German commentators and writers at the time.

> Our music has been called 'industrial folk music' . . . that's the way we see it. There's something ethnic to it; it couldn't have come from anywhere else . . . we are from the Düsseldorf scene, from Ein Ruhr scene, which is an industrial area, so our music has more of that edge to it. (Hütter qtd. in Gill, 1997)

Elsewhere on this theme, Hütter has also indicated that 'since we were into noise anyway, and we kind of liked industrial production . . . we had this vision of our music being like the voice of this industrial product' (qtd. in Trudgeon, 1981).

The fact that Kraftwerk embraced modernity, industrialization and urban culture that had long been viewed as the antithesis of notions of *Heimat* is significant, particularly when cast in the guise of industrial folk music or 'Industrielle Volksmusik' (Bohn, 1981, p. 32). Kraftwerk were partly juxtaposing their modern industrial music 'of the people', with the conservative product of the FRG's music industry, *volkstümliche*. This was a post-war contemporary folk-like music that appeared to 'construct a sense of 'Germanness' [that avoided] historical reality and responsibility' (Frith, 1998, p. v). As Schoenebeck (1998) suggests, the popularity of this music in the post-war period was partly due to its 'retrospective and regressive' values that fitted 'perfectly the political programmes and ideas of Germany's right-wing parties' (p. 290). Although leftist West German folk music influenced by the folk revival in the US did emerge in the late 1960s, and was used to soundtrack 'protest movements against things such as nuclear power plants' (Dirke, 1994, p. 67), terms such as *volksmusik* or *volkslied* still 'conjured up horrifying images of the Nazi past or neo-Nazi tendencies in the minds of historically

conscious people' (p. 66). This was in part due to the fact that in the early years
of twentieth-century German nation building, a nationalist German youth
movement or *Jugendbewegung* had pursued a chauvinistic music policy that
aimed to identify a *Gemeinschaftmusikkultur* (communal music culture), and
embraced German folk song among other forms. This was a strategy to mark
out a distinct German musical identity free from American popular music
and jazz, modernist music and commercial 'entertainment music', and that
contained marked strains of anti-semitism, and straddled both the Weimar
and Nazi eras (Potter, 1998, pp. 7–8).

Kraftwerk, by critically alluding to such tendencies, and by embracing
their Ruhr industrial *Heimat*, placed themselves in knowing opposition to
such right-wing and/or Nazi regressive representations of German people's
culture – and also to their hometown's own controversial musical history. The
National Socialists had mounted an exhibition of *Entartete Musik* (Degenerate
Music) in Düsseldorf in 1938 as part of a national festival of music, and further
wished to 'honor Düsseldorf as the official "Reich Music City"' (Potter, 1998,
p. 17). It is reasonable to assume that music audiences in the FRG were aware of
such historical resonances, even if they failed to travel beyond its borders.

It is also worth highlighting that Kraftwerk's appropriation of the term
volksmusik operated in parallel with a 1970s West German alternative culture
that had a 'strong interest in folk culture' (*Volkskultur*) that was 'quite surprising' as up until the 1970s 'folk culture had been a taboo for progressive
social forces' (Dirke, 1997, p. 145). However, whereas Kraftwerk deployed
the term in the context of an emerging aesthetic that seemed to parallel the
FRG's modernist and rationalist ethos in industrial production, alternative
culture 'rejected the aesthetic categories of the hegemonic institutionalized
culture – professionalism, high quality, originality, and stardom – in favor
of a somewhat vague idea of a culture of the people' (Dirke, 1997, p. 145). It
appears therefore that Kraftwerk's appropriation of *volksmusik* in the context
of the *industrielle* is also a critique of this alternative culture. The bands interest in high-quality, 'professional' aesthetic production sits in direct opposition
to the embrace of 'play, pleasure, and instant gratification' in alternative
culture (Dirke, 1997, p. 143). Since the late 1970s, *volksmusik* has taken on a
new set of meanings due to the rise of a more popular and populist version
of post-war *volkstümliche* that appears to have transcended earlier right-wing
connotations, though still conservative in its values (Benoit, 2007, p. 36).

On this evidence, Kraftwerk from the start have continually problematized
essentialist notions of Germanness and national identity. They have also
demonstrated their ambivalent feelings concerning a nationalistic attachment
to the FRG that was, as we now know, a transitory state without a clear identity other than one based on progressive industrial and consumerist modernity.
The FRG was afraid of its own history while being dominated by it, and was
awaiting a potential future resolution of the Cold War division of East and

West. Kraftwerk addressed the tensions and contradictions of the FRG within their music; however, they clearly also attempted to transcend it. Their embrace of a cosmopolitan outlook that was anyway a key feature of German history was perhaps the only viable response for leftist artists emerging from the anti-nationalist countercultural post-war milieu in the FRG (Kettenacker, 1997). It was potentially also a commercial decision to facilitate their escape from the confines of a restrictive West German music scene (Littlejohn, 2009). A more prosaic reason is suggested by Karl Bartos, Kraftwerk's electronic percussionist, who recently stated that on the US *Autobahn* tour

> we had been confronted by this German identity so much in the States, with everyone greeting us with the 'heil Hitler' salutes. They were just making fun and jokes and not being very serious but we'd had enough of this idea. (Bartos qtd. in Doran, 2009)

Kraftwerk therefore knowingly addressed German identity through a self-reflexive and playful representation of clichéd national stereotypes, and at other times critiqued into submission the simplistic portrayal of a defining and monolithic German identity presented to them by music journalists. They have also used the German language within their releases, though they have become polyglottic over the years. With this in mind, what is a little difficult to explain is that, despite Kraftwerk's clear engagement with aspects of their multilayered German/central European identity and the German language, they have largely been sidelined in studies of post-1945 German popular music.

For example, in Durrani (2002) Kraftwerk are briefly dismissed: 'Some rock groups, including Kraftwerk, have evidently been successful abroad and are recognized for their pioneering electronic techniques rather than for their lyrics' (p. 198), mistakenly assuming that Kraftwerk's German lyrics are an unproductive subject for further study. Larkey (2000; 2002) makes no mention of Kraftwerk at all. Burns and van der Will (1995) incorrectly state that the 'German bands which succeeded in attracting an international following did so *largely on the basis of instrumentals* [my emphasis], like the . . . synthesizer rock of Kraftwerk' (p. 312). Dirke (1994) simply mentions Kraftwerk in passing as an example of 'electronic German rock' (p. 65). More recently, Littlejohn (2009) creates a reductive thesis that ignores every aspect of Kraftwerk's *Gesamtkunstwerk* other than their language choice. On the basis of their move to a polyglottal vocal strategy and short-form compositions, he suggests that Kraftwerk sold out their Germanness and

> forfeited the element most clearly German about the group: its language. By changing [their] lyrics, language and form in a bid for commercial success, Kraftwerk turned [their] back on [their] national identity. This move away from Germanness is of no small significance for Kraftwerk

inasmuch as the band had previously kept its national identity very much to the fore. (p. 647)

However, it is very clear that Kraftwerk after *Autobahn* still continually addressed aspects of their national identity in media interviews, if not so directly in their music. It appears that Littlejohn like others before him have quickly dismissed Kraftwerk's German credentials merely based on the choice of language in their releases. That is, though Kraftwerk continued to produce German-language versions of their albums, they also produced English-language versions, used French in, for example, *Tour de France Soundtracks* (2003), and in tracks such as 'Numbers' from *Computer World* (1981) they simultaneously deployed several languages. In these studies there is an assumption that Kraftwerk's cosmopolitanism disqualifies them from being viewed as German popular musicians at all. This is despite Kraftwerk's choice of a German name (meaning 'power station') and the German titles they gave tracks on *Autobahn* that underpinned the presentation of themselves as ineluctably German. This seemingly simple fact should not be overlooked; the choice of the title 'Autobahn' clearly has a different set of national connotations than the terms *freeway*, *highway* or *motorway*.

A further crucial point concerning Kraftwerk's relationship to West German identity appears to have been missed by Germanist writers. That is, *Autobahn* and the following album, *Radio-Activity* (1975), can also be cast as a direct and knowing critique of West German populist and conservative pop in the form of *Schlager*. As Larkey (2002) indicates, *Schlager* (meaning 'hit') is a 'quintessentially German' form of pop music that in the post-war FRG 'reflected the optimism of the *Wirtschaftswunder* . . . by featuring lyrics that sentimentalized the *Heimat* . . . and extirpated unpleasant thoughts of the Nazi past' (p. 235). The music was culturally conservative, consumerist and always sung in German. In the documentary *Kraftwerk and the Electronic Revolution* (Johnstone, 2008), German cultural critic Diedrich Diedrichsen argues Kraftwerk's choice of German vocals for 'Autobahn' immediately placed them within the *Schlager* tradition for West German audiences. In the same film, musician and journalist Wolfgang Seidel states that *Schlager* portrays conventional themes of love and homeland in a sanitized, 'cold and rigid fashion' that has 'nothing to do with the emotions of real people'. He goes on to argue that

this is what Kraftwerk caricatured. This is how they were heard in Germany. [Kraftwerk's lyrics] were obviously senseless . . . they didn't even attempt to have any substance or value in such an obvious way that it became an artistic statement. It was a caricature of Schlager in the same way as their ties and their hairstyles were a caricature of the disciplined and ambitious German.

Kraftwerk, through this caricature of a sanitized, 'smooth, odorless and colorless' (Le Gloannec, 1994) FRG, ironically embodied Adenauer's call for the new nation to embrace '[r]enewal and modernisation [and] rationalization'. It is also significant that they portrayed themselves as disciplined and ambitious 'musik arbeiter' which alluded to Adenauer's notion that 'highly qualified skilled workers' were urgently required to underpin such renewal. They also potentially prefigured the turn to German in the work of late 1970s/1980s Neue Deutsche Welle artists who likewise satirically referenced *Schlager*, though in the context of punk and post-punk musical styles (Dirke, 1994, p. 71). As such, it appears that aspects of the satirical statement made in *Autobahn* were lost on international audiences. What was perhaps originally a parochial West German artistic statement became mistakenly understood through the filter of externally imposed stereotypes that failed to appreciate Kraftwerk's critical intentions. However, the mistaken perceptions of international media and audiences are telling in the manner in which they positioned Kraftwerk, as is the way the band positioned themselves within this feedback loop.

Kraftwerk and the iconography of the autobahn

Before exploring the music of 'Autobahn', it is important to consider the visual accompaniment Kraftwerk employed for their music that knowingly explored Germany and Germanness. The cover art for the *Autobahn* album and single releases was created by Kraftwerk associate and lyric writer Emil Schult.[2] The front cover is filled by a large painting, a rather kitschy comic book rendition of an autobahn surrounded by green nature. Bussy (2005) indicates that

> the front cover is a painting by Emil Schult that juxtaposes images of the countryside, mountains, an exaggerated sun, green grass, blue sky and floating clouds, against the most potent symbol of the industrial era – the motor car on the motorway. (pp. 54–5)

Schult's image is a direct visual representation of the lyrics of 'Autobahn' that simply describe the experience of driving on the autobahn on a sunny day through a wide valley, and reference the long concrete strip of road ahead, white road markings and the green borders to the road. Kraftwerk, as the occupants of a car, turn on the radio and hear their own song about travelling on the autobahn.

By the 1970s, the autobahns were a 'potent symbol' of the FRG's economic and industrial power, but also conjured up connotations of the Nazi era as it was one of Hitler's most prioritized projects. Spotts (2002) states that '[e]ven while under construction, these *Straßen des Führers* or *Straßen Adolf Hitlers* were heralded as one of the great manifestations of Hitler's genius, the vitality of National Socialism and the excellence of German technology' (p. 386). The autobahns were extensively used at the time for internal and external propaganda purposes. Zeller (2007) indicates:

> Hundreds of publications celebrated the roadways as a technological achievement of the highest order and as attractive structures, as an effective means of overcoming unemployment, and thus a contribution to a *Volk* community . . . [they were] depicted as uniquely German . . . given the dimensions and high degree of organization, these roads were possible only in Germany. (p. 63)

As Zeller outlines, there are problems and inaccuracies in these claims; however, a wide range of autobahn-related propaganda in 'newspapers, books, the theatre, movies, radio, public speeches, and even collectible pictures and board games' (p. 63) embedded the myths of the autobahn in the collective German psyche for many years to come. These myths also had a lasting impact outside Germany and, as Spotts indicates, 'the autobahn told the world that dictatorship was more effective than democracy and that Nazi Germany had reconciled technology and aesthetics, machinery and nature, the past and the future' (2002, p. 389).

The autobahns were not, as generally reported, built to rapidly transport troops and material in Hitler's planned war; as Spotts suggests, '[w]hat is not widely appreciated is that Hitler regarded these highways above all as aesthetic monuments' (p. 386). He also indicates the autobahns were designed to highlight the German countryside:

> Bridges and overpasses were designed and built not only to fit in with the landscape but also to be architectural achievements in themselves. Linked to beauty was sleekness. The roadways were to sweep through the countryside without intersections. (2002, p. 387)

Put simply, the autobahns were designed to show off Germany's natural landscape. For Hitler and the National Socialists, nature had a mythical status, and the racial superiority of the Aryans was based on a primordial rural myth of hunters, farmers and conquerors emerging from the deep German forests. In a study of propaganda in Nazi-era German movies, David Welch (2001) identifies two interpolated themes, namely '*Blut und Boden*' (blood and soil) and '*Volk und Heimat*' (people and homeland). These themes seem paradoxical: while Hitler used the autobahns in order to celebrate his country's modern technological achievements, the focus on the pre-modern remained strong. This paradox points to an intrinsic part of the Nazi ideology, namely linking a mythical past to a modern and expectedly bright future. This is of course a strategy that it shares with several other nation states – both democratic and dictatorial, past and present – but needless to say the ideological implications are not comparable in any way.

The front cover of *Autobahn* can be read as problematic in the sense that it conjures up the very same juxtapositions of modern technology and pre-modern nature that the Nazi regime identified with regard to the autobahns in the 1930s. In fact, it has a direct connection to a genre of propagandist autobahn painting popular in the 1930s. Zeller (2007) provides an example of the genre, which he describes in the following manner:

> The [Nazi] regime obviously saw itself in the form of the [autobahn] as a harmonious coexistence of nature and technology. The road itself in this painting leads into a far distance; in this vision, the autobahn project as a whole stood for a drive toward a modern, fast, and visually attractive future. In that sense, this painting is part of the promise that the roads would not be imposed on the German landscape, but merged with it. (p. 64)

This could easily have been a description of Schult's painting, and represents some of the sentiments of Kraftwerk, who represented the FRG-era autobahn (ironically, satirically or otherwise) in a similar manner. The sleeve not only alludes to an earlier set of autobahn-related myths, but also reflects the everyday realities of the mid 1970s for Kraftwerk. Although symbolically still linked to Hitler, increasing car ownership in the post-war era meant the autobahn came to constitute a major part of the everyday life of the FRG's citizens; the ones using it as a transit network (e.g. to and from Scandinavia, France, Italy, etc.) and later also for tourists. This banality is further amplified in Kraftwerk's stage performances of 'Autobahn'; intermingled with Nazi-era archive footage and Kraftwerk's own artwork are quotidian images of a more recent autobahn that now appears wholly unexceptional, looking like any other highway or motorway in Europe (Hütter and Schneider, 2005).

There are two other important points that should be considered concerning Schult's album cover. First, the naïve style suggests references to comic books and, therefore, a fantastical representation of the autobahn rather than a realist one. In addition, the photos of the four band members (just to the right of the car's steering wheel) inserted into this romanticized comic representation seem to subvert the *mise-en-scène* of the painting, and hint at elements of parody that seem to be lurking just beneath the surface. The second point concerns the potential gendered reading of the cover. It may at first seem too fanciful to suggest the two mountains can be read as a blunt reference to a woman's breasts, while the cars move along a road that represents a masculine technological drive to traverse and explore this landscape.

However, there is an interesting point to be made concerning a long history of implicit and explicit feminized representations of the German landscape in the context of *Heimat*. Blickle (2002) has suggested *Heimat*, as represented in literary and other texts, has often blurred representations of the feminine, nature and landscape, and he provides examples of where *Heimat* and 'male constructs of an ideal woman or mother' (p. 94) are closely connected. There is a possibility that Schult's naïve style is also referencing this gendered narrative and denotes an assumed male–female dichotomy to be found in the opposition between nature and technology.

Kraftwerk, rather than sustaining the nature–technology opposition, seem to place themselves in a space that questions it. Likewise their often camp and sometimes androgynous appearance questioned conventional representations of masculine identity. Zeller (2007), preferring the term landscape to nature, argues that we should be suspicious of the binary formation of landscape and technology, and suggests that

> it is useful . . . to posit landscape and technology not as a pair of opposites, but as a complementary continuum in which humans and nature have made a place for themselves. As David Nye has said: 'Technology is not alien to nature, but integral to it.' Landscapes . . . are not static places, but changing sites where new meanings are constantly emerging. (p. 14)

Kraftwerk appear to be aware of the contingency of the meanings mapped onto the German landscape, and seem to be operating from an indeterminate position on the landscape–technology continuum. The cover of *Autobahn* therefore represents this ambiguity and seems to chime with themes they spoke about in 1975 when they stated that 'you cannot deny technology . . . There was a tendency in the late Sixties to do so, to go back to the country, which is understandable. But technology is still there and you have to face it and live with it' (Townley, p. 20).

In facing up to and living with technology, for a band often represented as technophiles they appear to be surprisingly equivocal in balancing their interests in technology with their emotional responses to it. In 1975 they suggested:

> We are ambivalent about the impersonal nature of modern life . . . On the one hand we are excited by the colossal scale and coldness of modern technology. On the other hand, we can be repelled by it. What we try to do, however, is to stay right in the middle, drawing feelings from both aspects. (Dallas, p. 16)

Furthermore, they also appear to reference irrationalist and Romantic notions of spirituality in discussing their relationship to technology when stating that 'more than movements in music we are rather more aware of the more spiritual movements in general, in art or psychology, science and of course, general technology' (Dallas, p. 16). However, this ambiguity towards new 'general technology' proved problematic for Kraftwerk in the political climate of the FRG. From the mid to late 1970s, the countercultural and oppositional half of this divided society began to develop a 'German phobia about technology that was widespread', and that could be characterized as a 'deep fear of computers' and the associated growth of a surveillance society, and 'nuclear power' (Dany, 2003). Clearly, Kraftwerk's assumed ambiguity concerning nuclear power on *Radio-Activity*, and later a similar ambiguity concerning information and computers on *Computer World*, was at odds with wider fears in the FRG. Alternatively, it could be that Kraftwerk were raising awareness on these issues without proselytizing from a defined political viewpoint. With the later addition of the word 'stop' before 'radio-activity' in performances of the title track of *Radio-Activity*, along with the incorporation of anti-nuclear polemic in their visual projections, all such ambiguity has now lifted.

The Schult cover of *Autobahn*, in an ironic and satirical manner, reflects how Kraftwerk also ambiguously positioned themselves in the context of the FRG's rationalizing technological agenda. Post-war autobahn rationalization and expansion was viewed as important in the extension of the national communication infrastructure, and also symbolically crucial, so that FRG civil engineers could free

the autobahnen from the prefix *Reich-*, to turn them into federal superhighways ('Bundesautobahnen' rather than 'Reichsautobahnen') befitting a federal republic and thus to invoke instrumental rationality rather than the pet project of an unspeakable dictator . . . the autobahn was reduced to the function of an efficient transport machine. (Zeller, 2007, p. 237)

However, it is unclear if Kraftwerk's 'Autobahn' echoes this project of national reclamation, or problematizes it by implicitly and simultaneously alluding to pre-war Nazi propaganda imagery. Kopf (2002) feels that Kraftwerk do neither, and suggests that 'Autobahn' is

[a]s empty as the open road stretching out before it, its most remarkable characteristic is its blankness, its neutrality. The piece is as functional as the Autobahns it describes; as accurate a summary of the joys of driving there is. (pp. 144–5)

Contrary to this, we have to consider the national context within which *Autobahn* was created, and the ironic and satirical edge of Kraftwerk's music that, as previously suggested,was understood differently within the FRG than from the outside. In particular, Dany (2003) indicates that '[t]he Kraftwerk song with the familiar lines 'Wir fahr'n, fahr'n, fahr'n auf der Autobahn' was also an ironic play on the assertion, widespread in West Germany, that 'not everything Hitler did was bad, the Autobahn, for example . . .'

The autobahns and all their problematic connotations were still, in the mid 1970s, symbolically central to how the FRG was viewed by the outside world. Barr indicates they were '[t]he most visible symbol of modern Germany' that were 'a typical example of German efficiency' (1998, p. 83). Bussy (2005) echoes this when describing the link between industrial/economic power and German imagery in *Autobahn*'s cover art. He explains how images of nature are juxtaposed

> against the most potent symbol of the industrial era – the motor car on the motorway. The cover also juxtaposes two symbols of the world-wide economic success of post-war Germany. On the left a big black Mercedes symbolises a rich upper-class form of transport, whilst the white Volkswagen Beetle on the right typifies a mode of transport for the middle and working classes. (p. 55)

Therefore, what we might consider a simple appropriation of historical and contemporary stereotypes was actually a more complex visual strategy, alluding in an ambiguous ironic and/or satirical and/or blank manner to key myths of German identity.

Kraftwerk's strong visual presence – including cover art, films and videos, concert posters, advertisements and stage projections – were all implicated in the construction of the meaning of *Autobahn* by music critics, concert goers, media consumers and the 'listening' audience alike. The consistent combination of the visual and, as we shall see, the auditive create a very strong semiotic chain between Kraftwerk, the autobahns and therefore Germanness.

Autobahn – tracking the unfolding of time

> 'There is no beginning and no end in music . . . Some people want it to end but it goes on'. (Schneider qtd. in Townley, 1975, p. 20)

'Autobahn' is a sonic representation of a journey on the autobahn. The length of the track is 22:43 with large sections featuring highly repetitive and hypnotic grooves. There are two distinct tempi in the track. One around 80 bpm – with a laid-back, funky drum pattern, and one more energetic at approximately 160 bpm giving it a more propelling drive reminiscent of rock rhythms – with some similarities to compatriots Neu!'s *motorik* pulse. The first part of the song – after the intro consisting of car sounds and vocoded voices proclaiming 'Autobahn' – is based on a half-time bass line with a shuffle feel, which together with a half-time 2 and 4 on the snare drum gives the song a slow, rolling effect. Just before [3:20], a short three-note melody – that could be described as the 'roundabout' theme – signals an oncoming change of gear at the intersection of two segments of the track. At [3:20] the drums stop momentarily and a different, more rhythmically dense bass line begins, indicating a doubling of the time feel to roughly 160 bpm. After four bars, at [3:26], heavily phased drums re-enter affirming the new time feel by a propelling 2 and 4 groove at double the original tempo.

At this point, a new melody line enters, played simultaneously on flute by Schneider and electric guitar by Hütter. The electric guitar, played high on the neck with delay, continually echoes and doubles the flute melody and takes turns with the flute in the subsequent melodic improvisations. This section is reminiscent of Hütter and Schneider's earlier music and marks 'Autobahn' as a transitive work in more ways than one. This melodic line is probably the kind of melody, alongside those on earlier albums and on 'Morgenspaziergang' from *Autobahn* that relates to claims (e.g. Hemingway, 2003, p. 32) that they are based on German folk music. This interpretation could simply be a result of the connotations of the flute sound that evokes a certain kind of vague pastoral feeling. However, Kraftwerk's melodies that are often portrayed in this way appear to have further musical connotations. Hütter (qtd. in Gill, 1981), when asked about the 'fragments of Teutonic/Romantic classicism in Kraftwerk's melodies', suggests that these are allusions rather than direct musical quotations:

> I think that's our Germanic background, because we feel a lot of strength in this melodic richness, even though we use very few tones. But we have come up with a lot of harmonic melodies. In a lot of electronic music, there is a taboo about harmonics, so we try to bring certain things into harmony.

Whether Hütter is agreeing with or satirizing Gill's crude ethnic designation of aspects of their music, it is important to note that there are in fact no musical traits that indisputably belong entirely to German folk or 'Teutonic/Romantic' classical music. Potter (1998) makes clear that German composers, critics and musicologists in the nineteenth and twentieth century endeavoured to pin down German musical characteristics in an attempt to better understand the German character and national identity. However,

> [d]espite energetic attempts to isolate tangible German musical traits through race research, comparative studies of folk music, regional

studies, analysis of Gregorian chant, and close investigations of individual composers and their lives, musical Germanness [has] remained
elusive. (p. 200)

Claims concerning Kraftwerk's Germanic allusions therefore need treating
with scepticism.

At [6:38] another segment begins with a repetition of the line from the
original bass line, and the original bass intro re-enters – and with it, the
half-time feel. After four bars, the drums and main melody re-enter, together
with the vocals singing the chorus. At [8:17] a swooping panned synthesizer
sound resembling the Doppler effect of a passing car re-introduces the second
tempo. Now the song enters into a more experimental part, with car sounds,
car horns, and extensive phased electronic drum and percussion fills all
adding to a feeling of controlled frenzy. At [9:09] a new bass riff enters, with
a propelling dotted-quarter-note rhythm. The other embellishments also continue in a rather long stretch that lasts until [13:15], as the original bass line
enters for the third time, with a similar development as the last entering.

At around [14:15], however, a new element emerges. With static radio
noise as a backdrop, a strongly vocoded voice enters representing a broadcast
received on the car radio. The voice sings the song's refrain several times,
which after a while is overlaid by several voices, partly singing, partly proclaiming: 'Wir fahren auf der Autobahn'. The effect is chaotic but also joyful
– as if 'everyone' is joining in on the main refrain. Shortly before [16:00] we
again have a version of the 'roundabout' theme, which ends this section. At
[16:00] and onwards, the tempo slows drastically. Now we hear the voices,
slowly and quietly singing, repeating the refrain with a minimal musical
backing. After a while, the track returns to the 160 bpm feel that runs until
the end of the track.

One of the most interesting facets of the way 'Autobahn' unfolds is how
the two alternating grooves maintain the momentum of the track. The tonal
closures that are invoked in the melodic themes of the track are 'overpowered'
by the groove structures. Therefore, the closure effect on the harmonic level is
balanced by the groove, and especially the way in which the bass riffs propel
the track. The result is one of great listening complexity, which also is one
of the reasons why this 22:43 track does not get boring despite a sense of it
having no end.

When listening to *Autobahn* there are clearly echoes of the avant-garde
and electronic music experiments of Karlheinz Stockhausen broadcast from
the Westdeutscher Rundfunk (WDR) studios in Cologne in the 1950s and
1960s. This was music sponsored by the West German state and occupying
powers to enable the FRG to develop a new *de-Nazified* German musical
identity, and stood in direct Cold War opposition to the populist and anti-
formalist state music policy of the GDR (Kordes, 2002). Conny Plank, who

worked as a sound engineer at the studios in the 1960s, and was co-producer of *Autobahn* as well as Kraftwerk's earlier work, provides a creative link to this music. Hütter (1981) has also indicated that he listened to the WDR broadcasts when growing up, stating, 'We were boys listening to the late-night radio of electronic music coming from WDR in Köln . . . They played a lot of late night programmes with strange sounds and noise'. It was the overtly electronic aspect of the musical soundscape of 'Autobahn' that meant it was viewed by some as a distinctly West German musical statement, though the experimental soundscape of cars and horns has marked similarities to French *musique concrète*.

However, a close listen to the musical material of the song shows how deeply the Anglo-American inspiration had sieved in. The music shows traits such as the half-time shuffle groove that potentially evokes early African-American funk (see Danielsen, 2006). As has also been widely claimed the spectre of the Beach Boys looms large over 'Autobahn' due to the (intentional or coincidental) allusion to the songs 'Fun, Fun, Fun' (1964) and 'Barbara Ann' (1965) in the lyrics, vocal melody and harmonies. However, what isn't usually noted is that it also has segmented and multi-textural structural similarities to the songs 'Good Vibrations' and 'Heroes and Villains' (both 1967).[3] Speaking in 1976, Hütter's passion for the Beach Boys is clear when, in response to a question concerning a Beach Boys concert he and Schneider attended in Los Angeles in 1976, he states in a very fan-like manner:

> Yes, we have seen them in a big stadium. It was gorgeous, like a rebirth. There's a wonderful and very poignant song in their last album, 'Once in my life'. I'd like to dare to say once in my life what Brian Wilson says in that song. (Alessandrini, 1976)

This track, actually titled 'Just Once in My Life' and featuring a Moog synthesizer played by Brian Wilson, was not written by him; it was written by Phil Spector, Carole King and Gerry Goffin for the Righteous Brothers in 1965. Though mistaken about the provenance of the track, Hütter is here clearly demonstrating a predilection for American pop and the Beach Boys that he shared with Schneider.[4] Hütter has indicated that his passion for the band was related to 'the intelligence of their thoughts regarding American reality put onto records' (Alessandrini, 1976). Kraftwerk were clearly aiming to evoke a similar intelligence when they portrayed the everyday reality of the mid 1970s experience of living in the German Bundesrepublik or FRG through 'Autobahn'.

Sound production – the aesthetics of the mix

Another important factor, in addition to the programmatic unfolding of time in 'Autobahn', is the overall production of the song and the spatial dimensions of the mix. In 'Autobahn' the use of reverb and echo/delay is important to consider as they contribute to the creation of a complex sonic environment. Additionally, it is important to analyse how they affected the rhythmic structure of the track, the 'experience of time' and musical timings.

The heavy (and in the context of the 1970s innovative) use of echo/delay in the mix is crucial. It indicated that 'Autobahn' was a highly technological musical artefact that utilized cutting edge creative studio production techniques. Barr (1998) argues that Conny Plank's production work on *Autobahn* is crucial to understanding this. He was for all intents and purposes a collaborator on a par with Emil Schult in the 1970–75 period, and had taught Hütter and Schneider a great deal about the technological dimensions of studio production after working with them on all Kraftwerk's previous albums. Plank later described his role as a producer-engineer, stating:

> I'm more in the function of a medium and not as a creator who has a character and impresses this character on every note. I'm not a musician. I'm a medium between musicians, sounds, and tape. I'm like a conductor or traffic policeman. (Diliberto, 1987)

On *Autobahn*, he *virtually* became a traffic policeman. This arose in his successful attempts to corral the expansive autobahn and car travel themes and ideas, which Hütter and Schneider had recorded onto tape at their Kling Klang studio, into a finished work. Barr (1998) suggests that Plank faced no easy task, as

> [t]he complexity of the track built up over several months of improvisation and featuring several different melodic themes, was one obvious problem. Another was presented by the home-recorded feel of some of the material . . . Plank sat down with Hütter to carve some semblance of order from the mass of ideas, carefully balancing themes and counterpoints until the track conveyed the sense of movement that the group wanted to achieve. Then he set to work on building an astonishingly intricate web of echoes and reverbs around the instrumental parts, providing each sound with its own perfect separate space. (pp. 84–5)

It is difficult to specify exactly how Plank technically undertook this task, but there are clues to how the complexity of the sonic environment of 'Autobahn' came about. Petrus Wippel, an assistant in Plank's studio in the mid 1970s states that

[i]n Conny's hands, a simple tool always turned into a sophisticated instrument . . . [for] instance, a few channels on the [mixing] desk had a quadstick instead of a pan pot, but not because he did many quadraphonic mixes. He used them in his own way: routing the front channels into the main mixing busses while using the back ones to drive an effect such as an echo machine. This way he could pan an instrument left and right, as well as dry and wet, with only one fingertip, thus making a guitar solo fly through time and space during a mixdown session. (Strauss, 2004)

Therefore, it is important bear in mind Plank's 'spatial' production input, and it is also possible to suggest that the feeling of time induced by the use of echo/delay in Plank's production can be read metaphorically. As anyone that has ever driven on the autobahn knows, the road is often constructed by placing concrete blocks one after another, which provides a rhythmic sound each time one drives over it. The resulting sounds become echoes, similar to the sounds one hears as a train carriage passes over a rail track.

In addition, it is important to consider the extensive panning of sounds. Often, during the course of the track, we hear a heavy, almost distorted synthesizer sound that emulates a speeding car (e.g. at 9:48 and 10:00). This effect is achieved by panning the sound (from one speaker to the other) so that a feeling of real physical movement is evoked. In this case it resembles passing cars – either on the left lane of the road (which is the lane in which one overtakes the cars driving in the right lane), on the other side of the road (the opposing traffic), or the sound you can hear if you are taking a break at one of the many autobahn rest stops. The resulting effect adds to the feeling of temporality, as the studio production creates an imagined dynamic autobahn soundscape. In addition the vocoder, which is used most prominently in the part where it emulates the sound of a 1970s car radio playing the song, helps evoke the interior space of the car being driven.

The track's production is therefore important in two ways. First, it is crucial in marking out 'Autobahn' as an innovative electronic music landmark. Second, the production is not simply a matter of providing a hi-tech gloss to the music, but is an integrated feature of the narrative, which Kraftwerk and Plank wove around the notion of autobahn travel. The production of space created by the reverb and echo/delay effects does also have associative links to the fundamental purpose of the autobahn, namely space-time compression.

As we have already noted, the production of 'Autobahn' was the result of a painstaking and complex process utilizing what were at the time cutting edge technologies. The Minimoog synthesizer in particular was central to the construction of many of the band's signature sounds in the track. However, no sequencers or drum machines were used on 'Autobahn', despite the music appearing to have a regular rhythmic quality. The drumming on 'Autobahn' perhaps appeared machinic due to the use of electronic drums and their regularity and disciplined restraint in comparison to the then prevailing jazz and progressive rock stylings. The drums are therefore placed in the realm of controlled and rationalized music-making – both in terms of the very instrument that was being struck and the patterns that were played. It is interesting to note that under analysis the track's supposedly regular rhythms display a large number of tempo fluctuations, though these are not necessarily discernable when listening to the track. Nevertheless, this suggests that the narrative surrounding Kraftwerk as rigid, strict and machine-like in their timing constructs 'truths' about the band that did not exist until later technological innovations enabled them to work in a more precise rhythmic manner. Also, the use of echo/delay effects in creating a rolling sense of time (which is easily discernable in the bass line of the track) can be rather unstable which might have also added to the subtle time changes of the track.

Conclusion

'Autobahn' constitutes an act of world-making: the sounds transform what is a fact into a truth – the term 'truth' meant in a discursive way. We can sum up the facts of Germany in tables and statistics, make charts and track the birth of the autobahn network – but it is Kraftwerk that introduced the autobahn into a discursive truth about Germany in the late twentieth century. 'Autobahn' is how the FRG was expected to sound, and it is how it was expected to look. The metaphor of the 'soundtrack' seems most appropriate here, as it soundtracks a country carrying the burden of its horrific history while inexorably travelling forward. This was not only for itself, but also for its new partners in the Western world. With their use of technology – in itself a modernistic strategy – Kraftwerk had transformed the everyday experiences of an emerging nation and constructed an aesthetic counterpart to the other narratives present in this era of the FRG.

However, it should not be suggested that Kraftwerk simply and transparently deployed national clichés in constructing this narrative. This is clearly a danger if one does not manage to identify the ironic and satirical markers present in Kraftwerk's self-staging. In a critical analysis of music that transforms essentialist national stereotypes and clichés into national emblems, Connell and Gibson (2003) write:

> These appropriations and clichés, while never absolute, present simplified versions of nationhood, and ethnicity that 'stick' in global mediascapes, 'postcard' images that are as much related to national tourist campaigns as they are to sustained local cultures. (p. 126)

Kraftwerk and 'Autobahn' represent clichés of 'Germanness' in a knowing and complex manner. The band reflect on and appear to simultaneously critique the hegemonic values of the FRG and those of the counter/alternative culture, while observing the legacy of the National Socialists in their rear-view mirror. Kraftwerk's 'Autobahn' ironically and satirically balances on the very stereotypes they challenge.

The most important effect that the band's irony and satire has is that of potentially undermining the modernistic forward drive of the FRG through Emil Schult's kitschy painting. However, if we view Schult as representing a merging of *Heimat*/landscape and modernity, it may be productive to consider that Kraftwerk's seeming paean to the autobahn is potentially a shifting of notions of *Heimat* to the autobahn itself. In the FRG, the autobahn has perhaps become for Kraftwerk a further extension of a new technological *Heimat* in addition to their Düsseldorf home. Although this seems a controversial notion, it is clear that Kraftwerk's 'celebration' of the experience of the autobahn is intentionally close to the emotional effect of *Heimat*. This can best be seen through considering Eric Rentschler's statement that

> *Heimat* is an intoxicant, a medium of transport; it makes people feel giddy and spirits them to pleasant places. To contemplate *Heimat* means to imagine an uncontaminated space, a realm of innocence and immediacy. (Rentschler qtd. in Blickle, 2002, p. 148)

There appears little doubt that Kraftwerk similarly represented the autobahn as a trance-inducing space that they partly attempted to reclaim and decontaminate by blurring its National Socialist connections. This was therefore a realm that could once again be experienced as innocent – even if not historically cleansed. This realm also engendered an immediacy of experience that potentially attempted to wrench the FRG away from the troubled past that continually overshadowed Germans. There appeared to be a process of identity reconstruction and renewal that redefined the FRG in opposition to this past in 'Autobahn', while contradictorily alluding to it in the Schult cover. In attempting to define 'the sound of the German Bundesrepublik' Kraftwerk created a soundtrack that could potentially stand in for the FRG's tainted national anthem, and that confidently represented the modernizing, rationalizing and progressive industrial intent of this emerging but fragmented nation. In doing so, they constructed a 'tone-film' (Dallas, 1975, p. 16) that accurately characterized, ironically, satirically or otherwise, the Heimatklänge of the FRG.

The authors would like to thank John Shilcock, Stan Hawkins and Bas Jansen for their help with this chapter.

Notes

1. 'Heimatklänge', meaning the sounds of homeland, is the name of a track on Kraftwerk's pre-*Autobahn* album *Ralf and Florian*.

2. There are in fact two *Autobahn* sleeves: Schult's cover (http://bit.ly/180oLq) and a UK Vertigo version (http://bit.ly/13d9Tt) – featuring a cropped autobahn road sign similar to the cover of the 2009 *The Catalogue* release. Schult recently suggested the UK sleeve was based on a sticker he produced for the German release of the LP (Coulthart, 2009). British record sleeve designer Peter Saville said of the prescient UK sleeve, 'It was my introduction to semiotics and inspired a use of visual codes that I would develop later through Factory Records' (Saville, 2003).

3. The Beach Boys had a significant presence in West Germany in the 1960s. They recorded at least one German-language version of one of their songs – 'In My Room' as 'Ganz Allein (All Alone)' – in an attempt to break into the West German charts before 'Fun, Fun, Fun' reached #49 in April 1964. 'Barbara Ann' proved a major commercial breakthrough (#2, April 1966), later followed by 'Good Vibrations' (#8, January 1967) and 'Heroes and Villains' (#34, October 1967). Brian Wilson's reputation as an auteur-producer was cemented in the complex studio composition of these tracks, edited together from many hours of experimental recording – similar to the recording process of 'Autobahn'. Hütter and Schneider were perhaps also influenced by Wilson's single-minded studio experimentalism. Far from being geographically distant, the Beach Boys actually performed at the Düsseldorf Kongresshalle in December 1968 (see http://www.beachboys-germany.com/index.html).

4. According to Uem (2006), before Kraftwerk, Hütter played in mid 1960s beat bands the Phantoms, the Ramba Zamba Blues Band, and Bluesology who eventually emerged as the pre-Kraftwerk band Organisation (with Florian Schneider). Uem indicates their repertoire was influenced by contemporary Anglo-American pop, rock, jazz and blues music.

References

Alessandrini, P. (1976), 'Haute tension: Kraftwerk'. *Rock & Folk*, November, 54–7. http://www.thing.de/delektro/interviews/eng/kraftwerk/kw11-76.html (last accessed 5 March 2010).

Anderson, B. (1983/1991), *Imagined Communities: Reflections on the Origins and Spread of Nationalism*. (2nd edn). London: Verso.

Bangs, L. (1975), 'Kraftwerkfeature' in L. Bangs and G. Marcus (ed.) (1996), *Psychotic Reactions and Carburetor Dung*. London: Serpent's Tail, pp. 154–60.

Barr, T. (1998), *Kraftwerk: From Düsseldorf to the Future (with Love)*. London: Ebury Press.

Barton, G. (1975), 'Kraftwerk: 2 am Newcastle hotel "We not only try to brainwash people . . . we succeed"'. *Sounds*, 20 September, 22.

Benoit, B. (2007), 'That's all volks: how shrewd marketing helped one man transform German folk music'. *Financial Times*, 14 April, 36.

Blickle, P. (2002), *Heimat: A Critical Theory of the German Idea of Homeland*. Rochester, NY/Woodbridge: Camden House.

Bohn, C. (1981), 'A computer date with a showroom dummy'. *New Musical Express*, 13 June, 31–3.

Burns, R. and van der Will, W. (1995), 'The Federal Republic 1968–1990: from the industrial society to the culture society', in R. Burns (ed.), *German Cultural Studies: An Introduction*. Oxford/New York: Oxford University Press, pp. 257–324.

Bussy, P. (2005), *Kraftwerk: Man, Machine and Music*. (3rd edn). London: SAF.

Connell, J. and Gibson, C. (2003), *Sound Tracks: Popular Music, Identity and Place*, London: Routledge.

Coulthart, J. (2009), 'Who designed Vertigo #6360 620?', *feuillton* [blog post]. http://www.johncoulthart.com/feuilleton/2009/03/03/who-designed-vertigo-6360-620/ (last accessed 5 March 2010).

Dallas, K. (1975), 'Synthetic rockers'. *Melody Maker*, 27 September, 16.

Dalton, S. (2009), 'Album by album: Kraftwerk'. *Uncut*, Take 149, October, 68–71.

Danielsen, A. (2006), *Presence and Pleasure: The Funk Grooves of James Brown and Parliament*. Middletown, CT: Wesleyan University Press.

Dany, H.-C. (2003), 'Ich war eine Glocke'. *Afterall Journal*, (8), Autumn/Winter. http://www.afterall.org/journal/issue.8/ich.war.eine.glocke (last accessed 8 March 2010).

Diliberto, J. (1987) 'Man vs. machine: Conny Plank'. *Electronic Musician*, February. http://emusician.com/em_spotlight/interview_conny_plank/ (last accessed 5 March 2010).

Dirke, S. von (1994), 'New German Wave: an analysis of the development of German rock music'. *German Politics and Society*, 18, (Fall), 64–81.

—— (1997), *All Power to the Imagination!: the West German Counterculture from the Student Movement to the Greens*. Lincoln, NE: University of Nebraska Press.

Doran, J. (2009), 'Karl Bartos interviewed: Kraftwerk and the birth of the modern'. *Quietus*, 11 March. http://thequietus.com/articles/01282-karl-bartos-interviewed-kraftwerk-and-the-birth-of-the-modern (last accessed 3 March 2010).

Durrani, O. (2002), 'Popular music in the German-speaking world', in A. Phipps (ed.), *Contemporary German Cultural Studies*. London: Arnold, pp. 197–218.

Elias, N. (1997), *The Germans*. Cambridge: Polity Press.

Flür, W. (2000), *Kraftwerk: I Was a Robot*. London: Sanctuary Publishing.

Frith, S. (1998), 'Editorial introduction: Popular Music German issue'. *Popular Music*, 17, (3), October, v–vi.

Gellner, E. (1983), *Nations and Nationalism*. Oxford: Blackwell.

Gill, A. (1997), 'Kraftwerk'. *Mojo*, April. http://www.phinnweb.org/krautrock/mojo-kraftwerk.html (last accessed 5 March 2010).

Gill, J. (1981), 'Return of the Kling Klang gang'. *Sounds*, 27 June, 12. http://kraftwerk.technopop.com.br/interview_125.php (last accessed 8 March 2010).

Goldstein, T. (1977), 'Better living through chemistry thanks to Kraftwerk'. *New Musical Express*, 24 December, 37.

Hemingway, D. (2003), 'Tour de force'. *Record Collector*, 290, October, 30–35.

Hobsbawm, E. (1990), *Nations and Nationalism since 1780: Programme, Myth, Reality*. Cambridge: Cambridge University Press.

Hütter, R. (1981), 'Interview', *Beacon Radio, Birmingham, UK* [not Manchester], 14 June.

http://kraftwerk.technopop.com.br/interview_122.php (last accessed on 21 March 2010).

Hütter, R. and Schneider, F. (Prods/Dirs) (2005), *Kraftwerk: Minimum–Maximum*. [DVD]. 336 2949. Kling Klang/EMI.

James, H. (2000), *A German Identity: 1770 to the Present Day*. London: Phoenix.

Johnstone, R. (Prod.) (2008), *Kraftwerk and the Electronic Revolution*. [DVD]. SIDVD541. Sexy Intellectual.

Kettenacker, L. (1997), *Germany Since 1945*. Oxford/New York: Oxford University Press.

Kopf, B. (2002), 'The Autobahn goes on forever', in R. Young (ed.), *Undercurrents: The Hidden Wiring of Modern Music*. London/New York: Continuum, pp. 141–52.

Kordes, G. (2002), 'Darmstadt, postwar experimentation, and the West German search for a new musical identity', in C. Applegate and P. Potter (eds), *Music and German National Identity*. Chicago: University of Chicago Press, pp. 205–17.

Larkey, E. (2000), 'Just for fun? language choice in German popular music'. *Popular Music and Society*, 24, (3), 1–20.

—— (2002), 'Postwar German popular music: Americanization, the cold war, and the post-Nazi *Heimat*', in C. Applegate and P. Potter (eds), *Music and German National Identity*. Chicago: University of Chicago Press, pp. 234–50.

Le Gloannec, A.-M. (1994). 'On German identity'. *Daedalus*, 123, (1), 129–48. *Academic OneFile*. Web. 30 July 2010.

Littlejohn, J. T. (2009), 'Kraftwerk: language, lucre, and loss of identity'. *Popular Music and Society*, 32, (5), December, 635–53.

Lynner, D. and Robbley, B. (1976), 'A conversation with Ralf Hutter and Florian Schneider of Kraftwerk'. *Synapse*, September/October, 10–11. http://www.cyndustries.com/synapse/synapse.cfm?pc=35&folder=sept1976&pic=11 (last accessed 5 March 2010).

Özkırımlı, U. (2000), *Theories of Nationalism: A Critical Introduction*. Basingstoke: Palgrave.

Potter, P. M. (1998), *Most German of the Arts: Musicology and Society from the Weimar Republic to the End of Hitler's Reich*. New Haven and London: Yale University Press.

Saville, P. (2003), 'The inner sleeve: Kraftwerk: Autobahn (Vertigo) 1974 (uncredited designer)'. *The Wire*, 231, May, 89.

Schoenebeck, M. von (1998), 'The new German folk-like song and its hidden political messages'. *Popular Music*, 17, (3), October, 279–92.

Spotts, F. (2002), *Hitler and the Power of Aesthetics*, London: Pimlico.

Strauss, D. (2004), 'German producer Conny Plank defines Krautrock'. *Electronic Musician*, 1 August. http://emusician.com/remixmag/artists_interviews/musicians/remix_conny_plank/index.html (last accessed 5 March 2010).

Townley, R. (1975), 'Germany's Kraftwerk: metal of the road'. *Rolling Stone*, 3 July, 20.

Trudgeon, M. (1981), 'Interview: Ralf Hütter'. *Fast Forward*, December. http://kraftwerk.technopop.com.br/interview_120.php (last accessed 5 March 2010).

Uem, M. van (2006), 'Zum 60. Geburtstag von Ralf Hütter'. *die Heimat*, 77, 94–5. http://www.heimat-krefeld.de/website/dieheimat/2006/77_2006_gesamt/094-095_4c.pdf (last accessed 5 March 2010).

Welch, D. (2001), *Propaganda and the German Cinema 1933–1945*. London/New York: I.B. Tauris Publishers.

Welsch, W. (1996), 'Modernity and postmodernity in post-war Germany', in R. Pommerin (ed.), *Culture in the Federal Republic of Germany, 1945–1995*. Oxford/Washington, DC: Berg, pp. 109–32.

Zelko, F. (2006), 'Introduction', in *From Heimat to Umwelt: New Perspectives on German Environmental History*. Bulletin, Supplement. Washington, DC: German Historical Institute. http://webdoc.sub.gwdg.de/ebook/serien/p/ghi-dc-bu-supp/supp3.pdf (last accessed 5 March 2010).

Zeller, T. (2007), *Driving Germany: The Landscape of the German Autobahn*. Oxford/New York: Berghahn Books.

2

Kraftwerk and the Image of the Modern

David Cunningham

The culture of Central Europe was cut off in the thirties, and many of the intellectuals went to the USA or France, or they were eliminated. We are picking it up again where it left off, continuing this culture of the thirties, and we are doing this spiritually.

(Ralf Hütter)[1]

Among the most striking images produced by Kraftwerk, the 1978 album cover *The Man-Machine* has acquired a particularly iconic status. Four dark-haired men, uniformly dressed in red shirts and black ties, stand in line on the stairs of what appears a rather non-descript European apartment block. Yet, if the photograph belongs alongside the front covers of *Meet the Beatles* or the Ramones' first album in its power to present what Pascal Bussy calls 'the corporate mentality of the group as one whole' (1993, p. 101), its aesthetic is very different from the canonical rock 'n' roll image of the group as street gang projected by the contemporaneous image of the Ramones. The typography of *The Man-Machine*'s cover is all sharp angles; on its reverse face, simple architectonic geometric shapes float downwards in an abstract space across a stark white background, while, running at a contrary axis to its main text, the album's title is reproduced in Russian, French and German as well as in English.

The Man-Machine's design is, the inside sleeve informs us, 'inspired by El Lissitzky'. A Jewish Russian artist who was instrumental in the suprematist and constructivist movements that flourished in the immediate years following the 1917 Revolution, El Lissitzky was educated as an architectural engineer in Germany, where he would later serve as a cultural ambassador and exert a considerable influence on the Bauhaus. *The Man-Machine*'s restricted colour scheme of black, white, grey and red visually alludes to the 1919 poster *Beat the Whites with the Red Wedge*, a Bolshevik propaganda work produced during the Russian Civil War; the back cover's geometric, cuboid shapes are most reminiscent of his later, more purely abstract 3D forms called *Prouns*. Emblematic of the short-lived hopes for an International Constructivism that would embrace the new artistic and political possibilities of mass media, for El Lissitzky, the task of the modern artist was to construct 'a new symbol': 'not a recognizable form of anything that is already finished, already made, or already existent in the world' but 'a symbol of a new world' (Tupitsyn, 1999, p. 9).

Such a will to image a new world is rightly thought to be the most basic of modernist imperatives, and few artists of the late twentieth century have so emphatically or radically embraced such modernism as Kraftwerk. The desire to be 'absolutely modern' has seemingly functioned as *the* defining axiom of their career. Yet as the 'inspiration' provided for *The Man-Machine* indicates, the specific articulation of the modern generated by their work remains a complex one, tied up with a return to past motifs as much as with a creative destruction of the 'old', and with the ongoing, if discontinuous, legacies of twentieth-century European history as a whole. In part this is a function of what Theodor Adorno termed the aging of the modern, the recognition that the modern has acquired a history of its own that each new artwork must negotiate. But, more immediately, the will here to pick up again – 'where it left off' – some part of such a history, with its concomitant emphasis on the *recovery* of a lost, or at least catastrophically interrupted, central European culture of pre-war modernism, serves to identify Kraftwerk with a number of German artists working, across a range of media, from the mid 1960s.

As John Patterson puts it, for such a post-war generation, seeking to reinvent a cultural identity in the wake of Auschwitz, there was little choice but to assume the role of representatives of an artistic 'culture with no fathers (except the Nazis), only grandfathers (Murnau, Pabst, Lang)' (2004).[2] From New German Cinema's declaration that 'Papa's cinema is dead' to the search for pre-World War II artistic models in the works of artists from Bernd and Hilda Becher to Alexander Kluge, this motif of a 'fatherless' generation dominates much German culture of the 1960s and 1970s. In Hütter's own words:

> In the war Germany was finished, everything wiped out physically and also mentally. We were nowhere. The only people we could relate to, we had to go back 50 years into the '20s . . . But now with our generation it has begun again, with the films of Fassbinder, Herzog and Wenders or the writing of Peter Handke . . . we certainly represent the generation with no fathers. We have nobody to listen to, no old wise men or anything. We have to impose every question on ourselves and try to find the correct answer. (qtd. in Bohn, 1981)

Hütter's recollection of working out of a generational situation of total 'cultural emptiness' (2003) is emblematic, in this way, of a far more generalized feeling of inhabiting some *Nullpunkt* or *Stunde Null* (Year Zero) in post-war German culture. The fundamental question faced in a post-Auschwitz society of 'what it means to identify oneself as a German, what it means to say "*ich*" and "*wir*" in a Germany that still finds itself under the shadow of the Holocaust' becomes a search for what Eric Santer has usefully termed such 'stranded objects' as might yet be recollected from 'a cultural inheritance fragmented and poisoned by an unspeakable horror' (1990, p. xiii). As Arthur Danto writes of Kraftwerk's fellow Düsseldorf artist Gerhard Richter,

> [h]ow to be an artist in postwar Germany was part of the burden of being a German artist in that time, and this had no analogy in artistic self-consciousness anywhere else in the West. Especially those in the first generation after Nazism had to find ways of reconnecting with Modernism while still remaining German. (2002)

The singular *modernity* of this moment is one that must therefore be characterized, simultaneously by a look backwards to a series of modernist 'grandfathers' of the 1920s and 1930s (from the Bauhaus and early Frankfurt School to Lang, Döblin or Brecht) and a uniquely radicalized forward drive to some new beginning in European art.

In stressing their origins within this epochal moment, Hütter thus serves to frame Kraftwerk's own modernist practice in very specific ways. On the one hand, at the level of musical form itself, Kraftwerk's major works of the 1970s conform to, and acquire their intelligibility from, that general temporal logic of the 'new' which defines the meaning of the modern in its most basic sense. That is, they gain their meaning *as* modern from their dynamic relation to past works, through a determinate negation of what precedes them – most obviously, both the increasingly stagnant conventions of a dominantly Anglo-American rock or popular music of the late 1960s and those hegemonic forms of electronic 'art music' constituted within a post-serialist conjuncture by the likes of Karlheinz Stockhausen. At the same time, however, Kraftwerk's own articulation of this modernity, at the level of its accompanying *image* – both, that is, the music's minimal and montage-like lyrical content and the multi-faceted visual forms through which it is 'presented' – is more often than not dependent upon a certain non-synchronous reactivation of those stranded objects made up of *past* visual and conceptual motifs drawn from a specifically 1920s European culture.

The conjunction of these two enunciations of the modern can be observed in that complex repetition and re-functioning of *pre-war* motifs as a means of intervening within a specifically *post-war* cultural field, given an added geo-cultural dimension in its self-consciously European reworking of an essentially North American history and vocabulary, and emphasized, at the level of image, through a stripping away of the hegemonic signifiers of existing 'rock' culture. An obvious example here would be Hütter's adoption of a conception of the artist as technician drawn from the pre-war Bauhaus, El Lissitzky and productivism: 'We are not artists nor musicians. First of all we are workers [*arbeiter*]' (Bussy, 1993, p. 138). As *image* this is actualized in the group's favoured visual presentations from the mid 1970s onwards – a publicity shot for *Radio-Activity* (1975) has them posed in a nuclear power station wearing white lab coats – while *musically* it is given substance in their seemingly detached, 'deadpan' modes of expression and machine-led forms. The use of drum machines or sequencers as drivers of musical production is rendered equivalent to the 1920s 'New Vision' affirmation of Rodchenko's and Moholy-Nagy's photography, which realizes a fittingly 'machine age' objectivism and assault on Romantic sentimentality and decadent excess. If such a critique of 'the bourgeois concept of the artist' (Hütter qtd. in Barr, 1998, p. 138) self-consciously *repeats* an earlier attack on the subjectivist 'irrationalism' of early expressionism carried out by the more 'objectivist' avant-garde movements of the 1920s, it is also fundamentally *altered*, via its 1970s reinscription, not in relation to that earlier moment itself but as a determinate negation of a post-Dylan, post-Beatles, 'rockist' idea of the musician as expressive virtuoso, countercultural rebel or Romantic troubadour. What thus presents itself as a specific effacing of any gap between musician/composer on the one side and studio engineer/producer on the other simultaneously re-asserts, in relation to a very different context, the productivist demand of the 1920s to overcome the division between art objects and practices and those objects and practices characteristic of quotidian productive life itself.

As such examples suggest, these two aspects of their embrace of the 'modern' are especially apparent in Kraftwerk's use and presentation of advanced technology, both as practical means of musical production and as source of imagery in itself. Certainly, few artists have so consistently conceived of their own artistic logic in terms of its immanent engagement with the latest means of musical production. As Bussy comments, '[i]n effect, advances in recording technology would become the *raison d'etre* of the group's existence' (1993, p. 26). Yet, after *Autobahn* (1974), if not before, the power of the technological object as everyday emblem of a wider mass culture of modernity has played an equally pivotal role in their art: the car and motorway, radio and power station, the train, robot, computer. If this has frequently entailed a retrieval, too, of that fascination with the liberatory, democratizing possibilities of technology displayed by a pre-war modernist culture, then it also finds itself necessarily confronting the ambiguous character of such fascination in the context of German history in particular. But before we come to this, a little more needs to be said of what might be understood by the terms 'modern' and 'modernism'.

The music of modern life

As Tim Barr puts it, the 'thrill of the new is an integral part of pop culture's charm' (1998, p. 63). Nonetheless, how such affirmation of the new relates to what is customarily signified by the term *modernism* remains a difficult question. If nothing else, Kraftwerk's self-conscious references to, and borrowings from, a modernist culture of the twenties and thirties necessarily raise the question of in what an actual modernist *pop* music might consist of.

Such an issue has a particular resonance at the high point of Kraftwerk's career, insofar as it operates against the post-war backdrop of an increasing codification, both inside and outside of the academy, of an understanding of modernism that associated it precisely with the insistence on some fundamental boundary between so-called high culture and mass or popular culture. Reified in the form of an *ideology* of modernism, as Fredric Jameson terms it, constructed around the supposed 'autonomy of the aesthetic' (2002, p. 161), this conception was largely a belated 'product of the Cold War' period itself, which spelled, in the wake of Nazism, 'the end of a whole era of social transformation and indeed of Utopian desires and anticipations' that the likes of El Lissitzky had once reflected (p. 165). As Jameson points out, while this post-war ideology thus had as its aim the separation of 'art from non-art' – 'by purging it of its extrinsic elements, such as the sociological or the political; by reclaiming aesthetic purity from the morass of real life' – its simultaneous condition was also 'a radical dissociation' of the 'aesthetic', as identified with 'this or that type of daily life', from 'high culture' as such; an 'operation', he argues, that fully took place 'historically only at the very beginning of the television age' (pp. 176–7).

Unsurprisingly, more recent attempts to counter such a straightforward opposition have taken place in part, then, through the recovery of a number of pre-World War II models, which, far from attempting to sever any links between 'high' and 'low', laid great emphasis precisely on the capacity of new art forms to intervene within the terrains of mass culture and modern everyday life. Certainly this is a key aspect of not only Kraftwerk's retrieval of figures such as El Lissitzky but also of a far more general emphasis on art's immersion in the everyday that runs throughout their work:

> We just find everything we do on the streets. The pocket calculator we find in the department stores. The autobahn we find in the first five years of our existence, when we travelled 200,000 kilometres on the autobahn in a grey Volkswagen. So everything is like a semi-documentary. 'Autobahn' we made with the image that one day our music would come out of the car radio. (Hütter qtd. in Gill, 1981)

Technologically, this is manifested in a fascination with the modern mass-produced *object* as everyday image. But it also places emphasis on the everyday nature of the technological means of production of the actual music itself. Technology is thus both an object of the everyday and, for the artist as engineer-constructor, a means of reflecting on and intervening within it. In Hütter's words, 'When we started, electronics were either science-like – university, big academic titles – or space programmes. Our thing was always to incorporate from everyday life' (Toop, 1995, p. 204).

If this notion of modern(ist) art as bearing a 'semi-documentary' relation to the social and technological forms of quotidian modernity continues, then, to look back to and extend the ideas of constructivism, it thus also re-engages something of the conditions under which a recognizable concept of modernism first seems to have emerged in the work of the poet Charles Baudelaire during the mid nineteenth century – specifically, in his description, and crucially *affirmation*, of those modes of experience and time consciousness associated with *modernité*. Socially and culturally, far from 'reclaiming aesthetic purity from the morass of real life' (Jameson, 2002, p. 176), this connects what Baudelaire (1964) refers to as the 'special nature of present-day beauty' (p. 13) to the acceleration of social and technological changes during the nineteenth century: industrialization, new technologies of information, travel and communication. What Baudelaire calls the 'painting of modern life' has thereby both the quality of *being modern*, of being 'new' in a fundamental, historical sense, and of in some way immanently registering, within itself, those rhythms of movement and ceaseless change that characterize modernity in general.

It is not hard to conceive of Kraftwerk's work as a kind of music of modern life in something like this Baudelairean sense. The group's fixation not only on the production of qualitatively new musical works that would be themselves driven formally by advances in technology, but also on the artistic mediation of specifically modern everyday forms of social and technological *experience* would seem to place them squarely, and self-consciously, within such a tradition. Hence, the characteristic ways in which Hütter theorizes the 'travelling form' of much of Kraftwerk's music:

> Just keep going . . . In our society everything is in motion. Electricity goes through the cables and people – bio-units – travel from city to city. At one point they meet and then – *phwiit*. Why should music be at a standstill? (Toop, 1995, p. 202)

Formally, from 'Autobahn' onwards, this conception manifests itself in a musical form predominantly built around patterns of repetition constructed through the layering of short sequences of material (whether arpeggiated chords, 'riff-like' bass lines, or more abstract textures of electronic sound) which, liberated from the standard verse-chorus structures of 1960s pop, generates an impression of potentially infinite development (signalled in the titles of pieces such as 'Europe Endless' [1977] or 'Musique Non-Stop' [1986]). While tracing the evolution of such a form across Kraftwerk's work certainly suggests a debt to the minimalist music of American composers Terry Riley and Steve Reich, and to the increasingly extended works of rock groups like the Velvet Underground, Kraftwerk's 'travelling form' and use of repetition more explicitly connects such musical forms to specifically *social* forms, and hence suggests some homology between the two. (It is such a correlation that is, for example, also roughly indicated by the use of the term *motorik* to describe the distinctive musical structure and motorway-like experience produced by the music of their fellow Düsseldorf group, Neu!) This is further signified with an almost deliberate crudity (as judged according to conventional aesthetic criteria) by the incorporation of directly mimetic 'everyday' sounds into the structure of such pieces – the radio static of *Radio-Activity*, the engine and car horn noises that punctuate 'Autobahn', the electronic bleeps of 'Pocket Calculator', the synthesized moving train and bicycle-chain sounds used as rhythm tracks for 'Trans-Europe Express' and 'Tour de France' – which recall pieces such as Arseny Avraamov's *Symphony Of Sirens* (1922), composed using actual factory sirens, artillery fire, ships' horns and steam locomotives. Here the new soundworlds generated by machinery and technology function, above all, as a means of mediating fundamentally new modes of *social* experience within the very form of the music itself.[3] That is to say, they are 'modern' in the simple sense of identifying within the present those things that are 'new' (and as such representative of a modern life where 'everything is in motion') and making them constitutive of the artwork's *own* historical meaning and value.

It is such a desire to 'speak about our experiences' of 'industrial life, of modern life', at the level of new musical form itself which 'picks up again', then, the avant-garde ambition to melt artistic forms into the forms of the everyday. As Hütter puts it, 'the artistic world does not exist outside of daily life, it is not another planet' (Bussy, 1993, p. 88). Yet it is equally important to recognize that the re-functioning of such conceptions under the radically changed conditions of a post-war German capitalist culture simultaneously requires their fundamental *transformation* – not least because it attempts to redeem the promise of a modernist art that would 'attend us everywhere that life flows' (Gabo and Pevsner, 2000, p. 400) precisely on the terrain of post-war mass culture as such. An early twentieth-century conception of an art for which the 'streets are our brushes, the squares our palettes', as the Russian poet Mayakovsky once famously declared, thus becomes here an art forged around a new and ever more technologized post-war world of electronic media and computer networks – a modernity of 'time, travel, communication, entertainment' as 1981's 'Computer World' would have it – that must operate from inside the very mass cultural spaces of Jameson's television age.

The past as image

There are a number of obvious reasons why the Cold War ideology of aesthetic modernism should have, in the period immediately prior to Kraftwerk's emergence, assumed a particularly strong significance in Germany. As Danto (2002) argues, the first generation after Nazism had to find ways of reconnecting with modernism. In the new Federal Republic of Germany the drive to purge art of 'its extrinsic elements, such as the sociological or the political' assumed a particular importance, where 'the political' was associated, above all, with the Nazi past (or, increasingly, with the form of Stalinist communism being established in the German Democratic Republic, Germany's other post-war half). The modernism to which key post-war German institutions – such as Documenta, the modern art exhibition established in 1955 in Kassel, or what came to be known, in music, as the Darmstadt School – thus sought to reconnect was, unsurprisingly, a thoroughly 'depoliticized' one, grounded in modes of formalist abstraction.

It is against this backdrop that Kraftwerk's network of imagistic allusions must be understood: the attempt to reconnect with a very different cultural politics. In general terms, this is the terrain of what their contemporary Peter Bürger terms the *neo*-avant-garde (1984, pp. 53–4);[4] the tendency of post-war North American and western European artists to reprise 'such avant-garde devices of the 1910s and 1920s as collage and assemblage, the readymade and the grid' (Foster, 1996, p. 5). Certainly, while Kraftwerk may, from the mid 1970s at least, have operated within an apparently very different socio-cultural sphere to the likes of Daniel Buren or Hans Haacke, they undoubtedly shared a similar desire to locate 'historical alternatives to the modernist model dominant at the time' (p. 5). Yet, equally, this is where Kraftwerk's reworkings of such 'practices' on the terrain of pop music, and hence on the new media landscapes of mass culture, also assumes a crucial importance, insofar as, far from being a mere 'passive repetition' of some pre-war moment, they must thereby of necessity '*act* on the historical avant-garde' in significantly new ways (p. 4).

While Hal Foster discusses this 'retroactive effect' via the Freudian concept of *nachträglichkeit*, one might equally, given its extraordinary resonance within the late 1960s German Left, understand this in terms of the production of what Benjamin, writing on the eve of World War II, called a particular constellation of the 'Now' and 'Then'. Famously, in his posthumously published 'Theses on the Concept of History', Benjamin proposes a reconception of historical materialism organized around the concepts of *Jetztzeit* ('now-time') and of the past as 'image' (1992, 245–55). But, in broader (if looser) terms, Benjamin's 'constellation' attests to what Peter Szondi describes as a characteristic 'hope in the past' in general (see Leslie, 2000, p. 78) – not as simple backwards-looking nostalgia, but as a resource for past *futural* possibilities that were never actualized. In the context of a post-war German culture in which an earlier modernist history had not merely dissipated or 'failed' but had been brutally suppressed and ultimately erased, such hope evidently took on a very particular force. As in Benjamin's own work, technology plays a central role here:

> To revisit the past from the perspective of the now ... is undertaken because a return to the past will determine for us what has been lost, what has been betrayed and also what is yet possible, given the resources of *Technik* [technology/technique] ... [T]he act of interpretation, a reconstruction of what has been, formulates the possibility for change, by making the potential for transformation appear latent ... A political encounter with the past involves the theoretical re-encounter with initially utopian and progressive tendencies contained within technology. (Leslie, 2000, pp. 79–80)

Without straining the comparison *too* far, at the level of cultural politics (if not of actual revolutionary politics as such) it is, then, something like this encounter that would be articulated in Hütter's own will to the 'recovery' of an unrealized modernism as interruptive image:

> [V]isions and memories synchronise together and I think certain things from a little way back look more towards the future than things which are pseudo-modern today. The real modernism may be somewhere else, a different way to what we think is modern. (Barr, 1998, p. 127)

As a 'neo-avant-garde' practice, this has less to do with the kind of negative, anarchic thrust of the Dadaist attack on the 'institution of art' than with the recovery of that more 'utopian' and affirmative vision of the modern associated with the Bauhaus or elements of constructivism:

> To be able to feel any bonds at all, we had to go back to the Bauhaus school. It sounds strange but to continue into the future we had to take a step back forty years. The Bauhaus idea was to mix art and technology. An artist is not an isolated creature that creates for the sake of creation, but as part of a functional community. In the same way we are a kind of musical workers. The spirit of Bauhaus in electronic sounds. (p. 74)

If Kraftwerk seek to recover the avant-garde ambition to dissolve artistic forms into the forms of the everyday, they do so in terms of the desire for an art newly 'adapted to our world of machines, radio and fast cars', to cite Gropius, the first director the Bauhaus (Curtis, 1982, p. 309). Most profoundly, this looks to reconnect artistic technique to *Technik* at the level of the immanent logics of musical production, in a manner which may be indebted to the ideas of productivism or Benjamin and Brecht, but which is instantiated in a fundamentally new form.

As image, then, technology functions as a means of mediation between the histories of (artistic) modernism and those of (social and cultural) modernity. And it is certainly true that, at least prior to *Computer World* – in which the engagement with modernity moves in the direction of a far more immaterial world of 'business, numbers, people, money' – the use of technology as *image* tends to rely in Kraftwerk's works on a certain effect of anachronism: a characteristic combination of 'the newness of their musical ideas' with 'images, pictures and industrial design from a bygone age' (Bussy, 1993, p. 69). Such images – the car, train, power station – tend themselves to belong to an already 'outmoded' pre-computer era in which the machine as *object* was itself figurable in directly visual ways. This is 'the moment of futurism and of an excitement with the streamlined machines – the motorcar, the steamship, the airplane, the turbines and grain elevators and oil refineries of what Reyner Banham has called the "first machine age" . . . [in which] the energies of a now older capital seemed to have manifested themselves in visible, tangible, emblematic forms of a whole new object world in emergence, a whole new future already in view' (Jameson, 1998, p. 83).

Yet the use of such images in Kraftwerk is far from reflecting any simple *nostalgia* for the bygone; nor does it provide the basis for 'postmodern' pastiche. For its intent is not in fact primarily revivalist but rather entails an attempt to retrieve those 'initially utopian and progressive tendencies' contained within technology (Leslie, 2000, p. 80); the 'energies' of 'a whole new future' occluded by the forgetful nature of post-war West German consumer society. This is why it is the *constellation* of a 'Now' – the 1970s of post-war German consumer capitalism – and a specific 'Then' – the 1920s of avant-gardism and 'the first machine age' – that assumes such importance, since it is the conjunction of a past democratic and liberatory conception of the fusion of art and technology with a very contemporary use of *new* technologies of musical production that, above all, matters here.

Industrielle Volksmusik

Decried as 'un-German' by the Nazis, and regarded as a front for communist subversion, Hütter's assertion of Kraftwerk's affinity to the Bauhaus is of course itself political, once viewed through the lens of a post-war capitalism that was apparently as anxious to bury such past leftist currents of German culture as it was to erase its more immediate Nazi history. Yet this is not without its own forms of historical complexity. For if the Bauhaus idea 'to mix art and technology' constitutes one side of Germany's pre-war affirmation of 'modernity', this should not deflect from the extent of fascism's own involvements with the technologies and mass spaces of the 'modern'. Indeed, although official Nazi policy apparently privileged neoclassicism or the kitschy conservatism of *völkisch* vernacular, in other respects – from its engagement with new technologies of the masses in radio and film to the construction of the autobahns – its 'participation' in modernity was considerable:

> The human/machine interpenetration, the industrialized eye, is not abandoned in Nazi propaganda practice, despite their reinvention of a nostalgic nineteenth-century aesthetic in the realm of high art, and their ideological promotion of rural values . . . Its aesthetics respond to the changes in perception wrought by new technologies. Fascism acts upon the new machino-anthropos. (Leslie, 2000, pp. 162–3)

If Kraftwerk's search for historical alternatives to the modernist model dominant at the time is what propels their 'hope in the past' invested in the Bauhaus or international constructivism, their simultaneous refusal simply to *repress* Germany's more immediate and irredeemable past in Nazism – a refusal characteristic of a radicalized late 1960s and 1970s German youth culture in general – complicates any neat retrieval of an alternative modernist culture, particularly when resituated within the post-war spaces of capitalist mass culture itself. In this regard, Kraftwerk are scarcely unique. As Santer observes, the importance of film within German artistic culture of the period may, in part, have been because of 'the particular significance of the medium of film in the successes of German fascism to mobilize and sustain collective fantasies'. At the very least, this rendered cinema itself a highly charged and 'ambiguous site' (1990, p. xiii). Kraftwerk's movement away from the relatively constricted worlds of semi-academic electronic art music or experimental improvisation, and towards the cultural space of pop, similarly entailed a confrontation with mass culture's developments of forms of spectacle and the new media technologies underpinning them.

   Radio-Activity (1975) marks the group's engagement with some of these legacies most clearly. Utilizing established modernist techniques of collage on short tracks like 'News', alongside both disorientatingly abstract synthetic noises, and their developing mastery of pop form on the title track and (Beach Boys-indebted) 'Airwaves', the LP instantiates, in an entirely new form, Benjamin's observation that the 'mass is a matrix from which all traditional behaviour toward works of art issues today in a new form' (1992, p. 231). Yet, set in the context of German history, this fascination with radio's power as emblematic of a technology of information and mass communication also had, as Benjamin well knew, a rather more sinister potential. As overseen by Hitler's minister of propaganda, Joseph Goebbels, radio was explicitly deployed as a means of enforcing and sustaining Nazi political and cultural hegemony. In this light it is not immaterial (or untypical) that Kraftwerk's choice of radio set for the album's cover, as symbolically everyday, 'pop' technological image, should be one developed under the direction of Goebbels himself: a short-wave device designed to prevent the listener from receiving broadcasts from beyond Germany. The removal of the swastikas that would originally have adorned the set attests to the force of the post-war erasure of the troubling history lying behind the contemporary 'economic miracle' of West Germany's technological present.

As an image of modernity, this is therefore profoundly ambiguous. Similarly, while Kraftwerk's affirmation of the *menschmaschine* may primarily have been drawn from the Bauhaus and constructivism, even before the rise of Nazism in the 1930s the development of a veritable machine *aesthetic* belonged as much to the politically reactionary modernism of the Italian futurists or Wyndham Lewis's vorticists as to the Soviet productivists, Vertov, Picabia or Duchamp. Certainly, a figure like Marinetti found a ready audience among Germany's avant-gardes on both Left and Right during the 1910s and 1920s for his proto-fascist affirmation of war, 'the world's only hygiene', as much as for his celebration of 'the beauty of speed' (2009, pp. 21–2). A little later, Ernst Jünger, who, in books such as *Der Arbeiter* ['The Worker'] (1932), would go on to propound visions of a future state overseen by 'steel-nerved automatons', developed an indigenous German cult of the *menschmaschine*, derived in part from his experiences during the First World War (see Neaman, 1999). And while Jünger was at worst a fellow traveller of Nazism, never belonging to the party itself, the form taken by his specific brand of reactionary modernism at the very least serves to indicate that fascism's own relation to 'the modern' was, as a number of recent studies have shown, rather more complex than was once supposed (Hewitt, 1996; Griffin, 2007).

Something of this complexity is captured in Hütter's handwritten sign, pinned to a bedroom wall in the opening sequence of Chris Petit's first film, *Radio On* (1979):

> We are the children of Fritz Lang and Werner von Braun. We are the link between the '20s and the '80s. All change in society passes through a sympathetic collaboration with tape recorders, synthesisers and telephones. Our reality is an electronic reality.

From one perspective, the by now familiar conception here of a direct link between the 'Then' of the 1920s and the 'Now' of the 1980s might apparently work to bypass the Nazi era altogether. Yet the specific and deliberate citation of Lang and von Braun as parental figures for such a contemporary 'second nature' of technology, to use a favoured term of Benjamin, simultaneously indicates the difficulties entailed by this.

Fritz Lang's *Metropolis* (1927) – a constant reference point throughout *The Man-Machine* – is exemplary. While the half-Jewish Lang would himself go into American exile during the 1930s, its co-writer, Lang's then wife Thea von Harbou, would join the Nazi party in 1932 and become an enthusiastic propagandist for its regime. Moreover, the film itself, which has as its central iconic figure the female *Maschinenmensch* made by the inventor Rotwang, would come to be regarded by many later German critics, notably Siegfried Kracauer, as implicated in the emergent aesthetics of fascism (just as, much later, it would feed into the Hollywood-produced consumerist spectacles of *Star Wars* and other films).[5] If Lang is thus an ambiguous 'grandfather' for Kraftwerk, this is even more the case with von Braun. Hitler's chief rocket designer, responsible for the design of the V-2, after the war von Braun was one of those key German scientists taken to the United States as part of Operation Paperclip, going on to oversee the development of the technology that would ultimately result in NASA's 1969 moon landing.

It is not too much of a stretch to connect Hütter's citation of von Braun, with its implicit reference to the continuation of German wartime technology into Cold War capitalist production, with Kraftwerk's earlier fascination with the autobahn. In contrast to most of the approved neo-classical or pastiche medievalist architecture of the Third Reich, the autobahn was often strikingly modern in its design. (The Bauhaus's final pre-war Director, Mies Van Der Rohe, was among those who submitted designs for its bridges and service stations.) This had a wider cultural dimension, summarized by Hans-Jürgen Syberberg in his book *Die freudlose Gesellschaft*:

> We have become accustomed to smiling at the question of 'Hitler and Art' or relegating Nazi architecture, painting, literature or music to the second rank by comparison with the artistic avant-garde . . . [But one] can also see the artistic will of the Third Reich in quite other places, for example in the layout of its *autobahns* . . . [T]hey are the modern roads and arteries of a country which Hitler conceived of as a total artwork . . . [that] radiate[s] out across the landscape of mass industrial society. (cited Lacoue-Labarthe, 1990, pp. 62–3)

Significantly, Syberberg goes on to suggest a connection here with the Nazi fascination with the new technology of film itself, as, in some sense, the specifically techno-artistic actualization of a means of constructing, and *moulding* a mass audience.

Yet, far from repressing these resonances, and their own disturbing marriage of art, mass culture and technology, Kraftwerk's imagery for the *Autobahn* album rather subtly invokes them. Indeed Emil Schult provided a painting for the cover, the slightly kitschy pop pastoralism of which deliberately seems to recall Ernst von Demar's publicity images for the new KdF-Wagen (or Volkswagen) – KdF (*Kraft durch Freude*) stands for 'strength through joy' – made at the end of the 1930s: a sleek modern machine passing swiftly, via the autobahns, through Germany's natural landscape. In fact, it is the image of the Volkswagen, the technological object that derived from Hitler's instruction to Ferdinand Porsche in 1934 to design a mass-produced 'people's car' *for* the masses, and which is shown disappearing into the distance on *Autobahn*'s cover, that perhaps best encapsulates the complex historical, social and cultural contradictions at stake. First, because the Volkswagen perfectly emblematizes the contested histories of Germany's own cultural perceptions of new technology in the 1930s *and* their continuation into the post-war era. Second, because as a car for the *people*, the *volk*, it marks the complex histories of European attempts to make cultural and aesthetic sense of mass production and mass culture. Certainly it is hard not to hear Hütter and Schneider's favoured definition of their music as *industrielle Volksmusik* as containing an implicit allusion to the industrial *volk* of Volkswagen production.

Yet, like the 'folk car', the concept of *industrielle Volksmusik* is also an inherent contradiction, insofar as it is the very forces of industrial production that destroy the world of the *volk*; transforming it instead into that of the masses. The Bauhaus, for example, was often pulled between a desire to look back to and reinvent the 'folk' traditions of craft for a newly technologized 'mass' world, in opposition to the alienating effects of capitalist production, and an embrace of the destructive (and thereby creative) energies of such production. As much to the point, it is this that also defines the contrary pushes and pulls intrinsic to the development of pop music: a form born from the vanishing traditions of American folk music and the blues, but born into, and propelled by, the modernity of the industrial dynamics of mass commercial production and the new media landscapes of consumer culture.

In a 1991 interview, Hütter notes: 'We woke up in the late '60s and realised that Germany had become an American colony. There was no German identity, no German music, nothing . . . The young people were into the American way of living; cars, hamburgers and rock 'n' roll' (Barr, 1998, p. 74). While a fear of Americanization was common to much of post-imperial western Europe, it was felt far more profoundly in cities such as Düsseldorf, which was 'home to thousands of US and British troops . . . German radio was very quick to pick up on rock 'n' roll from the start . . . Like Japan, West Germany after the war was showered with so much aid that the culture of the aid-bringers inevitably left some pretty hefty thumb-prints on the people' (Cope, 1995, p. 5). As a response to such a 'culture' Kraftwerk's art is obviously ambiguous. While it is marked by a profound desire to re-establish a specifically central European identity – effaced once by Hitler and then in its displacement by 'the American way of living' – the medium through which it seeks to do so comes by way of American cultural colonization. By seeking to create its own new constellations, both from a 1920s avant-garde *and* a transfigured post-war form derived from imported pop culture, certain socio-cultural contradictions inherent to post-war German capitalism also return to their artworks. And if it is not within the power of any work of art to resolve such contradictions, insofar as they precisely *are* social, its power does lie in its capacity to reflect upon these as problems of form.

From Düsseldorf to the planet

As I have already suggested, Kraftwerk's movement towards the production of, and their reception as, 'pop', and away from their 'art' beginnings, might well be conceived of as a unique – certainly uniquely *knowing* – attempt to redeem the promise of a distinctively modernist art that would reintegrate artistic forms with the forms of the everyday on the terrain of mass culture; to uncover mass culture's own *utopian* moment. Yet, it does so under the changed conditions of both a post-war Germany that finds itself under the shadow of Nazism and of a fully fledged industrial *system* of mass culture, in which 'the mass' appear less as the active site of potential revolutionary transformation than as passive consumers of the new dreamworlds of advertising and celebrity.

It is this that marks the shift from the democratizing hopes once invested in new technologies of mass media by the Soviet avant-gardes of the 1920s, and by Benjamin and Brecht during the 1930s, to both the far bleaker perspective outlined by Adorno and Horkheimer in their studies of the 'culture industry', on the one hand, and the heavily ironized appropriations of mass cultural material by Warholian pop art, on the other. As Bürger argues, if the early twentieth-century avant-gardes sought the 'abolition of autonomous art' altogether, so as to reintegrate art 'into the praxis of life', in the post-war era such an overcoming of art's separation from daily life has seemingly happened only in the form of a 'false sublation' driven by an ever more intensified aestheticization of the commodity form itself (1984, pp. 53–4). Unavoidably, it is against such a background that Kraftwerk's own 'modernism' must thus be interrogated.

In his excellent *File Under Popular*, Chris Cutler argues that today

> [e]lectronic media occupy centre-stage . . . for it is their nature to make use of everything available – potentially for everyone – and at once . . . [Y]et, tied to commodity exchange, these same media are used to fuel and reinforce the very distortions which restrain them . . . [I]t is precisely those musics that are most intimate with the new media that embody most clearly the contradiction at the heart of these media; the same contradiction endemic in all areas of society, between the innate socializing potential of the new productive media on the one hand, and the restraining and distorting effect on them of private ownership or oligarchic control on the other. (1981, pp. 13–14)

Such a vision of the 'innate socializing potential' of new technologies returns us to the visions of Benjamin and productivism, and it is in their ultimate affirmation of this potential that Kraftwerk's utopian moment lies: the ambition to work *with* and *through* mass forms.

Part of the distinctiveness of art since the 1960s has been its compulsion to engage or 'appropriate' the materials, forms or practices of popular and consumer culture. Yet, to the extent that the critical *frisson* of such 'appropriation' has often been reliant upon a continuing situating of mass culture as art's *other*, it characteristically fails to allow for any real critical or emancipatory potential within those cultural forms which may actually emerge out of the technologies of mass production – that is, the modernist logics which are evidently at work, since the 1960s, within (certain practices of) popular music itself (see Cunningham, 2003). For better or worse Kraftwerk's distinctive 'avant-garde' gambit has been to produce a modernist form from a (quasi-autonomous) site inside the spaces of mass culture itself; to pursue the 'utopian' belief that, irreducible merely to the repetition of the new as the ever-same that characterizes commodity production, a 'thrill of the new' common to both modernism *and* the logics of 'pop' might still be conjoined in a collectivist desire for everyday forms of cultural emancipation.

Yet, this conjuncture may itself have been reliant on a very specific moment of the late 1960s and 1970s; a moment from which we are now distant. *Computer World* (1981) might well be Kraftwerk's most brilliant achievement – the launching pad, on its final two tracks, for almost the entirety of Derrick May and Juan Atkins's Detroit techno, and through this most of electronic music since, as well as an extraordinary prefiguration of a whole host of motifs, clustered around what the Spanish sociologist Manuel Castells calls the 'space of flows', that would come to dominate cultural theory a decade or more later. But the album also undoubtedly marks an ending. While the emphasis on the democratizing, liberatory powers of technology remains intact, *Computer World*'s turn to the increasingly abstract spaces of the global rather than the European (a world of electronic data and money symbolically materialized in the babel of distorted languages that closes 'Numbers', in which Japanese stands out just as clearly as the Russian of *The Man-Machine*) equally signals a growing detachment from the specific Benjaminian constellations of post-war German culture with 1920s modernism that had dominated the work of the 1970s. In its wake, the return to vague invocations of a European avant-garde coffee shop culture on *Electric Café* (1986) seems fairly unconvincing and unfocused.

Almost a decade and a half later, it is not hard to see why the commission to compose the 'theme' for the Expo 2000 'World's Fair' in Hannover might have tempted Kraftwerk out of what had come to look like an unofficial retirement. In principle the Expo was, after all, redolent of the early twentieth-century world's fairs that had provided a vital laboratory, and means of dissemination, for modernist art and design (from Mies's Barcelona Pavilion to Picasso's *Guernica*). Yet, in fact, events like Expo 2000 embodied the commodity aesthetics and commercial spectacle of a rather different world. In the face of this, the rejuvenated avant-garde project to locate a utopian moment in mass culture and production, against the legacies of its fascist exploitation (itself increasingly distant historically), risks becoming utopian*ism* pure and simple: an elision of social division and of the uneven, differentiated character of modernity itself in a fantasy of global capital. Musically seductive as it is, the mantra of a 'planet of visions' in the 'Expo 2000' (2000) piece – 'Man Nature Technology' – while in continuity with the Bauhaus-derived sentiments of the 1970s, appears here as more or less completely abstracted from its initially avant-garde impulses. Of course, as translated into the radically different urban contexts of, say, New York or Detroit, in which Kraftwerk's modernism has been itself renewed in its reception as a profoundly other, even culturally *alien*, instantiation of the 'new' – or in the global dissemination of what has become, via digitization, a kind of collective electronic resource of timbres and rhythms derived from Kraftwerk's music – such impulses are understandably and rightly 'forgotten' anyway, as a condition of their own re-mobilization as the basis for new modernist forms. But, in the twenty-first century that Hütter hymns on 'Expo 2000', the radical break that the recovery of a 'culture of the thirties' had once propelled has irreversibly dissipated. The image of the modern unfolds elsewhere.

Notes

1. Interviewed in Austrian TV documentary *Die Mensch-Maschine* (ORF 1982). Available online at: http://www.youtube.com/watch?v=c90DIwngylg.

2. The importance of such 'grandfathers' is evident in, for example, both Herzog's studied remake of Murnau's *Nosferatu* and Fassbinder's adaptation of Döblin's *Berlin Alexanderplatz* (for which Kraftwerk provide part of the soundtrack).

3. This is what would also seem to distinguish the incorporation of 'real world' sounds on *Autobahn*, and the albums following it, from the more familiar use of 'found sounds' on *Kraftwerk* and *Kraftwerk 2*, which appear more immediately derived from the avant-garde experiments of Fluxus or *musique concrète*.

4. Originally published in 1974, significantly Bürger's book defines its own context as one that 'reflects a historical constellation of problems that emerged after the events of May 1968 and the failure of the [German] student movement in the early seventies' and of the latter's belief that one 'could build directly on the revolutionary experiences of Russian futurism, for example' (p. 95).

5. Kracauer concludes his critique of *Metropolis* with a citation of Lang's own recollection of a meeting with Goebbels: 'He told me that, many years before, he and the Führer had seen my picture *Metropolis* in a small town, and Hitler had said at that time that he wanted me to make the Nazi pictures' (1947, p. 165).

References

Barr, T. (1998), *Kraftwerk: From Düsseldorf to the Future*. London: Ebury.

Baudelaire, C. (1964), *The Painter of Modern Life*. (trans. J. Mayne). London: Phaidon.

Benjamin, W. (1992), *Illuminations*. (trans. H. Zohn). London: Fontana.

Bohn, C. (1981), 'A computer date with a showroom dummy'. *New Musical Express*, 13 June, 31–3. http://kraftwerk.technopop.com.br/interview_124.php (last accessed 14 March 2010).

Bürger, P. (1984), *Theory of the Avant-Garde*. (trans. M. Shaw). Minneapolis: Minnesota University Press.

Bussy, P. (1993), *Kraftwerk: Man, Machine and Music*. (1st edn). London: SAF.

Cope, J. (1995), *Krautrocksampler: One Head's Guide to the Great Kosmische Musik – 1968 Onwards*. London: Head Heritage.

Cunningham, D. (2003), 'A time for dissonance and noise: on Adorno, music and the concept of modernism'. *Angelaki*, 8, (1), 61–74.

Curtis, W. J. R. (1982), *Modern Architecture Since 1900*. London: Phaidon.

Cutler, C. (1981), *File Under Popular*. London: ReR/Semiotext(e).

Danto, A. C. (2002), 'History in a blur'. *The Nation*, 13 May. http://www.thenation.com/doc/20020513/danto (last accessed 28 March 2010).

Foster, H. (1996), *The Return of the Real*. Cambridge, MA: MIT Press.

Gabo, N. and Pevsner, A. (2000) 'The realistic manifesto' (1920), in M. A. Caws (ed.), *Manifesto*. Lincoln: University of Nebraska Press, pp. 396–400.

Gill, J. (1981), 'Return of the Kling Klang gang'. *Sounds*, 27 June, 12. http://kraftwerk.technopop.com.br/interview_125.php (last accessed 8 March 2010).

Griffin, R. (2007), *Modernism and Fascism*. Harmondsworth: Palgrave.

Hewitt, A. (1996), *Fascist Modernism: Aesthetics, Politics and the Avant-Garde*. Stanford: Stanford University Press.

Hütter, R. (2003), 'Interview: Triple J Radio (Australia) with Richard Kingsmill'. 24 January. http://kraftwerk.technopop.com.br/interview_43.php (last accessed 28 March 2010).

Jameson, F. (1998), *Signatures of the Visible*. London and New York: Routledge.

—— (2002), *A Singular Modernity*. London and New York: Verso.

Kracauer, S. (1947), *From Caligari to Hitler*. Princeton: Princeton University Press.

Lacoue-Labarthe, P. (1990), *Heidegger, Art and Politics*. (trans. C. Turner). Oxford: Blackwell.

Lang, F. (Dir. 1927/2003), *Metropolis*. [DVD]. EKA40061. Eureka! Entertainment.

Leslie, E. (2000), *Walter Benjamin: Overpowering Conformism*. London: Pluto.

Marinetti, F. T. (2009), 'The founding and manifesto of futurism 1909' (trans. R. W. Flint), in U. Apollonio (ed.), *Futurist Manifestos*. London: Tate.

Neaman, E. Y. (1999), *A Dubious Past: Ernst Jünger and the Politics of Literature After Nazism*. Berkeley: University of California Press.

Patterson, J. (2004), 'A film without a cinema'. *Guardian*, 2 October. http://www.guardian.

co.uk/books/2004/oct/02/featuresreviews.guardianreview13 (last accessed 28 March 2010).

Petit, C. (Dir.) (1979), *Radio On*. [DVD]. BFI Publishing.

Santer, E. (1990), *Stranded Objects: Mourning, Memory and Film in Postwar Germany*. New York: Cornell University Press.

Toop, D. (1995), *Ocean of Sound*. London: Serpent's Tail.

Tupitsyn, M. (1999), *El Lissitzky: Beyond the Abstract Cabinet*. New Haven: Yale University Press.

3

Kraftwerk – the Decline of the Pop Star

Pertti Grönholm

Introduction

Another factor in the decline of the star has been the emergence of
computer technology in music, which bypasses the relation between
musicians and traditional instruments, on which a large part of the
star mythology was based. Music making has become an affair of
technicians and record producers. Kraftwerk, an electronic group, has
pushed this development to its logical conclusion by employing robots
as on-stage replacements. (Buxton, 1990, p. 437)

This quote from David Buxton is a typical commentary on the marriage of
technology and pop music in the late 1980s. Buxton claims musicians who
use modern technology have become enslaved by engineers and producers; implicitly, he also argues that digital technology has transformed the
performing artist into a computer nerd, no longer capable of truly artistic
creation. He contends that technology bypasses the relation between
musicians and traditional instruments, on which a large part of the star
mythology is based. Similarly to Buxton, the music press of the 1970s and
1980s often represented Kraftwerk as the ultimate antithesis to pop stardom;
placed alongside producers, sound engineers and the faceless machinery of
the music industry. However, this kind of conclusion is plausible only if we
look at Kraftwerk from the narrow perspective of its public image as a utopian man-machine. This approach tends to oversimplify the band's complex
relation to pop music, and obscures some important aspects of Ralf Hütter's
and Florian Schneider's ideal of an electronic pop group. This chapter will
examine Kraftwerk's relation to pop stardom and star imagery. In contrast
to Buxton, I shall argue that in the case of Kraftwerk technology has actually
liberated the artist. From the sound and imagery associated with the band,

to their touring schedules and marketing, Kraftwerk have learned how to gain control not merely over musical production, but over the whole chain of the music business – creating along the way their own particular way of communicating with the audience.

The question of how stardom manifests itself in Western popular music is a complex one; we are not only dealing with successful and prominent individuals, but also with a range of different actors and organizations all pursuing their own ambitions around the star. Mäkelä (2002) argues it is best to understand this situation as a network of stardom, a 'starnet', in which different actors in the music business are connected. This network consists of four major components (pp. 47–9). The first part is the star, and her/his public acts – recordings, public performances (live and in the media), interviews, statements and autobiographies (Shuker, 2001, pp. 67–89). The second is the music industry and its production and distribution of official star material, which aims either to create new stars, or to maintain the popularity of established acts. This material includes physical recordings and cover art, promotional photos, posters and newsletters. This branding has the effect of structuring 'continuities in consumer culture, where a sense of trust and security is indicated by certain symbols and companies' (Marshall, 1997, p. 245; see also Shuker, 2001, pp. 13–31). But the record companies are not the only actors in the music business; there are many others – musical instrument retailers, distribution companies, record shops, music media, royalties and licensing agencies, companies specializing in concert promotion, websites that stream music, and so on (Shuker, 2001, pp. 137–9). The third part of the network of stardom is the media in its entirety, understood not as a marketing channel for the industry but as commentators on stars and their public actions; and, as such, as mediators between star and audience. This includes not only critiques of the star's performances and recordings, but also news stories, columns, parodies, unofficial biographies, and so on (pp. 139–72). The fourth component of the starnet, and the most important, is the audience, which ultimately 'produces' the star by 'consuming' her/his products directly (through recordings and performances) and indirectly (by consuming the narratives created by the media) (pp. 173–89).

In the following, I will focus on Kraftwerk's relation to the first two components outlined above. In particular, the focus will be on Kraftwerk's relation to two features of stardom. First, commodity-related aspects such as star image and celebrity, and second, authenticity-related features such as agency and performativeness.

Musical workers in an electronic living room

The new German youth culture of the late sixties and early seventies, in which the taboos of the previous generations were questioned, seems to have left its ineradicable trace on both Hütter and Schneider. In the aftermath of 1968, the cultural environment of West Germany proved fertile ground for musicians and bands who sought greater artistic freedom. The impact of the youthful radicalism of the time can be observed in the way that these bands were formed and operated. Some, such as the original Amon Düül, resembled a sectarian commune more than a rock band.[1] Although many bands aimed at self-sufficiency, only a few groups other than Kraftwerk managed to achieve and sustain technical and financial independence. Bands like Tangerine Dream, Cluster, Can and Kraftwerk consisted of technically minded musicians: they experimented with electronics, built effect devices and – in the cases of Can and Kraftwerk – ultimately established their own recording studios. Accordingly, the roles of musician, sound engineer and producer merged. The recording studio became a creative instrument in its own right, drastically affecting the process of creating music. Cheaper recording, mixing and processing units enabled musicians to enjoy the potential of the studio; Can was the first major band to invest in a small-scale recording studio in the early seventies and Kraftwerk followed in 1973–74 (Bussy, 1993, pp. 25–6).

From apprentices to masters

The role of sound engineer and producer Konrad 'Conny' Plank in supporting many pioneering German bands was fundamental. Plank not only recorded a good deal of the new groups but also acted almost like an artist agency – his company, Rainbow Productions, was set up to support the new German rock music. Plank discovered Hütter and Schneider's first band, Organisation, in 1969; their album *Tone Float* was recorded for Plank's company, and he arranged its release by RCA in Britain. Plank's impact on the birth of the seventies German rock scene has been confirmed by a number of musicians who have collaborated with him. For instance, Klaus Dinger (Kraftwerk, Neu! and La Düsseldorf) has credited him as an invaluable mediator that gave musicians 'the freedom to fly high and wild' (Dee, 1998). Michael Rother (Kraftwerk, Neu! and Harmonia) has stated that Plank played a significant part not only in creating the sound of Neu! but also in producing bands such as Kraftwerk, Cluster, Harmonia and La Düsseldorf (Young, 2001). Rother has also suggested that

> Conny Plank had a lot of enthusiasm and understanding for our music, which was something rare at that time. He had a share in the financial risk with our first production and due to his personal authority; he was a most respected co-producer in the studio. Apart from his manual skills, Conny had a tremendous sensitivity for the music and psychological fine feeling. (Gross, 1998)

According to Christa Fast, Plank's late widow, Plank saw electronic music and the European avant-garde composers of the fifties and sixties as an expression of a new German art that was not in debt to Anglo-American culture. He was convinced that electronics and pre-Nazi German modernism would be a secure platform on which to build up an image and concept that was independent of the stereotypes of pop (Flür, 2003, p. 82).

Kraftwerk have always credited Plank as engineer and co-producer of the first two albums (*Kraftwerk* [1970] and *Kraftwerk 2* [1971]), but only as engineer for the following albums (*Ralf and Florian* [1973] and *Autobahn* [1974]). Hütter and Schneider have referred to him most often as an early collaborator and as a provider of technical aid. However, according to other associates and collaborators, Plank's contribution to the artistic concept of the band was essential. His belief in Hütter and Schneider's vision was so firm that he helped them sometimes at his own financial risk and for little or no remuneration. More importantly, Plank and his co-engineers taught Hütter and Schneider how to experiment with electronic sound, and to record and mix. These lessons aided their metamorphosis from rock musicians, to sound engineers and, further, to 'musical workers' (Bussy, 1993, pp. 29–30).

According to Christa Fast, Plank was confident that he would be credited as a co-producer on both *Ralf and Florian* and *Autobahn*. She recalled that the agreement between the three men was sealed with a handshake without any written contract, and stated, 'Konrad despised everything that stood between free musical workers, as he always liked to describe himself and the musicians more than everything' (Flür, 2003, p. 385). However, Hütter and Schneider did not credit Plank as a producer and, according to Fast, paid him only for his services as an engineer and for the rent of his studio and equipment. This not only led Plank's newly established studio into financial difficulties, but also marked the beginning of the gradual dissolution of their collaboration (Flür, 2003, pp. 382–3). As Fast also noted,

> Conny made his musical contributions, made offers, filtered and linked things together. Conny was very good at creating an atmosphere that gave the musicians free rein of their musicality, and they must have valued this quality or they wouldn't have worked with him for so long. (Fast qtd. in Flür, 2003, p. 385)

Flür interprets Fast's words on 'free musical workers' as evidence that the concept was hijacked from Plank by Hütter and Schneider (Flür, 2003, pp. 385–6). This may be an exaggeration, since Hütter and Schneider's quest for independence, and their detachment from conventional pop imagery, was widely shared by many of their contemporaries. However, they were also quick-witted in adopting ideas that they found inspiring. During the following years, 'musical workers' became one of Hütter's favourite phrases;

'We always thought of ourselves as workers in sound, as studio or musical workers, not musicians or musical artists. But as musical workers, going into the studio to work' (qtd. in Bohn, 1981).

Throughout the four decades of the band's existence, Hütter and Schneider have avoided or carefully sidestepped the question of Plank's contribution. The narrative of Kraftwerk's early stages became consolidated in 1975–76, when Hütter and Schneider gave several interviews in the music press and pictured the concept as their very own brainchild.

> We were not really interested in producers or any people that wanted to sell themselves to us, or sell some ideological thing that we should do. We knew right away what we wanted to do so we went to our studios and produced tapes and then later played for some people and they just took off from there. So we produced ourselves right from the beginning. There was never outside producers or anything like that involved in taking over our lives in our mind, telling us to play in C♯ or C minor. (Hütter qtd. in Lynner and Robbley, 1976)

In this narrative, Plank's place was among the numerous other people who collaborated with Hütter and Schneider. This demonstrates that, for them, establishing total control over both music and technology was vital in creating an aesthetic and conceptual (and, it could be argued, economic) framework for the band. Their desire for total control and self-sufficiency led them to split from arguably their most important mentor and collaborator. As Hütter put it in 1976,

> [w]e were fascinated by the creation of that concept and we tried to develop it by ourselves, without help of a producer. Anyone who is working in show business waits for someone else to create their specific image. We said to ourselves: we don't want to wait, we will discover ourselves alone. (qtd. in Alessandrini, 1976)

In the same interview, Schneider commented, 'Usually, behind the stars, there's always some Colonel Parker'.

Gardeners of electronic sound

Sales of the first Kraftwerk albums were around 60,000 each (Bussy, 1993, p. 36), which enabled Hütter and Schneider to invest in their Kling Klang studio, gradually transforming it into a real recording studio; most notably they acquired their first synthesizers in the shape of a Minimoog and an ARP Odyssey. They stated that the idea of a totally electronic band that plays not just instruments but an entire studio had attracted them for years, but only after the success of *Autobahn* in 1975 did the idea of a 'loudspeaker orchestra' become fully attainable (Smaisys, 1975). Kling Klang's completion meant that Kraftwerk were virtually independent of outside producers and engineers. As Hütter and Schneider had enjoyed financial security from the very beginning of their careers, they could control their creative environment and freely choose their collaborators.

> We have invested in our machines, we have enough money to live, that's it. We can do what we want, we are independent, we don't do cola adverts, even if we might have been flattered by such proposals, we never accepted. (Bussy, 1993, p. 68)

The hired 'electronic percussionists' Wolfgang Flür and Karl Bartos soon realized that they were not playing in a conventional band. Karl Bartos recalls:

> Equipment was never a problem, buying a new synthesizer or whatever. The good thing about being rich is that it makes you independent; you don't have to be part of the music business where everybody lives off you. You just deliver a tape whenever you want. (Bussy, 1993, p. 68)

However, Kling Klang was much more than just a base for musicians seeking independence from schedules and producers. From the mid seventies onwards, Hütter and Schneider described their studio as an 'electronic living room' and an 'electronic garden' – metaphors that reflect the symbiosis of humanity and technology:

> We call our studio also some kind of electronic garden, where we have some kind of biological biofeedback with the machines. And through the time they have been growing more and more complex and been growing different stages, and we have, since we started out, had complete control over all our material. (Hütter qtd. in Adrien, 1978)

Perhaps the idea of Kraftwerk operating from a private studio was not revolutionary by itself, but the way the studio was used, and its implications for the conceptualization of the band, was new. Kraftwerk were able to control their image and communication with the outside world; it enabled the band to identify themselves with their studio, dissolving all traces of individuality behind the concept of the man-machine. All in all, during the latter part of the seventies, Kling Klang and Kraftwerk melded together into a conceptual whole that not only dissociated the band from their *Kosmische Musik* contemporaries but also from much else that was happening in rock and pop.

Catching vibrations and musicians

Kraftwerk's first tour of America in spring 1975 was a watershed in the band's development. Flür and Bartos were successfully amalgamated with the founding duo. Furthermore, the concept of the man-machine (and the idea of the band as 'musical workers') started to evolve during the tour. 'Kraftwerk – Die Mensch Maschine' had already been printed in one of the tour posters. Karl Bartos has recalled that the initial idea was Hütter's:

> The initial image really came from Ralf. He wanted to make it clear that Kraftwerk were different from any other pop or rock group and he wanted this image of a string ensemble. I didn't like it that much, I thought I always looked like a banker. I liked it better when we changed to the black shirt and trousers. (Bussy, 1993, p. 64)

Interaction with the music media – interviews, reviews and public appearances – arguably had an effect on the maturation of the band's identity. Perhaps the most important effect of the US tour on the band's identity was the stereotypical image they encountered of Germans as unemotional, distant, rational, effective, well organized, mechanical, technically skilled and conformist. Hütter, Schneider, Flür and Bartos had to cope with their own ethnic and cultural background in a completely new way (see Albiez and Lindvig in this collection). This had an irreversible impact on the overall concept of the band, and on its music.

The machine that eclipsed the stars

As outlined above, the purpose of the Kraftwerk image is to keep the individual members of the band from the limelight and to avoid creating an aura of celebrity. In fact, the whole concept of Kraftwerk has embodied a critique of the *auteur*; that is, the domination of artistic practice by a single originating vision. In this and the following sections, I shall discuss the way in which the obsession Hütter and Schneider had with total control led them to refashion commodity-related (i.e. star image and celebrity) and authenticity-related (i.e. agency and performativeness) characteristics of stardom.

Originally the band sought to reject the type of star image and the commodity values that the music industry usually created and promoted. They sought popularity not as celebrities but for their ideas, messages, music and the concept itself. However, given the band's increasing success, it turned out that a 'faceless' collective and its associated signifiers, such as the robot torsos, were able to function as popular attractors.

Ian Biddle argues that Kraftwerk has used several rhetorical strategies in its critical and aesthetic agenda. These are identified as *ironic displacement* or a flattening of emotional dynamics and a subversive use of detached ironic humour; *dehumanization* through the deployment of 'industrial' automaton-like imagery to emphasize the 'flatness' of expressive means; *disengagement from traditional modes of authorship/creativity* by adopting an 'automatic' compositional process; *refashioning of 'antiquated' models of creativity in terms of zombiosis*, the crafting of 'artificially wrought agencies in which humans have some kind of rematerialized existence' (Biddle, 2004, pp. 83–4). Biddle employs his typology in an examination of Kraftwerk's treatment of the human voice, and gives an interesting account of Kraftwerk's aesthetic development. The way in which he connects the material and political conditions of 1970s West Germany to Kraftwerk's agenda is rather problematic; nevertheless, I have used Biddle's typology as a loose heuristic and interpretative tool through which to analyse some essential aspects of Kraftwerk's project.

Star images: from rejection to reconstruction

As David Chaney puts it, pop stardom focuses on the individual; at the core of the pop star image is the performer, who identifies him/herself with the audience, and consequently the individual in the audience identifies him/herself with the performer (1993, p. 104). In the pop music market, star images are commodities that can be constructed, reshaped, sold and utilized in selling other commodities. Hütter and Schneider realized that in order to operate within the market an image was required, even if it was based on anonymity or the creation of fictional characters.

In the beginning Kraftwerk did not stand out from the rest of the new German rock bands; many of them had rejected the clichés of 1960s rock and pop, and welcomed revolution in instrumentation, hairstyles and political thinking. Neither Hütter nor Schneider identified themselves with conventional rock performers. In addition, they were uncomfortable with publicity and became easily distant and reserved, especially in interviews. This prompted them to adopt an image that helped to create a mystique around their natural guardedness. In early 1973, in sharp contrast to their avant-garde contemporaries, Kraftwerk started to flirt with pop imagery; and mixed its conventions with influences from the pop art scene. In collaboration with the visual artist and designer Emil Schult, Hütter and Schneider retouched the band's image, to make it more humorous and approachable (Bussy, 1993, pp. 42–3). On the cover of *Ralf and Florian*, for example, the duo resembled eccentric scientists rather than musicians. In addition, the name of the album and the naïvely humorous cartoons (by Emil Schult) on the inner sleeve manifested that Kraftwerk had taken its initial steps towards the pop audience. Now Kraftwerk had an embryonic image, even though the music remained experimental.

After the unexpected international success of *Autobahn* in 1975, the band were placed in a completely new situation. Kraftwerk gathered an increasing amount of media attention, much of it due to their new record company, EMI, who promoted the band intensively. All this publicity demanded a group image (Bussy, 1993, pp. 74–5). Previously, Hütter and Schneider had adopted the imagery of mad German scientists, but now they wanted to break out of the stereotype. When the group became stable, Kraftwerk adopted a somewhat more conventional band image; however, rather than appearing as conventional pop musicians, placed at the centre of attention, they preferred to appear as classical musicians or as professional scientific researchers (rather than as unhinged experimenters). Hütter and Schneider had played with these images earlier, but now they adopted them more consciously, cultivating only such symbols and implications that suited the image of the band as 'musical workers'. This new image interestingly parallels Bennett's definition of the Romantic author, who also appears to be a person, who is 'ahead of his time' or 'beyond the human' (Bennett, 2005, p. 60).

Coping with success, and an identity crisis

As noted above, *Autobahn*'s unexpected success reshaped the image of the band irreversibly. Musically and technologically, *Radio-Activity* (1975) differed dramatically from their previous work; for the first time the instrumentation was completely electronic. The human voice, heavily altered by a vocoder and other effects, was used extensively. Most of the tracks featured lyrics sung (or spoken) in German and English, and song structures changed, coming closer to the verse-chorus structure of conventional 3–5-minute pop songs. Littlejohn (2009) claims that, due to the pressures of fame and a new record deal with EMI, this style change was an attempt to commercialize their music. The change can be partly explained by commercial pressures but, bearing in mind the experimental and conceptual background of both Hütter and Schneider, it is clearly an oversimplification. Unlike Littlejohn, I would argue that Hütter and Schneider did not simply try to cash in on the success of *Autobahn*; rather, they tried to balance the developing concept of the band against this new-found success.

Artistically, *Radio-Activity* was an ambitious project; in fact, it would be appropriate to view it as the first blueprint of Kraftwerk's *Gesamtkunstwerk*. It was the first album in which Hütter and Schneider used ironic displacement and dehumanization extensively; it was the first album in which Hütter and Schneider (in collaboration with Schult) succeeded in creating a coherent, all-embracing musical and visual concept, which blended together meditations on the medium of radio with an ironic critique of nuclear power and the history of electronic music. Metaphors, symbols, ambiguities, historical references and controversies, not to mention pure nostalgia and irony, permeated the criss-crossing themes. All this made the album intellectually extremely dense. The sound imagery was far remote from popular music of the time; it was electronic and filled with bleeps and sweeps reminiscent of Stockhausen and Varèse. In addition, *Radio-Activity* contrasted Kraftwerk's German identity with American mass culture, in the light of their experiences of the US tour. As Hütter and Schneider have explained, they were inspired by Brian Wilson's musical evocation of the Californian lifestyle; one of their goals was to create sound imagery that depicted their homeland, especially the Rhineland and Ruhr area. The album contains some very subtle comments about being German in a predominantly Anglo-American pop world. For example, 'Radio Stars' can be read as a metaphor of the cultural distance between Germany and the West. The quasars and pulsars mentioned in the lyrics may represent the pop stars that young German audiences only heard on radio stations run by the British and American occupation forces in the sixties; the culture evoked by these songs appeared as distant from Germany as the quasars are from Earth. On one hand Hütter and Schneider openly despised the way in which America valued radio only as a commercial and advertising medium; but on the other hand they and the whole band had been very impressed by the boost that the American radio stations had given to their music.

As Littlejohn (2009) has demonstrated, lyrics are an important but rarely used guide to Kraftwerk's complicated relation to identities, the iconography of stardom and the whole business of success. He argues that during the production of *Trans-Europe Express* (1977) and *The Man-Machine* (1978) the band experienced an identity crisis, caused by the growing demands of the market. These reflections may be plausible, but one has to bear in mind that Kraftwerk reshaped their image in the light of the public response to their work. One of the most interesting musical self-portraits of Kraftwerk is 'The Hall of Mirrors', which crystallizes the questions of celebrity and stardom. Just like showroom dummies, the greatest stars are constantly being watched and objectified; they live in a hall of mirrors that multiplies their reflections, creating false and distorted images. If the star identifies with the reflections, they eventually find they cannot live without the surrounding images. The hall of mirrors becomes their prison. The song is an attempt to process those reflections that were projected onto Kraftwerk by the media. The music press treated the band as aliens; they were (West) German, they were electronic, they were independent and they were distant and emotionless – and at this point the band felt that they grew into the image that the media had created. The story continues in 'Showroom Dummies'. The dummies, used to being looked at, break the glass of the showroom, go to the club and start to dance – putting themselves purposely on display once again. 'The Robots' and 'The Model' on *The Man-Machine* play with the same idea; songs by and about beings whose behaviour is determined by the people who watch and use them. All these tracks proclaim Kraftwerk's high level of interest in the mechanisms of stardom; and furthermore, they sought to introduce a more straightforward and intellectual relationship with the audience. As Hütter said in 1978,

> This is not the level of 'individual concentration' anymore. The point of view of the nineteenth century is over. The myth of the important artist has been overexploited. It doesn't fit anymore with the standards of modern society. Today, mass production rules . . . Everyone is a star. The spotlights search the stars . . . for a few seconds only. (qtd. in Adrien, 1978)

The dynamic described in the lyrics is played out in the interviews the band gave during this period; during the late seventies and early eighties the media had a remarkable effect both on the self-image and the public image of the band. In the mid seventies, Kraftwerk were greeted with inquisitiveness and confusion by the Anglo-American music press in particular (in continental Europe, the media response was usually much more favourable). For example, in 1981 *Sounds* journalist John Gill confessed that a few years earlier he had considered Kraftwerk as 'four clowns playing toy piano music or the dregs of the glam generation' (Gill, 1981). According to Flür, concert reviews typically described the band as unemotional, cold and unmoving; one American concert review described the band's music as 'like air conditioning' (Flür, 2003, p. 98). More seriously, some articles drew an analogy between Kraftwerk and the Nazis (see Albiez in this collection). Unsurprisingly, after this initial contact with American and British media, Kraftwerk became known for their elusiveness. The press had also marked Kraftwerk as outsiders in the music business as they had full artistic freedom and financial autonomy. In 1975, a *Record Mirror* journalist remarked, 'They don't do interviews, one is told, and they hardly do any concerts either because apparently they don't really need the money' (Sonnendecker, 1975).

However, from 1976 onwards the media's increasing attention had significant implications for the band's relation to publicity. While talking quite openly about Kling Klang and the man-machine concept, Hütter and Schneider avoided discussing the individuals behind the machines. In conversation they promoted a corporate image and adopted a style of response that bypassed all attempts to uncover their personal lives (Bussy, 1993, p. 64). Eventually this led to a situation in which Hütter became the spokesman for the band, and the minimal information his interviews provided was masked by repetitively used one-liners that continually offered the same official Kraftwerk narrative. The band also provoked the media further with *The Man-Machine* cover by adopting an ambiguous and uniform image, wearing make-up, red shirts and black ties in the context of artwork inspired by El Lissitzky (see Cunningham in this collection). Moreover, as Flür (2003, p. 143) indicates, the decision to construct the lookalike 'robot' dummies in 1977 came in response to a number of articles and reviews in which the band was described as puppet-like, cold and robotic; consequently, the puppets inspired the band to realize the man-machine concept that had been evolving in the minds of the members for several years. As a culmination of this media reaction, Kraftwerk replaced the 'musical workers' with dummies in a press conference in Paris in 1978.

It is ironic that a band that has saluted technological progress, especially in communication, has closed almost all of the normal channels of communication between musicians and the media. According to Hütter, this reflects their 'musical workers' philosophy; they communicate with the audience only through their work – the recordings, their imagery and their performances:

> We don't think of ourselves as musicians, but rather as people who create out of the different media or ways of expressing yourself, whether it is painting, poetry, music, or even film. The ideal is to communicate with people. (qtd. in Smaisys, 1975)

Agency: authors in disguise

As the very concept of 'musical workers' implies, Kraftwerk emphasized the importance of social interaction in the process of artistic creation – extending the concept of creativity to include the contribution of music technology in the process. In the Kraftwerk universe, human potential is inseparable from its material environment, the creative space and the instruments of creativity. By stressing this Kraftwerk has also sought to question the Romantic concept of the artist as individual genius:

> A good electronic music studio doesn't make good electronic music. So that's why we've created this word 'The Human Machine' or 'The Man Machine' or 'Kraftwerk', which it stands for. At one time we are machinery but at the same time we are human. So we're neither simply humans or machines. It's a symbiosis. (Hütter qtd. in Lynner and Robbley, 1976)

During the 'classic' line-up of Kraftwerk the image of anonymous 'musical workers' could not hide the music's real authors, but it managed to obscure the connection between the images of the 'musical workers' and identifiable persons behind the roles. While the average listener could read out the credits from the label or the back sleeve, it was difficult to recognize individual band members; the connection between the images and the data was broken. Nonetheless, it would be unfair to claim that the collective image intentionally disguised the band's inner power structures. For example, Bartos and Flür still refer to their former group as 'we' and unhesitatingly identify themselves as important contributors to the music, the band's imagery and the technology used in the studio and in performance.

Hütter envisioned a collective in which individual 'musical workers' would be totally immersed in their duties at Kling Klang. In interviews, Hütter claimed that they spent almost all of their time in the studio and had no life outside the band: 'There is really nothing else we do apart from Kraftwerk and related things. We have no other choice than going totally into that thing' (Bohn, 1981). This kind of narrative is a manifestation of one of Kraftwerk's rhetorical strategies. Dehumanization was one way to detach the band from the idea of the pop star as Romantic artist. Instead of heavenly inspiration and the poetic contemplation of the self, Hütter claimed that Kraftwerk's music was a result of disciplined commitment to, and seamless interaction between, the studio and its crew. This official narrative enabled Hütter and the band to deflect any attempts to tease out information about their private lives. While in some sense Hütter's narrative was truthful, the image that the music press circulated has revealed to be heavily mystified and exaggerated. Bartos, Flür and Schult have confirmed that, although in the mid seventies they lived in a commune, they enjoyed parties, music, food, sex and various refreshments – much like 'ordinary' rock and pop musicians (Flür, 2003, p. 127).

Performance: distancing the audience

In 1975 Hütter was asked, 'Why do you not make a show?' He answered, 'Only one year ago we had long hair and jeans. Now we appear in black suits, white shirts, ties and short hair. That is our "show"' (Smaisys, 1975). This statement not only illuminates how Kraftwerk reconstructed its identity, but it also worked as a clever argument against the standard expectations of the pop audiences and the music press. In Western popular music, audiences and journalists usually consider qualities such as presence and immediacy as prerequisites for the authenticity of the performing star. However, the ego-driven performer as the centre of attention was, for Hütter and Schneider, one of the most distasteful parts of pop stardom; the band have employed various strategies to distance themselves from this kind of (apparently) direct, revelatory performance. One strategy, as Biddle (2004) has demonstrated, was the use of voice-altering devices, such as the vocoder, filtering and other effects ('Ananas Symphonie' from *Ralf and Florian* was the first Kraftwerk track that featured a vocoder). Hütter and Schneider have admitted that recording their own voices was a problem because of their timidity; before the mid seventies, they suffered from 'tape paranoia': 'for nine years we were afraid to put our voices on the tape . . . It [the tape] discovers things within ourselves we wouldn't have known before' (qtd. in Schober, 1976).

Soon they discovered that technology was not only a way of distancing themselves from the conventional notion of performed authenticity in rock music but it also helped them to adapt themselves to live performances. Neither was especially good at singing; therefore, they equalized the performative status of the vocals down to the level of other instruments. Hütter used the term *Sprechgesang* – something between speaking and singing – to describe their style.

> We use language also as a musical instrument. It's like when we sing. People say, it's too low, we cannot understand the singer. But we are not singers in the sense of Rod Stewart, we use our own voices as another instrument. Language is just another pattern of rhythm, it is one part of our unified sound. (Bussy, 1993, p. 56)

In live performance Kraftwerk adopted an extremely static, expressionless performance style (see Pattie in this collection). However, for the band, a static presence was itself expressive; it signalled an alienation from, and a critique of, the idea of engaged, authentic performance. For example, during 1975–76, journalists suspected that the band played tapes on stage – the ultimate insult to the audience; in other words, machines on stage destroyed the illusion of the quasi-Romantic rock musician described above. The band explained that they were playing their instruments and making music on stage, but they did so in line with the overall conceptual framework of the band.

> If we play a tape, we play a tape, and we show that we play a tape. Most conventional entertainment is just playing a tape but people pretend to be very live, they shout and sweat but if you come to the essence of it, it's just a tape that's being produced. We play a tape, we do not sweat and when we play music or make up music then we show what we do. (Hütter qtd. in Lynner and Robbley, 1976)

In the course of the late seventies and early eighties, Kraftwerk also abandoned some other conventions that usually maintain the illusion of authenticity. One of these was the symbiotic relationship between the star performer and his/her instrument. When the first sequencers and drum machines entered the Kling Klang studio and the stage, the roles of the four members changed. Although Hütter remained the main vocalist and Schneider specialized in sound modification, vocoders and speech synthesis, the 'electronic percussionists' became multi-tasking personnel who took care of many things from playing to the design of parts of the stage.

It is also worth noting that Flür and Bartos were hired primarily for their ability to adapt themselves to Kraftwerk performative aesthetics. They could discipline themselves, playing expressionlessly and without emphasis. It is ironic that Flür, who played the first electronic drum kit in a ZDF television performance in 1973, felt that due to his drums he became the centre of attention or the star (Flür, 2003, p. 66). It is more likely though that it was the drums themselves that drew the TV camera's gaze. Hütter and Schneider considered Kraftwerk's members not to be instrumentalists but instrumental parts of the machinery of the band. In this performance, the machinery itself became the star.

An exceptional demonstration of Kraftwerk's anti-star aesthetics occurred during the 1981 tour. During 'Pocket Calculator', the band appeared on the edge of the stage, and played little hand-held instruments and controllers; they even invited the audience to play some random tunes. In addition, they gestured and danced in a 'robotic' manner; Schneider even played his mini keyboard behind his back, mimicking rock guitar players. As expected, the audience went wild. This may now appear to us just as a simple gimmick; Kraftwerk had found some cheap musical toys and consumer items, such as a Stylophone and a Casio FX-501B calculator, and wanted to have fun with them. Hütter explained that they wanted to show how the group used everyday items from 'street level' (Bussy, 1993, p. 119). However, the performance achieved more than this. First, it functioned as a sarcastic mocking of standardized rock performance. While approaching the audience Kraftwerk simultaneously revealed their fundamental otherness. They did not want to ridicule the audience; rather, they invited the audience to participate in a deconstruction of the performative myth of the rock performer. This myth stated, as Hütter put it, that '"you have to watch them – they are super-important people!" which isn't the case, it's all rubbish. Musicians are not important people' (Gill, 1981). Second, the irony of this 'anti-spectacle' reflected back on Kraftwerk themselves; it worked by ridiculing the 'musical workers' for their own shortcomings, as dancers and performers.

Overall, Kraftwerk's live performances have been predicated on the idea that complicated technical devices could also function as aesthetic attractions. This manifested itself fully on the 1981 tour, when the band used hand-held mini-instruments for the first time, and even replaced the 'musical workers' with lookalike dummies during 'The Robots'. Furthermore, the idea of Kraftwerk as a *Gesamtkunstwerk* was re-enforced by the fact that the stage actually consisted of the equipment of the Kling Klang studio. Later in the nineties, partially moving robot torsos replaced the dummies and the hand-held devices were abandoned. During the late 1990s and early 2000s, the mobile Kling Klang studio has transformed into four laptops and visual projections have become the main stage attraction (see Brocker in this collection).

Conclusion

It seems that Kraftwerk have deliberated the concept of pop very analytically. Hütter, Schneider and other Kraftwerk members and associates understood pop music as something that is not only a clever combination of all-too-familiar melodies, chords and rhythms, but as a network of ideas and images through which a performer's cultural environment, its past, present and future, are mediated. Kraftwerk have also used many rhetorical tools, as Biddle (2004) has indicated, through techniques such as ironic displacement, dehumanization and critical disengagement in order to challenge, broaden and revise the conventions of pop music. As I have attempted to demonstrate, rather than proving to be an extreme example of anti-pop stardom, through their technical skills and artistic vision the band managed to convert its disguised collectivist image, aesthetics and intellectual message to an effective marketing tool. This has allowed Kraftwerk to both reach a substantial popular audience and to maintain a distinct artistic identity through a fully worked-out intellectual and aesthetic concept; all of the music and visual iconography they have produced stands as a manifestation of a distinct and finely crafted *Gesamtkunstwerk*.

The author would like to thank Bruce Johnson for his help with this chapter.

Note

1. In the turbulent years of 1967–69 Hütter and Schneider, while studying at the Düsseldorf Conservatory, had occasionally performed in art school happenings. For example, Schneider played in a short-lived collective, Pissoff, that was an avant-garde jazz-rock combo.

References

Adrien, Y. (1978), 'Interview: Ralf and Florian'. *Rock and Folk*, June. http://kraftwerk. technopop.com.br/interview_113.php (last accessed 25 March 2010).

Alessandrini, P. (1976), 'Interview: Ralf Hütter and Florian Schneider'. *Rock and Folk*, November. http://kraftwerk.technopop.com.br/interview_25.php (last accessed 25 March 2010).

Bennett, A. (2005), *The Author*. London and New York: Routledge.

Biddle, I. (2004), 'Nostalgia, irony and cyborgian vocalities in Kraftwerk's Radioaktivität and Autobahn'. *Twentieth-Century Music*, 1/1, 81–100.

Bohn, C. (1981), 'A computer date with a showroom dummy: Kraftwerk feature'. *New Musical Express*, 13 June. http://kraftwerk.technopop.com.br/magazines_england_80. php (last accessed 25 March 2010).

Bussy, P. (1993), *Kraftwerk: Man, Machine and Music*. (1st edn). London: SAF.

Buxton, D. (1990), 'Music, the star system and the rise of consumerism', in S. Frith and A. Goodwin (eds), *On Record: Rock, Pop and the Written Word*. New York: Pantheon Books, pp. 427–40.

Chaney, D. (1993), *Fictions of Collective Life: Public Drama in Late Modern Culture*. London and New York: Routledge.

Dee, M. (1998), 'Interview: Klaus Dinger'. *Pop* (Sweden), October. http://www.dingerland. de/Talks/pop_int.html (last accessed 3 August 2010).

Flür, W. (2003), *Kraftwerk: I Was a Robot*. (2nd edn). London: Sanctuary Publishing.

Gill, J. (1981), 'Return of the Kling Klang gang: Kraftwerk interview'. *Sounds*, 17 June. http://kraftwerk.technopop.com.br/interview_125.php (last accessed 25 March 2010).

Gross, J. (1998), 'Michael Rother interview'. *Perfect Sound Forever*, March. http://www. furious.com/Perfect/michaelrother.html (last accessed 25 March 2010).

Littlejohn, J. T. (2009), 'Kraftwerk: language, lucre, and loss of identity'. *Popular Music and Society*, 32, (5), December, 644–9.

Lynner, D. and Robbley, B. (1976), 'A conversation with Ralf Hutter and Florian Schneider of Kraftwerk'. *Synapse*, September/October, 10–11. http://www.cyndustries.com/ synapse/synapse.cfm?pc=35&folder=sept1976&pic=11 (last accessed 5 March 2010).

Mäkelä, J. (2002), *Images in the Works: A Cultural History of John Lennon's Rock Stardom*. Academic Dissertation. Turku: Cultural History, University of Turku.

Marshall, P. D (1997), *Celebrity and Power: Fame in Contemporary Culture*. Minneapolis and London: University of Minnesota Press.

Schober, I. (1976), 'Interview: Ralf Hütter & Florian Schneider'. *Musik Express*, December. http://kraftwerk.technopop.com.br/interview_49.php (last accessed 25 March 2010).

Shuker, R. (2001), *Understanding Popular Music Culture*. (3rd edn). London and New York: Routledge.

Smaisys, P. (1975), 'Interview: Ralf Hütter & Florian Schneider'. *Triad*, June. http://pages. ripco.net/~saxmania/kraft.html (last accessed 14 April 2010).

Sonnendecker, M. (1975), 'Interview: Konrad Plank'. *Record Mirror*, 17 May. http:// kraftwerk.technopop.com.br/interview_101.php (last accessed 25 March 2010).

Young, R. (2001), 'Langer atem. Junkmedia speaks with Michael Rother of Neu!' *Junkmedia*, September. http://www.junkmedia.org/index.php?i=37 (last accessed 25 March 2010).

4

Authentic Replicants: Brothers between Decades between Kraftwerk(s)

Simon Piasecki and Robert Wilsmore

Seeking the essence of consciousness ... will consist in rediscovering my actual presence to myself ... Looking for the world's essence is not looking for what it is as an idea once it has been reduced to a theme of discourse; it is looking for what it is as a fact for us, before any thematization.

(*Merleau-Ponty, 1970, p. xv*)

This chapter deals in assignation. That is to say, this chapter deals in the assignation of authenticity between siblings and the manner in which this might be an index to a crucial yet paradoxical shift in the authenticity of Kraftwerk between *Autobahn* (1974) and *Computer World* (1981). It also marks a shift between the 1970s and the 1980s, and between the musical and cultural investments of elder and younger brothers. We have written this chapter collaboratively, and with the energy of a conversation through which common ground inevitably emerged. We both became increasingly aware of the unifying issue of authenticity – as listeners who ascribe this quality, as sufferers of accusations of inauthenticity by elder siblings, as observers and participants in a time caught in the uneasy coexistence of a decaying modernity and an emergent postmodernism. We argue that Kraftwerk shift from one mode of authenticity to another but that conflicting ascriptions remained which divided followers – and, in both our cases, divided brothers – where opposing parties both lay claim to owning the real Kraftwerk.

First Person (1)

Simon

In the mid seventies, while I was still playing 'Blowing in the Wind' on a red Bontempi with a single finger, my elder brother exposed me to Hawkwind, Gong and Black Sabbath. But he also added a significant album by Kraftwerk – *Autobahn* – to his collection. In many respects, despite the repetitive chant of the title, 'Autobahn' the track reminded me of Hawkwind. Certainly at that age I didn't ponder the differences between musical genres and, for the purpose of this chapter, I might argue that there was none. 'Autobahn' was a 22-minute track that, certainly in length, fitted the progressive rock scene. However, Kraftwerk seemed to eschew the mythology of a Romantic past, embracing instead the cool rationality of technology. As a rational product, notwithstanding its original politics, the notion of the 'autobahn' was a perfect metaphor. For me though, at that time, there was far too much space between the catchy repetition of the chorus and everything else. I wondered how my brother listened to these epic works and whether he actually enjoyed them. I was also not equipped to separate them thematically from the space rock of Hawkwind, which he also played and in whose music I heard similar qualities – a 'wind-rush' velocity, and a similar stretching of time.

When I was thirteen and shifting through my third musical incarnation (1. Osmonds versus Yogi Bear, 2. Punk, 3. New Wave versus Ska revival), I would visit the record section of the public library in Tamworth. The notion of borrowing records from the library filled me with a sense that my musical taste was somehow a display of intelligence, an expression of a developed musical taste, and of social and artistic aspiration. In there I found a more experimental or audacious will to look further than my existing musical boundaries. I discovered the Yellow Magic Orchestra, Eloy and Kraftwerk – a Kraftwerk quite different to the one that I had listened to my brother play. The first album that caught my attention was *Computer World*. Something fundamental had happened to the group, who were now producing shorter tracks rather than grand orchestrations. This shift is gradual: *The Man-Machine* (1978) has a 9-minute track ('Neon Lights') and *Computer World* has a 7-minute title track. Even so, there is also a shift towards commercial melody, and this was certainly part of my attraction at that point. Pascal Bussy writes that the development and trajectory of Krautrock from the mid seventies was related to a German preoccupation with technology and efficiency (2002, p. 28), but there are factors at work that have to do with the closure of a gap between the band's conceptual and commercial status; hence the understandable accusation of a lack of depth in my taste, from my elder brother's perspective.

Robert

As a second son benefiting from the advantages that come with the more relaxed parenting style of those that tested their worries on the first born, I tagged along as a young teenager to Motörhead, Iron Maiden, Saxon and Sabbath with my brother (four years my senior). This was an age when the studio album claimed artistic primacy and live performance was an attempt to recreate this phenomenon – a reversal of the traditional idea that a recording stands as a representation of the performance. Philip Auslander (2008) notes that 'there is no question that rock exists primarily as recorded music and that rock culture is organized around recordings' (p. 75). Tours were tours of the latest album, and with luck (or, rather, absolute certainty) previous hits and favourites would also be played. That the album's multi-tracked illusion of unity 'performs' as the needle hits the record presented different problems for artists attempting to recreate this live at the time. Different solutions were offered, from pre-recording material, to attempting accurate replication via synthesizers, to doing something obviously not the same – thus emphasizing the liveness of the event. Replication, as if it were a Hegelian idea with a life of its own, began to seep out through the fissures between live and recorded music and try out various guises so that it might come to know itself.

But what authenticity might be ascribed to a group centred on replication, on the robot, the simulacrum, on a preoccupation with machines and clones? Ironically, it is through the working of inauthenticity that Kraftwerk's later authenticity is perhaps revealed. The 'progress' in progressive rock finds a location in the epic form, in the sense that longer compositions are more sophisticated. Coupled with this is a sense of complexity of musical elements that encompass difficulty and virtuosity; with this the sympathetic listener might have attained an elevated sense of their importance – a notion that 'I' must also have made progress and am on a higher musical plain than those who listen to music that is not progressive. But a paradigm shift occurs at some point in the 1970s that moved the status of technology, complexity and length from expansive progressive rock virtuosity to the cool neo-modernism of electro-pop. In the evolution of the music of Yes in the 1980s, (when, for example, their producer Trevor Horn was part of the futurist-inspired The Art of Noise at the time of working on *90125* [Warner, 2003, p. 91]) we may see a direct connection and a logical progression from progressive rock to neo-modernity to postmodernity.

Electro-pop irony and the aesthetics of the everyday

It is the 'real' as opposed to the representational that ascribes authentic-ity, by expressing 'the truth of the situation' (Gilbert and Pearson, cited in

Moore, 2002). In contrast to progressive rock, *Autobahn* and *Trans-Europe Express* (1977) had epic proportions but banal themes; if we take Rush's *2112* (1976) as an example of the treatment of technology in progressive rock, the technology of the time, as heard in the opening, sweeping synthesizers, is a signifier of the future (similar to the theremin in 1950s sci-fi movies). Yet the Priests of *2112* also refer back to some former mythological time, and their future is also regressive. Conversely, Kraftwerk's technologies are ironically mundane; they deal in the everyday (the road, the train) rather than in futurist visions of heroic technology. The representation of the future through synthetic sound in *2112* may seem to our ears now to be quaint and dated: these signifiers no longer carry the same currency as they did to sympathetic audiences of the time. Kraftwerk have fared rather better in this respect. The appreciation of their technological soundscapes now is not one of nostalgia for past representations of the future but one that remains current, or at least holds firm as bearing witness to reality. It operates ironically, in that it is deeply self-conscious and critiques its own existence (though even Kraftwerk, when in literal mode, were capable of cringe-worthy word painting at times – take, for example, the extra musical wobble as the picture distorts in 'The Hall of Mirrors').

Somehow though, even earlier examples of *musique concrète* to which the band are indebted (such as Pierre Schaeffer's 1948 *Etude aux Chemins de Fer* – a piece constructed from train sounds) seem to lack this irony. *Musique concrète* may be paradigm-breaking, but the progressive label of progressive rock suggests succession rather than a break with tradition, enforcing an existing paradigm rather a new starting point (see Sternberg, Kaufman and Pretz, 2002). In the context of the time (the simultaneous rise of punk and disco) the thinking listener needed the thinking pop group. This is not to ridicule the Romantic epics of progressive rock or the coexistence of punk and disco, but to speak for us of the banality of the rhizomatic expansion of all things mediatized, and the difficulty of constructing meaning from the plethora of things coming our way. As Baudrillard writes, '[w]e live in a world where there is more and more information, and less and less meaning' (1994, p. 79). Kraftwerk offered an alternative to the escapist ideology of progressive rock, the anarchy of punk or the absurdity of disco, and asked us to stop and construct meaning from our new technological age.

In the same manner the technology of reproduction – the vinyl record – was treated differently. The length of a record side had become a governing factor of progressive rock albums (*Meddle* [Pink Floyd, 1971], *Close to the Edge* [Yes, 1972] *2112* [Rush, 1976] – and *Autobahn*). While it is worthwhile noting that a strain of art rock prized the shorter song (Bowie, Roxy Music, *et al.*), somewhere in the mid seventies a shift occurred, and length was in itself less of a mark of quality. The constraint of the single vinyl side gives way to the internal workings of the song. Kraftwerk, post *Trans-Europe Express*, took a step further into a popular coding (see Stephanie, cited in Middleton, 1990, pp. 175–6) that maintained, indeed increased, its dual posture as simultaneously ironic and sincere.

First Person (2)

Robert

My brother gave me a Uriah Heep badge (or maybe I took it, I can't quite remember). I didn't know any of their music but I knew the name was acceptable – that it could sit alongside Motörhead – and that was all that was needed to take the decision to wear it. School uniform was strictly suit and tie but there was little restriction on what might be painted on one's canvas rucksack. So every six months or so a new album cover was lovingly traced and painted on the flap, the only externally visible expression available to communicate an 'I' between home and school. One occasion sticks: walking back from a bus stop, two girls were walking towards me. They giggled and said, so that I might hear, 'Bet he likes Beethoven'. They were audibly surprised to see Rush's red figure in a star emblazoned on my rucksack. A small victory – except that I did like Beethoven. I hadn't noticed that turning up to my piano lessons in full Heavy Metal-badged armoury with a Beethoven sonata tucked under my arm was in any way unusual. The two musics occupied different 'I's; not consciously – there was just no reason for them to meet, no shared point of connection. Kraftwerk bridged such divides; and my brother recalls that at *Rock-Night* on Thursdays in Yate in the early eighties Kraftwerk were often played. They were accepted within the rock paradigm, a legitimate (if unspoken) part of the rock 'I'.

Simon

My brother gave me nothing but a hard time, as far as my musical tastes were concerned. I would gaze at the patches that covered his denim cut-off jacket and those of his friends; the back was usually reserved for a larger patch of the favourite group and the most significant to me was the figure within the star that signified Rush on his friend's cut-offs. As an undergraduate, I would come to love everything they produced. However, Rush fail to look forward on tracks such as 'Red Barchetta', for example, because its quasi-futurist celebration of the speeding car is so firmly framed in the technology of the past; the bleak technology, and indeed the laws of the future, cannot hold a feather to the throaty roar and rebellion of an old car. Kraftwerk are much more taken with the infinite expanse of road than with the vehicle, and even with *Trans-Europe Express* the real promise has to do with traversing architectonic space, rather than the nostalgia of the train journey.

Ironically, I had at this point begun a series of long coach trips to Germany with school friends on an exchange system. On these trips the prerequisite, in the period just preceding the Walkman (for us, at least), was a radio cassette recorder. This was another key difference between my brother and I: my interest in music was portable, transferable and dependent upon a weekly recording session between 5 and 7 p.m. on a Sunday, when I would sit with my finger hovered over the record, play and pause buttons while I dubbed the Radio One charts onto cassette. It was a rugged-looking Ferguson with a shoulder strap and a PA facility. It wasn't a stereo, but it had a loudness button and it sounded fabulous. This was how I really got to grips with *The Man-Machine*. In some respects, and given the length of the trips to and from Westfalen, *Autobahn* would have been the relevant choice, but these trips were for group singing and displays of contemporary credibility. Everybody liked *The Man-Machine* (well, two tracks on it). Everybody liked the charts. Apart from the Germans. The German kids were predominantly into rock, and rock seemed to be all that I could hear in bars and discos there. I remember this as a vivid difference between the social spaces of West Germany and England; this was certainly part of an attachment to the examples of a sixties generation that had attempted to distance itself from the rational horrors of the previous decades. My peers in Germany, not too far from Düsseldorf, dressed as my brother had done but were listening to the Scorpions, not Kraftwerk.

The knowingness of post-production

Kraftwerk's pared-down ironic electro-pop style allowed it to be read as both popular music and art music. The simple triadic structures that formed the basis of a number of melodies both subversively and respectfully pay homage to classical composers such as Schubert and Beethoven as well as situating the group comfortably alongside (and usually ahead of) contemporary New Wave bands. Such knowing intertextuality lends itself to an ascription of authenticity that might combine both first and third person in Moore's terms (Moore, 2002) given that both expression and execution are sincere and borrowed (a dual positioning). Nicholas Bourriaud picks up on the music and film industry terminology of *post-production* (see Bourriaud, 2007) from which we may infer a notion that an artist's material is already created, already produced, and that they then deal with this anew; and we might now re-appropriate the term back into music production with its newly acquired inflection. In this sense there can be no first person originality (as all is third person in origin) and so another dual position arises, an ironic one that produces a third-first hybrid where the distance between third and first person authenticities is compressed to nil. First person authenticity here is a synthesis of third persons; a designation only, a name assigned to the phenomena that appear when these extant

parts come together, and authenticity is located in the acknowledgement
of the synthetic. If we apply Derrida's position that there is 'nothing outside
the text' (1976, p. 158), then we might consider that the Kraftwerk of *The
Man-Machine* is authenticated by the genuine awareness of its replication, its
engagement with the simulacrum (Baudrillard, 1994), its postmodernism,
as opposed to the authenticity of *Autobahn* which is located in a classical, almost anti-pop tradition. Yet the lived experience of listening to *The
Man-Machine* is to say 'this is Kraftwerk', but through othering themselves
they become Other (third person becoming first person and vice versa in
an asignifying system – for example, the wasp becoming orchid [Deleuze
and Guattari, 2008]). One observer, sympathetic to *Autobahn*, may ascribe
authenticity here and see the shift to pop, commerce and reproduction as
inauthentic (see Littlejohn, 2009), while another may ascribe authenticity
precisely to the knowing engagement of these qualities (Mark Prendergast
notes 'they played the pop game to the hilt' [2000, p. 297]). The inauthenticity of playing the game demonstrates a lack of integrity; but the
authenticity of playing the game is where the game itself is scrutinized and
critiqued within its own framework. One brother's meat is the other brother's
poison.

In an age of reproduction, Kraftwerk re-present themselves as musicians
and as marionettes. As Benjamin wrote, '[i]n principle a work of art has
always been reproducible. Man-made artefacts could always be imitated by
men' (1969/2002, p. 217). Kraftwerk in the late seventies became experts at
mimicking themselves, or, rather, mimicking themselves as machines. But
Kraftwerk also confounded Benjamin's predictions concerning original value
in the technologies of reproduction. Benjamin had described a dilution of
value in the art object, as an inevitable consequence of the process of reproduction; the value and authenticity of the unique artwork was a cause célèbre
of conceptual work since Duchamp's *Fountain* (1917) and Warhol embraced
reproducibility as an art form in and of itself. That Kraftwerk's transformation
into simulacra occurred when it did is also an interesting correlation with
the reproduction of punk themes, a wider commitment to experimentation,
and the ironic embracing of commerciality in New Wave (cf. the Pop Group,
for example). The emphasis for Kraftwerk was on establishing authenticity
in reproduction (of everything from a pulse to a haircut), always with the
promise of non-dilution; a repositioning of authenticity as plural in an age
of mechanical reproduction, with each successive unit the same as its pre-
decessor, each original and yet each homogeneous. This is an act of cloning.
Benjamin suggests that

> one might generalize by saying: the technique of reproduction detaches
> the reproduced object from the domain of tradition. By making many
> reproductions it substitutes a plurality of copies for a unique existence.

And in permitting the reproduction to meet the beholder or listener in his own particular situation, it reactivates the object reproduced. These two processes lead to a tremendous shattering of tradition which is the [opposite] of the contemporary crisis and renewal of mankind. (Benjamin, 1936, cited in Harrison and Wood, 1995, p. 514)

Kraftwerk hark back to the point in modernism in which Benjamin and Adorno had begun to grasp the cultural significance of new reproductive technologies. Kraftwerk grasp the working of mimeticism, an active *doing* of repeating rather than a passive mirroring of the individual object; as Gary Peters puts it, 'The mimetic act does not copy the world, it copies other mimetic acts . . . Mimeticism imitates the working not the work, the saying rather than the said' (Peters, 2009, p. 101). Michael Bracewell considers the proximity between Warhol's and Kraftwerk's treatment of the art object:

After Autobahn, [Kraftwerk] became Germany's Andy Warhol: artists dedicated to expressing the quotidian landscape of a Mass Cultural age, and doing so in a manner which was itself a further expression of mass cultural technology. (Bracewell, 2006)

This influence, or perhaps this awareness, was certainly present before *Autobahn*; on the cover of the 1970 album *Kraftwerk*, a single traffic cone is outlined and printed in flat colour on a plain background – a direct reference to Warhol's *Campbell's Soup Cans* (1962), and to the banana on the front cover of *The Velvet Underground and Nico* (1967). But Kraftwerk's reference is not without humour – here an industrial legisign replaces the consumable item, and banality replaces the promise of consumption and enjoyment. The Factory becomes the power plant; and instead of the consumable being the homogenized object of our attention, we are ourselves homogenized in the system of our own production.

In Kraftwerk's version the emphasis therefore shifts from freedom to consume the repetition to a symbiotic relationship of mimetic equality in the work's constant re-production, re-production, re-production. I *am* a robot. I *am* the operator. In this sense it's not surprising that the work shifted easily from an industrial reworking of the epic-length tracks of space rock to shorter post-punk products that readily embraced the commercial. It follows the logic of their own discourse, echoing Peters (quoted above) in imitating the 'working not the work'; so that, for example, the Barbara Ann-esque vocals of 'Autobahn' parody the aspirational lifestyle of the Beach Boys in a fun ('fun, fun, fun') self-mocking way. Even at the start of the track the vocal harmony mimics the building of the major chord in 'Ba-ba-ba, Ba-bar-bara-Ann' but this harmony, similarly tonal, major and triadic in construction, is seemingly a single voice made multiple by a vocoder, rather than 'real' and multiple voices. The One attempts to replicate the Many. The human–technology synergy here is strongly affirmed; but this strength is re-evaluated when the vocals come in (in their 'unmediated' form) with 'fahr'n, fahr'n, fahr'n'. These voices are thin and weedy, frail in comparison with the precision of the surrounding synthetic music, yet they are unapologetic; like the driver of the car, they are in control. However, the last word on the album goes to the people, not the technology, with a humanized version of a melody taken from the first track (a kind of symphonic second subject). Here the recorder (the woodwind instrument as opposed to the tape machine) makes the point that the human, a poor instrument of replication in comparison with the computer, can be the most effective interpreter. Like the frailty of the voices, the recorder and the less-than-concert-tuned piano carry a sense of humanity. *Autobahn* is beautifully human.

Intermezzo: replication in Simon's brother's Kraftwerk

The working of repetition in relation to reproductive technology may be explored beyond the more obvious observations; the thousands of copies of *Autobahn* or *Trans-Europe Express*, or of the thousands of playings of these recordings – all of which purport to *be Autobahn*, to *be Trans-Europe Express*, and as such fall within their ontologies. The technology of non-acoustic (synthetic) instruments is to the fore, the band's images directly refer to replication, the lyrics to cloning – even the track 'Autobahn' hears itself on the radio. But we might also see how a different mode of repetition in the age of technology plays out in the traditional world of tonality, that seemingly eternal playground of composers. The technology of Bach's time (c.1700s) produced an equal-tempered system that allowed composers to shift comfortably around the keys of the cycle of fifths and modulate in and out of distantly related keys. This was liberating; not that harmonic movement and modulation were absent pre-Bach (very far from it), but it became an even more prominent feature. Harmonic stasis took a back seat while harmonic movement and modulation enjoyed their liberation. Harmonic progression within this tonal hierarchy had to conform to the hierarchy; where a triad is sounded on the tonic of a major key and moves up a tone to the supertonic (the chord of the second note of the scale), the chord would necessarily be minor not major.

In the first subject of 'Autobahn' (that which accompanies the main vocal section 'farh'n, farh'n, farh'n') we are rooted to a harmonically static chord (as with much Kraftwerk). This is tonic and major. The chord then changes, shifting up a tone. Within a tonal hierarchy the chord ought to conform and alter its inner semitone relations and become minor, but the next chord is also major – no modulation, no conforming to an implied (present but absent) tonality; the schema is replicated, the technology has replicated the unit and the unit has maintained its integrity. The cloning of the schema has triumphed over the demands of tonality; the Platonic blueprint retains its singularity and independence even in, indeed because of, its repetition. Deleuze describes the qualities of repetition in identical elements by noting discrete elements in two different forms of repetition:

> [O]ne is inanimate, the other carries the secret of our deaths and our lives, of our enchainment and our liberations, the demons and the divine. One is 'bare' repetition, the other a covered repetition, which forms itself in covering itself, in masking and disguising itself. One concerns accuracy, the other has authenticity as its criterion. (2010, p. 27)

The shift in 'Autobahn' from one chord to the next attempts to disguise its repetition; the pitch has shifted so it is not 'identical' in that sense, but that is its cunning – it mimics humanity but gives itself away as technological replication. 'Autobahn' is beautifully *un*human.

We find something similar in 'Trans-Europe Express', the counterpart of 'Autobahn'. At the opening and as a recurrent gesture a chord builds up in a series of fourths. The interval of the fourth is another guise (a repetition) of the fifth; the fifth descends to resolve itself and becomes 'perfected' in the perfect cadence, and likewise the fourth ascends to the same effect. Taking the replication of the Platonic blueprint, as discussed through the 'Autobahn' chords, the rise of a fourth to a new destination (the second note of the two-note sequence) takes that destination as the end of one unit and the start of the next. Deleuze notes, 'They [the artists] do not juxtapose instances of the figure, but rather each time combine an element of one instance with another element of the following instance' (p. 154). This dissymmetry reveals itself only where the repetition stops. In this instance the repetition of fourth on fourth is snared by a tonic and brought into line; the starting note firmly establishes itself as a root, but the sequence moves away from it a fourth up at a time until it comes 'too close' to the gravitational pull of a tonic, as the sequence of fourths brings the note to (what might best be described as) a flattened ninth. The close proximity to a nearby tonic only a semitone away permits a resolution that intervenes with the unit's desire to replicate itself *ad infinitum*. There is some human control here then, or at least someone or something to prevent infinity – such as the desire for the tonic to replicate itself being a greater force, a stronger Platonic idea, than that of the fourth.

First Person (3)

Simon

I remember enjoying Kraftwerk because I sensed a sardonic humour that was sincerely meant, rather than a sense that they were actually being serious. It was a little like the deliberate pretension of Devo and their flowerpots, or the lesser-known Yellow Magic Orchestra; it was also true of Laurie Anderson's 'O Superman' (1981) – clever like an intelligent and warm joke. I loved it in complete ignorance of her status as a long-established performance artist, in complete ignorance of the influence of classical operatic works (Massenet's *Le Cid* [1885]) on its structure. I was also completely unaware of any political meaning in the work; rather, it had a current relevance that I wanted to aspire to – the work had a clarity about it, strong in colour and optimism, at least so far as its surface was concerned. Rockwell argues that Anderson's repetitive and 'rhythmically charged declamation' in addition to her 'reliance on pitch choices not bound by diatonic scale and on the subtly exact rhythmic articulation of her texts, speaks directly to the musical concerns . . . of her time' (Rockwell, 1983, p. 60). I lived in a depressed Midlands town, with a looming recession, and so Kraftwerk, Devo, *et al.*, felt akin to the clean production of pre-eighties science fiction, rather than the retrograde dirtiness of what followed. I wasn't a realist. But now I'm confused. I thought that Kraftwerk were the realists that survived the death of Romantic progressive space rockers – but then what was actually real about this precision electro-puppetry? To an unsure youth, in an unsure world, Kraftwerk seemed sure.

Robert

As gravity bends light, so passing time bends reality. Laurie Anderson's knowing post-9/11 re-singing of the line '[h]ere come the planes. They're American planes, made in America' (lyrics in Anderson, 1984), reinforces a sense of authenticity and belief in the voice of the artist, validating with hindsight our own original cleverness in recognizing their status. Similarly it is hard to straighten the path back to seventies Kraftwerk, to our eighties use of Kraftwerk, or to revisit with any certainty the time as it actually was. Confusion is a positive response, as certainty would poorly represent the human authors of Kraftwerk's struggle with identity (humans pretending to be dummies becoming human). Besides, at the time I could only display a belief in the gestural medium of rock expression; the screaming guitar, the excruciating wailing vocals, the angst-ridden woe-is-me depression of the lyrics, all these resonated with what it is like to be me. To have outwardly shown any belief that Germanic electro-pop held any such similar significance would have cast doubt on the certainty of my identity (that is, the rock 'I' rather than the Beethoven 'I'). But listen to it I did, particularly the bits that sounded like Pink Floyd and that was fine – an acceptable, or at least unchallenged, contradiction – and besides, other headbangers listened to it as well, we just didn't pin it to our denims. But now I'm confused. I thought rock expression was real but the grand dramatic gesture looks childish and theatrical now, and its current value only that which nostalgia is prepared to lend it.

Hin und Zurück on the Trans-Europe Express – tracks, journeys and time

Trans-Europe Express sits between borders both gesturally and literally. It stands as a literal biography of Kraftwerk's experiences at the time of its recording, constantly travelling between Düsseldorf, Paris and the south of France by rail; but it also charts a significant departure and an arrival. There seems to be a liminality in the space of this record, wherein certain contexts will change irrevocably. The work retains some of the windy sweeping gestures of 'Autobahn', a major motif throughout being a Doppler-effect pitch drop suggesting the passing of the train from a static perspective. There are decisions to be made here; and it is as if the work itself represents the space of their consideration.

During this period the arrival of punk, although not quite the tectonic shift in popular music history that it might have appeared at the time, ironically represented something economically plausible – short, anthemic and polemic tracks with an exciting dynamic and an anarchic heart. Relative to this, *Trans-Europe Express* appears undecided; on the one hand there are shorter track lengths, but several of the tracks, 'Trans-Europe Express', 'Metal on Metal' and 'Franz Schubert', for example, are fairly seamless and form a good 18 minutes regardless. In this way the group are still looking back in the direction of 'Autobahn' and their point of departure, while considering shorter subdivisions of material that might imply a new consideration of what constitutes a Kraftwerk product. That's not to suggest that there is an absence of the former reflective space here – that progressive space in 'Autobahn' into which the listener, or indeed traveller, experiences the immersion of the journey. This is a quality, inherited from the concept album, which Kraftwerk would take and reforge as the machined repetition that would lead to trance (see Rietveld in this collection).

The permanence of octaves (similarity and difference across the divide)

As revered an opera as *Fidelio* is, it might often be overheard in conversation during the intervals between acts that Beethoven's music does not facilitate the representation of different individual voices; its driving force is musical argument, the discourse of the syntagmatic chain, not the conflict of multiple and independent subjective motivations. There is a paradigmatic breach between Simon's brother's Kraftwerk (*Autobahn* and *Trans-Europe Express*) and Simon's Kraftwerk (*The Man-Machine* and *Computer World*) but for the most part the band's sonic identity remains constant, or at least very similar, and differences are often structural rather than timbral, in the lyrics rather than in the sound, in the politics rather than the modalities. But the trademark bouncing octaves remain, the melodies of 'Europe Endless' and 'Neon Lights' both flitter lightly around the sweet major sixth, and both carry the same vulnerable human voice. There are a number of small differences between worlds: one lengthens and the other shortens, one is liminal while the other situates, one extols the rhythm of the machine, the other the rhythm of dance (one is the wheels of the train and the other is Donna Summer), one is symphonic and nostalgic for its beginnings, while the other cares little for its genealogy.

While still retaining a 9-minute track, *The Man-Machine* (1978) unapologetically compacts and condenses the form and shortens the time between the notes and the space between harmonic shifts; the casual effect is that of shorter track lengths, quicker tempi and increased harmonic movement. The album is melodic, driving and visually iconographic. The sleeve was inspired by early Soviet-era Russian suprematism, but controversial in its deployment of black and red (the colours of Nazism), but then the group look to their left, or eastward, in a further reference to the Soviet Union (future and production). The first track deploys Russian, declaring that 'I'm your slave, I'm your worker', leaving a question in the air as to whether this is a critical observation or an admirable example. So while there is sincerity here, there is also perhaps a sense that we have to accept a compromise in our humanity if we are really going to meet the machine with the efficiency of mutually assured production (or reproduction) (see Pattie in this collection). We are workers but we are slaves, and our proximity to the machine, our growing automatism, requires some reduction of the individual.

Herein lies the early modernist debate between the individualist and the universalist, typified by Franz Brentano in his Viennese lectures at the turn of the twentieth century. Brentano was well regarded for the brilliance of his lectures that attempted to reconcile science with faith (characterized by individualism and universalism respectively) out of which sprang Gestalt Theory and Phenomenology (see Watson, 2000, p. 30). Having said this, the mood throughout the album is upbeat, victorious, as forward-marching as it is backward-facing. 'Spacelab' begins by literally beaming us up to the heavens; the track unfolds with an adrenalin surge of excitement in its driving beat, while from this vantage point we look upon something much softer, clear, blue and heavenly in the melody. Back on earth the clock is ticking in the 'Metropolis'; the track is almost identical in length to 'Spacelab', and it is also similar in shape, beginning with something of a dawn before the upbeat electro tempo takes hold. Here again is that future presented in the here and now; but the track also enacts mimesis – in this case, of a German past. There is more than the reference of the title to Fritz Lang's 1927 film. The clock-tick beginning not only parallels the presence of clocks in the film, but also the Heart Machine that powers Lang's *Metropolis*. 'Neon Lights' dissolves architectural space; the space is reconstituted, but instead of buildings, the city is made of light. This is hauntingly mesmeric; instead of ending, its lyric and body acts only as an exposition to set up a long exposure of the city at night. We wait by and reflect upon the exposition while this exposure runs its course for the remainder of the track. Fritz Lang's film surfaces throughout the album in fact; 'Man-Machine' itself is a simple reversal of the film's *Maschinenmensch*, which of course is a robot, an automaton that is created to replace the human. This replacement juxtaposes the running themes of capitalist class struggle, between the worker (slave/robot) and the owner. As a track, 'The Man-Machine' shares something of the same provenance, with the simple juxtaposition of 'pseudo' and 'super' human beings. Technology and machine cultures make us great; we become Nietzsche's *Übermensch*, we hold the God card, but in so doing we also relinquish something of our human authenticity – we are *ersatz*, counterfeit. The *Maschinenmensch* is also a cold object of exquisite female beauty, as the lyrical description in 'The Model' makes clear.

If *The Man-Machine* has something of the pre-war vision of the future about it, *Computer World* shifts to more postmodern concerns. It's as if the sums are finally adding up and, in building again on the economy of the previous album, *Computer World* accurately predicts a major shift in personal, social and state relationships to technology. Retaining the symmetry of six tracks (in practice, 'Numbers' and the reprise of 'Computer World' are one track), longer track lengths are finally rejected. Part of the reason for this is that a short album is sonically better, at least on vinyl – the shorter tracks mean that the grooves on the album are not crowded together. It begins by identifying the cornerstone aspects of this new world – crime, travel, communication and entertainment – with a juxtaposition of organizations that represent these and the objective interests of business, numbers, money and people. The German lyrics are quite different to the English, with additional references to travel, time and medicine; they also refer to the state collection of personal data and tax. When one considers the huge global shifts in social culture and state governance between 1981 and the present, the apparently *naïve* simplicity of this focus is counterpointed by an astonishing predictive accuracy. 'Pocket Calculator' has a childlike simplicity, with lyrics constructed around verbs to do with operation, with being an operator. Here our interface with available technology is celebrated as a form of choice and freedom. The sum is the result of our decisions, of our choice, and we are rewarded with our own private melody. This is not *we* anymore, however; it is *I*. The pocket calculator might now be replaced with the mobile phone, the PDA, the iPod, the Netbook, the Game Boy or any number of variations, because the point here is the magic of our interface with these personal technologies and the resulting way in which our immediate and intermediate worlds are affected. From its outset the success of the Google search engine has to do with the manner in which it employed programmers to write numerical algorithms to suit a search that would only produce the results that were desired. Kraftwerk recognize the coming global significance of numbers in the track of the same name; in their interweaving of numbers said in six languages there is recognition of the emerging importance of an operator as programmer that underpins 'Home Computer'.

In the sequence of these numbers and the interweaving of languages, we are invited to participate in a dawning age of global information. Kraftwerk aren't able at this point to separate the operator from the user, which is hardly surprising, but there are two significant further observations, in the gentility of 'Computer Love', and in 'Home Computer', that are certainly prescient. First, there is a clear recognition that the computer would connect us all to the world and the future from the comfort of our living rooms; but there is also something of the dualism referred to on *The Man-Machine* in 'Computer Love', with a lyrical recognition of the remote but public isolation of being at home but connected, of being at once alone and in company. The final track then borrows a slogan from classic pinball machine gaming – 'It's More Fun to Compete' – replacing the last word with 'compute'. The mantra is repeated throughout the track, and the listener again falls into an undecided space between parody and sincerity; is this a message that is the given of an advert or authority, or is it expressed with the sincerity of the user? The dichotomy certainly reverberates in the contemporary meta-spaces between our spreadsheets, our e-mails, our gaming and our online shopping. It's more fun to compute.

Conclusion: binarisms

Younger brothers are duplicates, they are a repetition, they wish to replicate their elders yet also want differentiation and difference. Albums are similar – the band wishes to progress, develop, change, differentiate; attempting to replicate too closely a previous success would lack integrity – and the band would be accused of pandering to external demand rather than intrasubjective drives. Brothers, like the albums of a band, need to be similar but different, to share genealogy but to maintain independence. Kraftwerk is shared here by brothers, but a subtle divide occurs between *Trans-Europe Express* and *The Man-Machine* that allows a difference of identity to exist while continuity of identity is maintained. So much of what we have written, and indeed the manner in which we have written in this chapter, has a binary quality: Simon and Robert, our brothers and us, parody and sincerity, long and short. The essence of the digital is binary, information stored as a sequence of on-offs, of zero-ones, of flipped coins; how is it then that this vehicle of our writing is also a quality that permeates the consistencies and contradictions of Kraftwerk's music and history, but also forms the fabric of a digital age? The prescience and ascription of authenticity of Kraftwerk's music reverses the normal order of social technology. While emerging digital technologies have attempted to replicate analogue qualities, they began with an inauthentic analogue interpretation of the digital. Kraftwerk were sounding digital long before the digital world attempted to sound analogue, long before the scratchy quality of vinyl was digitally recreated to lend a nostalgic authenticity to trip-hop. During the New Wave we thought that we perceived a parodic humour in the articulation of their look and their compositional form. We thought that this referred to a past vision of a future, or a sardonic and baseless fantasy of a world full of robots and pseudo-humans. In many respects they used the analogue as the herald of its own obsolescence; when we now consider authenticity, we are now fully engaged in a culture of the pseudo-authentic wherein the documents of our life are recodified as binary facsimiles and conveyed along the internet super-autobahn.

Dedicated to Wayne and Stuart, elder brothers.

References

Anderson, L. (1984), *United States*. New York: Harper & Row.

Auslander, P. (2008), *Liveness: Performance in a Mediatized Culture*. London and New York: Routledge.

Baudrillard, J. (1994), *Simulacra and Simulation*. (trans. Sheila Faria Glaser). Michigan: University of Michigan Press.

Benjamin, W. (1969/2002), *Illumination*. London: Random House.

Bourriaud, N. (2007), *Postproduction: Culture as Screenplay: How Art Reprograms the World*. New York: Lukas & Sternberg.

Bracewell, M. (2006), 'Wired for sound'. *Frieze*, 98, April. http://www.frieze.com/issue/article/wired_for_sound/ (last accessed 26 March 2010).

Bussy, P. (2002), *Kraftwerk: Man, Machine and Music*. (2nd edn). London: SAF.

Deleuze, G. (2010), *Difference and Repetition*. (trans. Paul Patton). London and New York: Continuum.

Deleuze, G. and Guattari, F. (2008), *A Thousand Plateaus: Capitalism and Schizophrenia*. (trans. Brian Massumi). London and New York: Continuum.

Derrida, J. (1976), *Of Grammatology*. (trans. Gayatri Chakravorty Spivak). Baltimore: Johns Hopkins University Press.

Harrison, C. and Wood, P. (1995), *Art in Theory 1900–1990: An Anthology of Changing Ideas*. Oxford: Blackwell Publishers.

Lang, F. (Dir. 1927/2003), *Metropolis*. [DVD]. EKA40061. Eureka! Entertainment.

Littlejohn, J. T. (2009), 'Kraftwerk: language, lucre, and loss of identity'. *Popular Music and Society*, 32, (5), 635–53.

Merleau-Ponty, M. (1970), *Phenomenology of Perception*. London: Routledge & Kegan Paul.

Middleton, R. (1990), *Studying Popular Music*. Buckingham: Open University Press.

Moore, A. (2002), 'Authenticity as authentication'. *Popular Music*, 21, (2), 209–23.

Peters, G. (2009), *The Philosophy of Improvisation*. Chicago and London: University of Chicago Press.

Prendergast, M. (2000), *The Ambient Century: From Mahler to Trance – the Evolution of Sound in the Electronic Age*. London and New York: Bloomsbury.

Rockwell, J. (1983), 'Laurie Anderson's music', in J. Kardon (ed.), *Laurie Anderson: Works from 1969 to 1983*. Philadelphia: University of Pennsylvania.

Sternberg, R., Kaufman, J. C. and Pretz, J. E. (2002), *The Creative Conundrum: A Propulsion Model of Kinds of Creative Contribution*. New York and Hove: Psychology Press.

Warner, T. (2003), *Pop Music, Technology and Creativity: Trevor Horn and the Digital Revolution*. Aldershot, UK, and Burlington, VT: Ashgate.

Watson, P. (2000), *A Terrible Beauty: A History of the People and Ideas That Shaped the Modern Mind*. London: Weidenfeld & Nicholson.

5

Kraftwerk: Technology and Composition

Carsten Brocker (translated by Michael Patterson)

Introduction

No musical form is as dependent on instrumentation for its texture as popular electronic music. Thus, any consideration of its musical structure must examine the development of the electronic instruments themselves; in this area of music practice, composition and technology form an unending reciprocal relationship. This chapter therefore sets out to analyse the influence of technical development on Kraftwerk's style of composition, and on the texture of their overall sound. Although the character of the band's music has changed considerably over the years, one can nevertheless trace a clear development from album to album. In addition to technical innovations only the most significant compositional elements will be discussed on the basis of selected examples, since an explicit analysis of all Kraftwerk's pieces would go far beyond the confines of this book.

At this point it is important to draw attention to the critical state of research with regard to the band. The frequently quoted story that the early Kraftwerk recordings were created on instruments developed by the band has, as a result of poorly researched and self-repeating music journalism, led to a host of myths, which with the growth of the internet has only been added to over the years. Supposedly authentic information is based solely on the photographs, video stills and details of equipment given on record sleeves. Primary sources are difficult to access as core Kraftwerk members Ralf Hütter and Florian Schneider have been fiercely protective of their privacy. Moreover, in interviews with individuals associated with Kraftwerk one discovers significant discrepancies in factual information;[1] a typical example is Wolfgang Flür's (1998) totally incorrect account of the functioning of the Matten & Wiechers Synthanorma sequencer (pp. 152–3). Because of these variables it is difficult to give a precise picture of technological components,

since even the simple addition of effects makes it difficult to establish the
source of the original sound. Some information in this chapter has therefore
been based on personal communication, and offers an approximation of the
technological dimensions of Kraftwerk's music rather than solid fact.

Early experiments: Organisation and Kraftwerk – from *Tone Float* to *Kraftwerk 2*

Tone Float (1970)

The pre-Kraftwerk Organisation album *Tone Float* may well appear musically
and technically very different from the music one associates with Kraftwerk.
Nevertheless it is worth a brief look as it was Hütter and Schneider's first
recording and represents the beginning of Kraftwerk's musical development.
The album, both with regard to its conventional instrumentation (percussion instruments, bass guitar, Hammond organ played by Ralf Hütter,
flutes played by Florian Schneider) and its musical texture is exemplary of
Krautrock. It is similar to the recordings of West German contemporaries
Can or Amon Düül II. Well-constructed melodies, typical of Anglo-
American rock and pop music, give way to long improvisational passages.
The compositions can be perceived as ambient soundscapes. Underlining
the experimental character of the music, there are many rhythmically free
and atonal passages, which, in part due to their epic length and their occa-
sionally ethereal sounds, indicate a certain affinity with the 'Berlin School'
(Tangerine Dream, Klaus Schulze, *et al.*).

The most important elements of *Tone Float* are the improvisations since
it is here that one learns something of the style and melodic preferences of
Ralf Hütter – Kraftwerk's main composer from the mid 1970s. For example,
a significant element is the use in the title track of the Dorian mode. The
Dorian mode's major sixth, occasionally exploited in the improvisations,
was to become a stylistic characteristic of later Kraftwerk recordings. On
'Noitasinagro' sporadic blues elements can be heard in Hütter's solo. Hütter,
however, defined the musical style of the album differently by stating:

> We did not have any real strategy; we just took the leap into creating
> industrial music and so abandoned all that had gone before – our edu-
> cation, our musical training. For us it was a completely new departure.
> (Bussy, 1995, p. 24)

'A completely new departure' is an exaggeration, since *Tone Float* has similarities to Krautrock of the period.

The technical production of the album contains no revolutionary effects
even though produced by Conny Plank, who carried responsibility for

all Kraftwerk recordings up to and including the *Autobahn* album (see Grönholm and Albiez and Lindvig in this collection). Alongside Schneider's sonic experiments, which will be discussed in greater detail below, Plank exerted a decisive influence on the musical texture of Kraftwerk's early period, and on the music of other Krautrock bands such as Kluster. Plank had worked as a studio engineer with, among others, Karlheinz Stockhausen and Mauricio Kagel in the 1967–69 period and gained new perspectives on working with sound materials from them. However, though he acknowledged the important influence of Stockhausen, he personally felt restricted by the confines of academic electronic music and indicated that in his own early experimental studio work.

> We often worked with cheap toys and used them in a strange way. We distorted a lot of things and filtered sounds very radically but we didn't call ourselves electronic musicians. We used any scratch on guitars, or noises on an instrument . . . we used pianos and scratched the strings and put echoes on them, and tried to find drastic or attractive elements that turned us on. (qtd. in Diliberto, 1987)

Plank's links to Stockhausen support the commonly held view that Stockhausen functioned as a kind of guru to experimental German rock music at the end of the 1960s. Kraftwerk themselves acknowledged his influence, but also indicated he was one of several influences on their music and Krautrock as a whole (Lynner and Robbley, 1976). This does not mean that the whole range of the contemporary avant-garde was explored; central principles of Stockhausen's composition, like seriality or – in the case of his electronic works – the use of augmented sound synthesis, cannot be found in Krautrock. Similarities with the contemporary music of the post-war period can be found rather in the frequent use of tape-recording effects, which form a musical bridge to *musique concrète*. In fact, the frequent naming of Stockhausen as a source of inspiration – both by the press and the musicians themselves – perhaps stems from an attempt to raise the status of rock music by giving it an academic and artistic gloss. The main thrust of Plank's activity, typical of Krautrock, was to embrace musical experimentation and so create improvisational rock and pop music that broke with existing forms. Moreover, as with Organisation, and later with Neu!, he bought shares in the production and so helped to minimize any financial risks (Rother, 2009).

Generally speaking, the improvisational and experimental character of Krautrock depended to a great extent on recording conditions. Since experimental compositions required a considerable amount of time, some bands built their own studios because they simply could not afford the fees demanded by commercial studios. This self-reliance gave birth to a new kind of musician; one who apart from his musical ability had to be a sound technician. By extending their range of skills, the bands also extended the range of their sounds. For example, Can (who began from 1971 onwards to produce recordings on very basic equipment in a castle called Schloss Nörvenich) rented a cinema in Weilerswist near Cologne, where they built their Inner Space studio and worked until 1978; their bass guitar player Holger Czukay acted as sound technician and editor. Similarly, Kraftwerk developed their own Kling Klang studio in Düsseldorf from 1970 onwards. Beginning as a rehearsal room with only limited recording facilities, the studio was repeatedly augmented, so that more and more post-production work could be carried out on recordings made in rented studios (Barr, 1998, pp. 52–3). By 1975 their technical resources had been sufficiently expanded for all later Kraftwerk albums, beginning with *Radio-Activity*, with the exception of mixing and mastering, to be produced in the Kling Klang studio. Ralf Hütter has summarized the importance of the studio stating, 'The studio actually preceded the band. Everything could be traced back to the studio, as to a mother ship' (Bussy, 1995, p. 34).

Kraftwerk (1970)

Conny Plank's working method can be best established by considering the first Kraftwerk album, which Hütter, Schneider and the two percussionists Andreas Hohmann and Klaus Dinger recorded in Cologne from July to September 1970. The sound technician Klaus Löhmer describes his collaboration with Kraftwerk and Conny Plank by stating:

> 'Nobody knew what we were actually doing . . . we played around . . . It was great that we were always experimenting like this . . . Conny was open to everything'. (Johnstone, 2008)

On considering the individual tracks, one is aware of repeated elements of sound and composition that are characteristic of Kraftwerk's music, and which reappear in different forms on later albums. Thus, 'Ruckzuck' ['Snappy'] begins with a flute solo opening with intervals in fourths in A, which can also be heard in similar form on the 'Strom' ['River'] track from *Kraftwerk 2* as well as the beginning of 'Trans-Europe Express'. Note also the percussive keyboard accompaniment, which consists of one beat using the minor seventh and the major sixth, which shifts the piece into Mixolydian mode – a mode which can be found on other albums. Also typical of the whole album is the track's harmonic and melodic reduction; with the exception of a D major chord with the bass in A in the interlude, all the other chords in 'Ruckzuck' remain within the tonic. The musical emphasis rests totally on rhythm and sound texture; as with *Tone Float*, distortion, wah-wah and delay are prominent. It is also worth mentioning the use of phasing and the application of ring modulator effects to the keyboard's Tubon sound,[2] which gives the music an industrial quality.

This industrial sound is most obvious on the tracks 'Stratovarius' and 'Megaherz', which in the manner of *musique concrète* use tape recordings of machinery and everyday sounds, and served as a prototype for the industrial genre which emerged in Britain in the mid 1970s (for example, Throbbing Gristle's work reveals obvious parallels to the first Kraftwerk album). Surprisingly, 'Stratovarius' (alongside elements of *musique concrète*) uses some of the techniques of serial music. After 10 minutes there is a violin melody reminiscent of chamber music, played in a free rhythm. Apart from E-flat and G this is played on an almost complete twelve-tone scale. If one were to count in the tonal foci of the preceding parts – in the first part consisting of chords on the keyboard, the frequency of which varies within a full tone, it is E-flat; in the second part, dominated by percussion, it is G – the series would be complete. Lastly, 'Vom Himmel Hoch' ['From the Heavens Above'] begins with pulsing sounds that are treated with wah-wah and delay. This may well indicate the use of the often-mentioned oscillators that Kraftwerk built themselves. The musician Klaus Röder, who later played the violin and guitar in the *Autobahn* recording sessions, emphasized Conny Plank's role:

Ralf and Florian always had the right friends who were skilled technicians. Conny was one . . . Conny had a decisive role in the recordings. Ralf and Florian always had these acquaintances, people who worked in studios or who made their own stuff and could deliver the techniques that were needed . . . Electronic equipment was also built. (Johnstone, 2008)

There is clear evidence of the use of oscillators, since in the course of the piece the frequency is altered more strongly than would have been possible to achieve on the Hammond organ or the Tubon. The sound is reminiscent of a World War II bombardment. On the one hand, the change in frequency sounds like a falling bomb; on the other, faster modulation creates the effect of an air-raid siren. The whole effect is reinforced by the intermittent sound of explosions.

After the percussionist Andreas Hohmann left the band during the recording of *Kraftwerk*, the line-up continually changed. When Ralf Hütter left temporarily towards the end of 1970, the group was reduced to Schneider, Dinger and Michael Rother on guitar. Apart from various bootlegs, only a few recordings from this period have been preserved: a live extract from the track 'Rückstoss Gondoliero' ['Gondoliero Reverse'] in the Beat-Club, Bremen, on 22 May 1971, as well as an undated extract from the track 'Köln II' ['Cologne II'] from Westdeutscher Rundfunk in 1971. Recordings made with Conny Plank were never released (Barr, 1998, pp. 56–7). According to

Michael Rother, Kraftwerk's music at this point was founded on improvisation, based on agreed tempi and sound styles (Rother, 2009). Thus, in 'Rückstoss Gondoliero', the harmonic reduction to one basic keynote together with Klaus Dinger's drumming (see below) is typical of Kraftwerk's music at this time. Again according to Rother, the intention was that by restricting themselves to a few notes they would invest them with greater significance. This structural simplification can also be heard on 'Köln II', where the unrelenting tempo is also based on a single chord. Klaus Dinger reported, 'It's difficult to say when Michael and I found our music but it didn't happen on live TV. It was, however, heavily influenced by the live-concerts we had played with Florian' (qtd. in Dee, 1998). Dinger's drumming is based on eighth notes, which, by combining a pulsating bass drum pattern with minimal snare drum on the second and fourth beats, creates a dynamic marching sound. This style of monotonous percussion, described by parts of the music press as *motorik*, can be heard on Kraftwerk's later albums from *Autobahn* to *The Man-Machine*.

Kraftwerk 2 (1971)

The most significant technical innovation on *Kraftwerk 2*, besides the use of a Farfisa Professional Piano, was the introduction of a drum machine, which was acquired through necessity. Hütter complained in several interviews (for example, 1981) that it was impossible at this time to find a percussionist who was prepared to work with drums that were amplified by contact microphones. Hütter described working with this electronic substitute by indicating that '[i]n 1971 Kraftwerk was still without a drummer, so I bought a cheap drum machine giving some preset dance rhythms. By changing the basic sounds with tape echo and filtering we made the rhythm tracks for our second album' (qtd. in Beecher, 1981). Despite his claim to have treated the percussion with tape echo and filtering, the synthetic sounds of the drum machine lack precisely these enhancements.

A further significant development can be heard on the first track, 'Kling Klang'. In addition to already familiar sound experiments, the quality of the sound and the music are altered through the different playing speeds of tape recorders. Thus, in the introduction, some of the metallic percussion instruments are played at a relatively slow speed, giving the whole sound a synthetic character with low frequencies. After two minutes the pattern of the drumming is matched to the one-beat cadenza motif of the bass; the speed of the master tape is altered shortly afterwards, so that together with a minimal change in tempo a half-tone slide from G to A-flat is achieved. This procedure is maintained throughout the whole piece, which finally climaxes in B major. After the introduction there is an accompaniment in the major key on the Farfisa piano, with the occasional suggestion of the subdominant. This light-hearted style of accompaniment stands in obvious contrast to the dark, industrial sound of their previous album. Reinforced by the banal, repetitive percussion of the drum machine, it evokes a gently trivial atmosphere that anticipates the primarily major key sounds of *Ralf and Florian* and *Autobahn*.

The sound of transition: *Ralf and Florian*

Ralf and Florian (1973) is particularly significant, in that it represents the transition between early experiments and the characteristic Kraftwerk sound. Above all, it saw the acquisition of analogue synthesizers – the Minimoog and the EMS Synthi A.[3] Up to this point, apart from the oscillators, the Kraftwerk sound was derived from the innovative manipulation of traditional rock instruments (keyboard, drums or guitar), together with acoustic instruments (flute and violin). Now, however, they had the opportunity to create music based entirely on electronically generated and modulated signals – a development that, given bands like Mother Mallard, Tangerine Dream or Popol Vuh were already using the technology, Hütter and Schneider arrived at relatively late. Equally important is the use of speech on 'Ananas Symphonie' ['Pineapple Symphony'], which is manipulated by a twelve-track vocoder built by Peter Leunig and Knut Obermayr.[4] After the success of *Autobahn* these machine voices became Kraftwerk's stock-in-trade, and their introduction into popular music was regularly ascribed to Hütter and Schneider.

If we consider the compositional element of the album, it is clear that while many tracks, by using tape-recorder effects and major harmonies, reveal a clear link to 'Kling Klang', there are also well-developed melodies. According to Barr (1998), this change in direction was above all due to the influence of Emil Schult:

Schult's impact on the group had an immediate effect on the album … Though he was untrained as a musician, he had an instinctive ear for melody. The simple but effective phrases he picked out during the improvised sessions and concerts which he was involved in were largely a result of his limited facility on the guitar and violin but they intrigued both Hütter and Schneider who began exploring ways of simplifying their own melodic ideas. (p. 66)

'Kristallo' is especially notable as it reveals the adoption of this new melodic element, and it anticipates techno by combining the drum machine with a sixteenth-note bass pattern, created by the synthesizer. The track's short, repeated fragment of a melody references the minor third as the highest note (deriving from a minor 7/9 chord based on the fifth) and ends on the tonic. What at first appears banal is developed into an important stylistic element featured on later Kraftwerk albums. For example, the motif recurs on 'Radio-Activity', 'Hall of Mirrors', 'Showroom Dummies', 'Computer World' and 'Expo 2000'.

Electronic pop music: from *Autobahn* to *The Mix*

Autobahn (1974)

Autobahn was completed, after initial pre-production work at Kling Klang, in Conny's Studio in Cologne with Hütter and Schneider joined by Wolfgang Flür and Klaus Röder.[5] This album completes Kraftwerk's transition from experimental Krautrock to electronic pop music. Apart from the occasional melody played on the flute or guitar, all essential musical elements are created on the synthesizer or drum machine, and the simplicity of the underlying melodies and harmonies point to pop music. Another important feature is the introduction of lyrics; while speech was introduced in 'Ananas Symphonie' as phonetic colouring, this is the first time that language is used for communication. Karl Bartos regards this as the major characteristic of Kraftwerk's transition (Johnstone, 2008), stating, 'They [Hütter and Schneider] came from this classical angle, that's how I see it, and then they moved to pop music by adding lyrics. There is no pop music without lyrics apparently'. However the lyrics provide little evidence of intellectual profundity. Karl Bartos (qtd. in Piltz, 1998, p. 53) suggests that '[a]part from a few exceptions, the texts are descriptive rather than meaningful. If for example the text consists of a single word, this leaves plenty of room for interpretation'. The German musician and journalist Wolfgang Seidel goes further in seeing Kraftwerk's lyrics as a parody of German pop music and their image as a caricature of the disciplined and industrious German (Johnstone, 2008). (See Albiez and Lindvig in this collection.)

By contrast, Hütter regarded the introduction of lyrics merely as a way of extending the sound spectrum, by indicating, 'We use our voices as an additional instrument. Words simply provide a different pattern of rhythm; it is a part of our unique sound' (Bussy, 1995, p. 72). Because of the vocal limitation of Hütter and Schneider we have the basic impression of *Sprechgesang*, a vocal technique between singing and speaking, which through monotony reinforces the sensation of driving on an autobahn.

The most important technical element of the album is phasing – also found on *Ralf and Florian* (if not to the same extent). Since there is virtually no phasing on *Radio-Activity*, which was the post-Plank recording, it could be surmised that phasing was Plank's idea. Although Hütter and Schneider are credited as producers on the sleeve and Plank is credited as the sound engineer, Röder indicates Plank's contribution to the musical structure and to the overall sound of the band was considerable by stating that

Conny Plank played a decisive role. He mixed everything and assembled individual sounds into a whole. That was, I believe the last time that Conny did that. He then told me that he did not know what Kraftwerk would sound like when he was no longer there. (Johnstone, 2008)

The title track, 'Autobahn', was a milestone in Kraftwerk's development, both musically and commercially. Despite many innovations, though, familiar fragments of sound and composition can be distinguished; for example, the use of taped sounds like the car starting up at the beginning of the track or, later, noises from a radio. However, the musical building blocks combine to create new elements that are developed in subsequent albums. One example is provided by the sound of the vocoder at the beginning of the track, which recalls 'Ananas Symphonie' and presages the vocoder passage on 'Trans-Europe Express'. Similarly, the minimal automated percussion playing is reminiscent of Klaus Dinger's drumming with Neu! and of the drum machine of the previous albums. The same relationships can be found in the bass riffs, based on fourths and fifths, on 'Autobahn', 'Kristallo' and 'Klingklang'. This is possibly due to the fact that these all arose in long improvisations (hence also their slightly changing structure) and that their rhythmic and melodic patterns are determined by the ease with which jumps of octaves, fifths and fourths can be played on the keyboard. Through the use of delay synchronized with the tempo the sequence achieves a lively, rhythmic quality – a trick which is later fully exploited in *Computer World*.

The best way of indicating how the musical texture of 'Autobahn' is determined by technicalities and by the limitations of the available instrumentation is by examining the use of the synthesizer and the harmonic structure of the music. The theme consists of two melodies created on the Minimoog, which are split to the right and to the left sides of the mix. On the right track the three oscillators are set at thirds, the highest note of which corresponds to the basic note of the underlying chord. Using a monophonic synthesizer there was obviously no possibility of playing polyphonically and this had a direct effect on the composition. Thus all harmonies have to be in the major key, deriving from the models of pop music composition which because of their monotonality allow only three major chords in the diatonic scale. These three indeed do appear in a major cadenza as the main melody (F major, B-flat major, C major and finally F major again), which eventually shifts to G major. There then follows a change in the dominant to D major. Because of the aforementioned limitations, the thirds remain on the tonic, while the Mixolydian melody is taken over by a percussive sound on the synthesizer. The harmonic sequence, which breaks free from all restraints and is again taken up by the Minimoog, concludes with a shift (again in thirds) in whole notes through B-flat major, C major and D major. It is interesting that, although 'Autobahn' can be categorized as pop music, the melodic focus actually rests with the synthesizer and the passages of song are supplementary. This reliance on instrumentally realized hooks represents one of Kraftwerk's major stylistic characteristics.

Radio-Activity (1975)

If *Autobahn* represents the turning point in Kraftwerk's move towards pop music, *Radio-Activity*'s purist electronic instrumentation and the ambiguous technical meaning of the title act as a launch pad for the familiar image we have of the group. The album was recorded by Hütter, Schneider, and Flür, together with percussionist Karl Bartos, who had joined them for the US tour in the spring of 1975 (a line-up which remained fixed until 1987). Walter Quintus acted as sound engineer and Peter Bollig as technician in the Kling Klang studio. According to Wolfgang Flür, the concept for *Radio-Activity* arose as a result of the many radio interviews which Hütter and Schneider had given during their US tour, stating that '[w]hen we were on the flight back [from the US to Germany], I heard Ralf and Emil [Schult] speaking about "Radio activity is in the air for you and me."' (Flür, 2001)

The track 'The Voice of Energy' may, however, have another source. In 1949, Werner Meyer-Eppler had recorded an example of synthetic speech entitled 'Die Stimme der Energie' in which a text is distorted by a vocoder (Ungeheuer, 1992, pp. 98–9); the Kraftwerk version uses an almost identical text. There are also parallels to Meyer-Eppler on other tracks. For example, 'News' filters several news items into different frequencies, a technique used by Meyer-Eppler in his piece 'Gefilterte Sprache' ['Filtered Language']. The origin of these similarities can possibly be found in the night-time programmes broadcast by Westdeutscher Rundfunk. Hütter has indicated that, when growing up in the 1950s and 1960s,

[w]e were boys listening to the late-night radio of electronic music coming from WDR in Köln, where there was one of the first electronic studios in the world. They played a lot of late-night programmes with strange sounds and noise. So it was like our dedication to the age of radio, and radiation at the same time, breaking the taboo of including everyday political themes into the music. (Hütter, 1981)

Inspired by this, *Radio-Activity* embarked on a new confrontation with phonetics and language and created an aura for the group as pioneers in the use of phonetic experiments in pop music. However, as we have seen, Kraftwerk's sound is not entirely reliant on their own artistic achievement and clearly reveals evidence of external sources.

With regard to individual distortions of language, it is clear that 'Radioland',

'The Voice of Energy', 'Radio Stars' and 'Ohm, Sweet Ohm' used the vocoder. The speech on 'Uranium' points to the use of a Votrax speech synthesizer, which Ralf Hütter often called a 'singing typewriter' (qtd. in Schober, 1976). Further evidence for this is provided by the unrhythmic series of individual phonemes characteristic of the Votrax and by a lack of any audible filtering, typical of the vocoder. In addition to these phonetic elements there is a significant use of electronic equipment in the creation of sounds. Thus, almost every track is enriched and indeed sometimes dictated by the filter frequency modulations achieved on the EMS Synthi A and the ARP Odyssey, purchased prior to the US tour (e.g. 'Radio Stars'), which sometimes occupy the highest range of audible frequencies. Moreover, polyphonic sound textures are generated by the orchestron (purchased during the US tour and used on *Radio-Activity* and *Trans-Europe Express*). This instrument used optical discs to generate string and choral sounds, rather than the tapes used in the mellotron. There are also frequent ethereal vibrato sounds from the synthesizer, reminiscent of a theremin.

This album has two different strands. There are experimental pieces, consisting of linguistic distortion rather than harmony or melody ('Intermission', 'News', 'The Voice of Energy', 'Radio Stars' and 'Uranium'). There are also pop music structures of a length suitable for broadcasting and that utilize a verse-chorus form. Lyrics are also used more plentifully, and many texts are sung in both German and English ('Radio-Activity', 'Radio Land', 'Airwaves').

Although *Radio-Activity* was initially produced in Kling Klang, with Walter Quintus, one must not underestimate the contribution of the technician Peter Bollig. He was involved in the band's technical innovations from the mid 1970s, up to the rebuilding of the Kling Klang studio from 1978 onwards. He was responsible for the photoelectric percussion device known as the 'cage' – a cube-like frame constructed out of metal pipes by Bollig in 1976. On the sides photoelectric cells were mounted; when their contacts were broken, this triggered the sounds of the drum machine. Bollig was also responsible for Schneider's electric flute, which consisted of a flute-like metal pipe attached to a tripod. On the pipe were electronic buttons that could activate a synthesizer (Flür, 1998, pp. 131–4). Once again Klaus Röder's statement rings true, that the frequently lauded position of Kraftwerk as innovators of music technology actually came from the skills of their colleagues.

Trans-Europe Express (1977)

Trans-Europe Express is the first album in which all the compositions, with the exception of 'Endless Endless', are by Hütter who is therefore responsible for the album's move from experimental sounds to formal structures and melodies. Also, the introduction of the Matten & Wiechers Synthanorma sequencer lends a mechanical precision to music which persists to this day.

Hütter's compositions on *Trans-Europe Express* work within the technical limitations of the sequencer; this is evident on the first track, 'Europe
Endless'. It begins with a three-note major arpeggio driven by the sequencer
and repeated through the whole piece; this is played with a percussive
sound, and with delay. This use of a major sequence means, however, that
the minor chords played in real time are introduced only with great difficulty – just as with the use of the Minimoog on *Autobahn*. Such a harmonic
sequence can therefore be introduced only in cadenzas.

The band deals with this problem by employing a harmonic shift. While
the introduction, the main melody and the following song are all in G major,
the second part of the song is in B major. There is here neither a transitional
melodic or harmonic modulation nor an introductory drum break. The
F-sharp major middle section, which follows the repeat of the two parts, is not
musically introduced either. This juxtaposition of thematic elements reinforces
the monotonous machine-like quality of the constantly repeated synthesizer
sequence. The drum pattern is simple, with quarter-note changes on the
bass and snare drum beats and on the hi-hat on the off beats, and also in the
structured build-up in the introduction of the piece, with successive elements
being added. This repetition, as well as the never-changing drum pattern, tie
the different elements together and so lend the piece certain uniformity. The
main element of the melody, besides the relentless use of the three chords, is
the frequent use of the major sixth both in the synthesizer theme and in the
two song sections and their connected vocoder parts. The synthesizer melody
in the linking passages manipulates this thematically by using major seconds
and fourths; an improvisation develops from this, building from the third to
the fifth and finally to the minor seventh. The most notable aural effects besides
the use of the orchestron for polyphonic choral harmonies are synthesizer
vibrato (as in *Radio-Activity*) and the use of the EMS Vocoder (used here for
the first time, and further used on subsequent albums).

The title track structurally unites the first three compositions on the
album. It is based, like 'Europe Endless', both on harmonic shifts and on the
formal patterning derived from the use of the new sequencer. However, it also
has a pop song structure, with verse and chorus (like both 'Hall of Mirrors'
and 'Showroom Dummies'). Here the main rhythm (provided by two ostinato
drum patterns) is taken over by a hi-hat sound, with phasing and a sixteenth-
note delay. This rhythmic motif alludes to the sound of a railway carriage as it
passes over the joints in the rails. The melody is based on two themes, both of
which are played on the orchestron. The first melody is based on the layering
of six fourths. The second theme is notable above all for its use of the minor
ninth, which was to be taken up several times on the 1981 album *Computer
World*. Structurally, it is significant that the phrase 'Trans-Europe Express'
is repeated 32 times at the end of the piece. This structural device bears out
a statement by the DJ Grandmaster Flash, for whom 'Trans-Europe Express'

is one of the few pieces that he would never scratch, break or extend since it was already mixed (Toop, 1992, pp. 205–6).

The Man-Machine (1978)

Musically *The Man-Machine* continues on from where *Trans-Europe Express* ends. Again, both sequencers and vocoder are used extensively, and the compositions display the type of harmonic shifts and synthesizer melodies that played an important role in the band's work since *Ralf and Florian*. Here for the first time Karl Bartos is named alongside Hütter and Schneider as composer. Since Bartos collaborated with Hütter on all subsequent compositions until his departure in 1990, it is worthwhile looking more closely at his description of Kraftwerk's working methods:

> [O]ne of us would write the introduction, another the ending, we would then improvise, jamming for three or four hours . . . Florian would work above all on the sound and with the machines; he is not someone I would necessarily call a musician, he is an artist rather . . . He actually is not familiar with musical chords, his inspiration is more oriental: playing around for hours lost in thought. (Bussy, 1995, p. 126)

According to Flür, synthesizer sequences ran for days in the studio with only minimal variations, just to test their effect (1998, p. 157). The machine-like precision of the percussion was achieved with a special device, made by Matten & Wiechers; this was a console with six rows of switches for the Synthanorma sequencer, which controlled individual percussion sounds (Matten, 2009). Since *Autobahn*, the drum machine had been augmented by various sounds created on the synthesizer. Now, very short filter sweeps with high resonance frequency, synchronized with delayed bass sequences, lent a pulsing rhythmic background to the sparse percussion. Furthermore, in addition to the vocoder voices and the theremin-type synthesizer sounds already familiar from *Radio-Activity*, a filter-frequency-modulated polyphonic synthesizer – a Polymoog – is used for the first time (Matten, 2009). In their syncopated synthesizer and drum machine sequences both 'Neon Lights' and 'The Man-Machine' anticipate the rhythmic complexity of *Computer World*. By contrast, other tracks continue the minimalistic linearity of *Trans-Europe Express* through the simple augmentation of the drum pattern, in the form of relentless quarter notes and the playing of the snare drum on the second and fourth beats. The drum pattern of 'Metropolis' is particularly noteworthy: not only do the consistent quarter notes of the bass drum have a disco feel but also the use of white noise in conjunction with the snare drum sounds almost like a sample of the snare drum used in Giorgio Moroder's 'I Feel Love'. These similarities together with the sixteenth-note bass pattern suggest – at least with regard to the sound aesthetic – a link with Moroder's recordings; the vocoder passage at the beginning of Moroder's 1977 piece 'From Here to Eternity' suggests a reciprocal influence.

Although many tracks on the album use pop song structures, the use of the sequencer and the resulting harmonic shifts reveal the same patterning as *Trans-Europe Express*. One of the few exceptions, containing a harmony tied to a sequence of notes is 'The Model', which is the most pop-music-like track on the album. Its length (3:44) makes it suitable for broadcasting, and it fulfils the usual criteria for the pop song by using an untypical long, discursive lyric. A central element is the 2-bar-long bass rhythm, which is reinforced by an accompanying chord that consists of eight notes based on A minor and E minor. This provides the basis for a melody alternately sung and played on the synthesizer as in 'Radio-Activity'.

By using brass-like sounds, powerful synthesizer melodies and strong rhythms, the album contributed to the development of synthpop in England in the late 1970s. Early releases by British bands such as the Human League, Soft Cell, Depeche Mode, Ultravox, New Order and Visage show clear parallels both in structure and melody to *The Man-Machine* (see Albiez and Witts in this collection).

Computer World (1981)

Computer World was released three years after *The Man-Machine*. The (then) relatively long period between the two albums was due to two factors: the gradual growth in the range of instruments and the increasing technical difficulty of performing their music. This meant that after the release of *The Man-Machine* Kraftwerk did not tour (see Pattie in this collection). To enable them to perform again, they redesigned and rebuilt the Kling Klang studio so it could be transported in modules and assembled with relative ease on stage. Wolfgang Flür and Matten and Wiecher technician Joachim Dehmann undertook most of the work. The decision to integrate the studio into their performances emphasizes the importance to the band of the technological aspects of their music, and how complex the textural dimension of their sound was becoming. Traditional compositional considerations, such as harmony and melody, tended to be pushed to one side. As Hütter put it, '[w]e spend a month on the sound and five minutes on the chord changes'(qtd. in Beecher, 1981).

Because of this growing complexity, it is harder to establish exactly what equipment was used to create individual sounds. The only detailed source of information about the equipment in the Kling Klang studio is provided by a technical article in *Electronics and Music Maker* (Beecher, 1981), published in conjunction with the *Computer World* tour in 1981. There were new additions from Korg (in particular the PS-3300) and Sequential Circuits (the Prophet 5), together with a Sennheiser Vocoder VSM-201. According to Hütter, this was the model specially developed for Kraftwerk in the early 1970s. However, in view of the use of the vocoder developed by Leunig and Obermayer, this seems unlikely (Barr, 1998, p. 153). The concept of the album is further supported by the use of several appliances from the computer and toy industry: a Casio pocket calculator, a Dübreq Stylophone, a Bee Gees Rhythm Machine toy keyboard made by Mattel, and voice-producing appliances from Texas Instruments. The complex layering of sounds in the music is reflected in the juxtaposition of several synthesizer sequences and drum patterns that are delayed and syncopated. Perhaps this reflected the band's growing interest in African-American music that had clearly developed apace since their US Pop Music Disco award success in 1977 (p. 126). This would explain some of the similarities in the synthesizer sequences on *Computer World*, which, in their tendency to mesh sounds together, fulfil the same rhythmic function as guitar or clavinet licks in funk.

The first track, 'Computer World', offers a musical and sonic cross-section of the album. In the introduction the quarter notes of the bass drum and the high resonating filter sweeps as substitute snares (because of its synthetic, percussive character this sound will henceforth be termed 'synclick') followed by the hi-hat on the offbeats still display characteristics from previous albums. However, with the addition of the main theme on the synthesizer, and the varied synthesizer sequences and broken drum patterns, the track develops a rhythmic sophistication missing from *The Man-Machine*. This is supported by the bass pattern, which consists of two notes, which are played on the first beat and the second eighth of the second beat. The syncopation of the third beat that results from this operates as the central rhythmic element of the whole album. Together with the use of the vocoder for the chorus, the Speak & Spell educational toy from Texas Instruments is used for the first time in the bridge. This, again, is characteristic of the album as a whole, which is notable for the frequent use of manipulated or synthetically generated voices – an echo of the phonetic experiments on *Radio-Activity*. On both albums the innovative use in a musical context of products from the entertainment industry, like the Votrax voice synthesizer or the Speak & Spell, is due to Florian Schneider.

The linked pieces 'Numbers' and 'Computer World 2' are notable for their drum pattern, which, through the syncopation similar to the bass sequence of 'Computer World' on the second eighth of the second beat, together with a consistent snare drum pattern on the second and fourth beats, arguably serves as a blueprint for 'electro' drum rhythms. In addition on both tracks there is, besides the strongly modulated synthesizer sounds added to the bass and snare drum passages of 'Numbers', a permanent synclick sequence which undergoes gentle rhythmic changes based on sixteenth notes, substituting for a hi-hat pattern. The embedding of the synclick sound into the percussion not only became a central element in 'electro' but also appeared in many pop recordings of the 1980s.

Tour de France (1983) and Techno-Pop/Electric Café (1986)

Electric Café, the album that followed *Computer World*, had various working titles including *Techno-Pop*. Apart from two bootlegs circulating on the internet (alleged demo versions of the tracks 'Techno-Pop' and 'Sex Object'), the only official release available from early production sessions was the single 'Tour de France' (1983). Here Kraftwerk embarked on a new musical phase, using sampling for the first time. At the beginning of the piece sampled sounds of breathing are heard (on the B-side of the Maxi version these are joined by sampled bicycle sounds), but also sampled instrument sounds like a slap bass or an arpeggiated harp. In addition to familiar stylistic elements, like the spoken rather than sung text and the synthesizer melody that acts as a chorus, there are much harder sounds in the percussion. These are closely allied to 'Numbers' and 'Computer World 2' and are produced mainly on a LinnDrum, found in many recordings at that time.

By using sounds that had become standardized industrial products, Kraftwerk were now seemingly neither musical nor technological leaders in their field, and their music began to merge with a familiar sonic backdrop developed in recent pop productions. They would be judged against recordings that had reached the new standard of sound aesthetic set by *Computer World*. Barr (1998) considers this the reason why in 1984 Hütter decided to undertake the final mix of the still analogue recordings of *Techno-Pop* in The Power Station studio in Los Angeles – a studio that seemed to have its finger on the pulse of the day (pp. 173–4). However, Bartos (in Johnstone, 2008) indicates that neither Hütter nor Schneider were satisfied with the final mix, so they further altered the 'final' recordings, which were not released until 1986 as *Electric Café*. According to Hütter,

> [t]his *Techno-Pop* LP was just about ready, but we then worked on it some more. This was happening while we were switching from analogue tapes to digital technology. With all these changes and sampling like mad going on, we dithered, and things got delayed. We have not used recording tapes for five years. (qtd. in Reinboth, 1991)

The individual tracks are notable for the application of FM and wavetable synthesis and the programmatic use of sampling, which resulted from the acquisition of new equipment: the NED Synclavier, the E-mu Emulator sampler and the PPG Wave synthesizer (Barr, 1998, p. 172). The emphasis on rhythm was intended primarily to place the music in the context of the dance floor; this can be heard on the first three tracks, which are linked thematically. 'Boing Boom Tschak' begins with a collage of manipulated speech samples, which create a changing rhythm by using varying reverbs and delays with different tempi. In addition there is significant use of synthetic speech created mainly on a Votrax speech synthesizer. The strong patterning of 'Boing Boom Tschak' is continued on the following track, 'Techno-Pop'. Here the percussive sounds and fills are united by a recurrent G-sharp minor melody. Since this melody is so fragmentary, the musical essence of this very repetitive piece is to be sought, alongside the voices in several languages and Hütter's singing, in the varied sounds of the synthesizers and their selective manipulation (with reverb, delay, reversing and flanging).

The track 'Musique Non-Stop' forms the conclusion of this rhythmically and melodically linked trilogy. Here the main feature is a variation of the melodic motif already encountered in the linking passage of 'Techno-Pop'. This theme is rendered by samples of a synthetically generated female voice, underscored by a loop of one of the samples treated with an echo effect. In addition to the percussive sounds of the Linn drum machine, a Roland TR-808 drum machine was used that was also manipulated with delays and artificial reverbs.

The Mix (1991)

During the production of *Electric Café* the Kling Klang studio was reconstructed once again. Digital equipment was acquired and computer processing introduced, and the band digitized their analogue multi-track recording tapes. Fritz Hilpert undertook this work – he had replaced Wolfgang Flür in 1990 after the latter's gradual withdrawal from the group between 1987 and 1989. After *Electric Café*, the band considered releasing a 'Best of' album using digitized material, but then, fearing that this might be seen as succumbing to commercial pressure, decided instead to create a remix album. *The Mix* can be seen as a concession to the popular genres of techno and house; the cool, digital atmosphere of *Electric Café* resurfaces here but is treated with effects or replaced by contemporary counterparts. Besides sampling the car sounds on 'Autobahn' or several percussion samples on 'Metal on Metal', the most notable feature is the use of a particular bass drum, which at the end of the 1980s was a characteristic element of techno and house and was produced on the Roland TR-909 drum machine. This would seem to have been an attempt on many of their tracks to adapt the former trailblazing Kraftwerk sound to a contemporary recording aesthetic by combining a bass drum pattern based on quarter notes together with an offbeat hi-hat. This closeness to electronic dance music is reflected also in the style of composition: the mainly organ-like chord patterns of 'Computer Love', 'Pocket Calculator' and 'Dentaku' are on almost every track accompanied by syncopated bass lines. The best known of these is surely the synthesizer sequence of 'The Robots' – a key feature of Kraftwerk's live shows (see Pattie in this collection).

Further techno and house elements can be found in the structure of the tracks. For example, while 'Autobahn' or 'Trans-Europe Express' were shortened, and tracks like 'Pocket Calculator', 'Dentaku', 'Home Computer', 'It's More Fun to Compute', 'Boing Boom Tschak' and 'Musique Non-Stop' were mixed to emphasize the main theme, other tracks were lengthened by the addition of percussion and atonal effects, which offered DJs more scope for mixing. In addition to textual changes like the omission of the third verse of 'Trans-Europe Express' and the insertion of an explicitly anti-atomic power message on 'Radio-Activity', there was another technical innovation: as on *Electric Café* almost all vocoder-like voices were produced by the Votrax speech synthesizer, or at least the vocoder-manipulated voices on the original albums were replaced with synthetic versions. This was achieved by the Robovox speech synthesis system, which, unlike on *Electric Café*, was recorded in real time. In 1990, Florian Schneider applied for a patent at the European Patent Office for this 'System for and method of synthesizing singing in real time'.[6] This functions as follows: the Votrax chip (SC-02) provides the sound, which is controlled by a midi and a phonetic keyboard; the Doepfer-modified phonetic keyboard controls the individual phonemes of the Votrax, which at the same time are altered in pitch and length by the midi keyboard. Although the use of the Robovox represents a significant element of the group's style and all of the tracks on *The Mix* can be heard in similar form in concerts to this day, this does not disguise the fact that technically the album has a slightly anachronistic feel.

The twenty-first century: *Expo 2000, Tour de France Soundtracks* and *Minimum–Maximum*

Expo 2000 (2000)

The 1990s saw a different line-up and a long gap with no new recordings but the band made some interesting technological changes. Their collaboration with Doepfer continued with the development of the Midi Analogue Sequencer MAQ 16/3 as well as the Vocoder A-129 in 1992 and 1997. 'Expo 2000' (2000) was commissioned by the world exhibition of the same name. Originally this consisted of a melody fragment in six languages generated with synthetic voices. Because the piece is technically much more complex than *The Mix*, it is hard to establish how the individual sounds were created. It seems likely though that a PC system was at the centre of the production. Steinberg are credited on the single, therefore it is probable a version of Cubase (Steinberg's audio and midi production platform) was utilized alongside VST instrument and effect plug-ins. The creation of the synthetic voices – probably through a mixture of Robovox and vocoder – is similarly complex. 'Expo 2000', with its syncopated drum pattern and use of synclicks contains typical 'electro' elements; on the other hand, in its use of powerful reverbs, strong delays and the manipulation of the sound spectrum, it reveals some of the characteristics of 'IDM' (Intelligent Dance Music). In any case, compared with *The Mix*, it reveals a significant development in technique and anticipates the sound of *Tour de France Soundtracks*.

Tour de France Soundtracks (2003)

Tour de France Soundtracks was released in August 2003. Consistent with the ongoing computerization of the Kling Klang studio, it has been suggested – with information apparently gleaned from manufacturers' sites and publications (Anon. 2003) – that it was produced on a networked computer setup with Sony VAIO laptops utilizing Steinberg's VST System Link technology. The laptops had Steinberg Cubase SX and TC Works PowerCore PCI cards (enabling high-quality effects plug-ins with dedicated processors to be accessed and controlled from Cubase SX) at the heart of the system. All sounds were generated in the computers using virtual instruments (VST) such as the HALion virtual sampler and various Native Instruments applications. On this adoption of a fully integrated music production computer system, Fritz Hilpert commented:

> We've been trying a lot of new things, and the virtual technologies were key to that . . . We all have an 'old-school' studio background where lots of cables and complex connections are required before anything goes. Working with virtual setups has changed all that. (Hilpert, 2003)

Whether, in addition to this concept of virtual sound, creation and control, there was also recourse to external sound sources when recording *Tour de France Soundtracks* cannot be ascertained. The sound texture of the many synthetic voices indicates again that the Robovox system was used, alongside the TC-Helicon VoiceModeler. For example, Hilpert (2003) indicated the latter was used 'to create these whispery voices in the chorus on the track "Elektrokardiogramm" . . .'. The affinity to IDM noted on 'Expo 2000' is here continued, reflected not only in the manipulation of the sound spectrum through a heavy use of filtering effects but also in the selective use of delays and reverbs (created according to Hilpert by the TC MegaReverb plug-in). The programmatic use of effects is seen primarily in the first five thematically linked tracks ('Prologue', 'Tour de France Étape 1–3' and 'Chrono').

At the centre of this is a pattern of chords, appearing in two variations, based on a percussive pulsing sound that is manipulated with reverb and delay and passed through a high-resonance filter. Harmonically based on F minor, it moves between F minor and C minor chords underscoring the minor seventh. The rest consists of various thirds, based on an F minor chord enriched with the minor seventh and the major ninth, which are counteracted by a third consisting of B and D notes. This tritone-like motif is a recurring compositional element in these pieces. Rhythmically it is notable that, despite the fact the bass drum is played consistently on the quarter notes, there is no gimmicky technical colouring. Rather it develops complexity through utilizing a minimalist and middle-frequency bass drum sample combined with the recurrent offbeat playing of the hi-hat.

Minimum–Maximum (2005)

Although *Minimum–Maximum*, to date Kraftwerk's only live album, contains no new compositions, it is worthy of mention here, not just for the sake of completeness but also because like the 1991 *The Mix* it presents the best-known pieces since 'Autobahn' in a contemporary manner. Since it is also their most recent album, it offers the most up-to-date insight into Kraftwerk's technical development. The album comprises extracts from the concerts of their 2004 world tour, the sound aesthetic of which displays strong similarities with *Tour de France Soundtracks*. As well as manipulation of sound by selectively executed delays and reverbs there is above all excessive filtering with powerful resonance and frequency cut-off pitch shifting. Moreover, many melodies are enriched with the familiar crystalline sine wave sounds created by multilayered oscillators found on the previous album. Although some tracks in their texture are based on *The Mix* version, some have been revised in order to get rid of the somewhat trivial technical gimmicks of the 1990s. Just as 'Home Computer' returned to its original sampled sounds and to its syncopated drum pattern instead of the relentless four-note pattern of *The Mix*, so too the first part of 'Radio-Activity' uses the drum pattern of the original 1975 version.

The future?

It is difficult to predict how Kraftwerk's future compositions will sound. Although the band has always maintained a certain disciplined continuity, which remained unaffected by the departure of Karl Bartos who had been strongly involved in all compositions from *The Man-Machine* to *Electric Café*, founder member Florian Schneider's departure in April 2009 may be harder to overcome. It was above all his influence in introducing synthetic voices and his inspiration in developing the band's sound texture that helped to create Kraftwerk's unique character and allowed the band to claim a major place in the history of electronic music.

The author would like to thank Michael Rother, Ludwig Rehberg, Dirk Matten, Rüdiger Barth and Peter Leunig who were interviewed for this chapter.

Notes

1. In Lynner and Robbley (1976), to the question, 'When you were at the academy, were you studying music and composition?' Ralf Hütter replied 'Yes'. However, Flür (1998, p. 63) and Eberhard Kranemann (http://www.e-kranemann.de/kraftw1/start.htm [last accessed 21 March 2010]) indicate Hütter studied architecture. Bussy states that Hütter studied the electronic organ at the Düsseldorfer Konservatorium – Frank Stadler, chief librarian at the Robert Schumann Hochschule in Düsseldorf, insists no such course existed.

2. The 'Tubon' is a manual organ-like instrument made by the Swedish firm Joh Mustad AB.

3. Flür (1998, p. 54) maintains Schneider owned an ARP Odyssey controlled by a foil touch screen. It is more likely that it was an EMS Synthi A, with a KS control (seen on the back of the *Ralf and Florian* cover). Dirk Matten, says the ARP Odyssey was bought after the completion of *Autobahn*.

4. The EMS and Sennheiser vocoder had not been introduced in 1975, so it must be assumed the Leunig and Obermayr vocoder was also used for this album (Matten, 2009).

5. The credits of the 2009 *Autobahn* re-master state Hütter and Schneider played almost all the instruments on the album, with Flür contributing 'percussion' only on 'Kometenmelodie 2' and Röder 'electric violin' on 'Mitternacht'.

6. The first page of the patent application, naming Florian Schneider, Gert Ott and Gert Jalass, can be viewed at http://kraftwerk.technopop.com.br/data_technology.php.

References

Anon. (2003), 'Tour de France Soundtracks and new technologies . . .' Kraftwerk Related News. *technopop.com.br*, 25 August. http://kraftwerk.technopop.com.br/news.php (last accessed 21 March 2010).

Barr, T. (1998), *Kraftwerk: From Düsseldorf to the Future (with Love)*. London: Ebury Press.

Beecher, M. (1981), 'Kraftwerk revealed!: interview with Ralf Hütter'. *Electronics and Music Maker*, September. http://kraftwerk.technopop.com.br/magazines_england_80.php (last accessed 14 April 2010).

Bussy, P. (1995), *Kraftwerk: Synthesizer, Sounds und Samples – die ungewöhnliche Karriere einer deutschen Band*. Munich: Piper-Verlag.

Dee, M. (1998), 'Interview with Klaus Dinger'. *Pop* (Sweden), October. http://www.dingerland.de/Talks/pop_int.html (last accessed on 14 April 2010).

Diliberto, J. (1987), 'Man vs. machine: Conny Plank'. *Electronic Musician*. February. http://emusician.com/em_spotlight/interview_conny_plank/ (last accessed 17 March 2010).

Flür, W. (1998), *Kraftwerk: Ich War ein Roboter*. St. Andrä-Wördern: Hannibal Verlag.
—— (2001), *Pop I Fukus*, [TV programme, Sweden]. http://www.youtube.com/watch?v=h
   Te2J8ceUJw&feature=related (last accessed on 14 April 2010).
Hilpert, F. (2003), 'Interview'. *TC Electronics*. http://kraftwerk.technopop.com.br/
   interview_93.php (last accessed on 21 March 2010).
Hütter, R. (1981), 'Interview'. *Beacon Radio, Birmingham, UK* [not Manchester], 14 June.
   http://kraftwerk.technopop.com.br/interview_122.php (last accessed on 21 March
   2010).
Johnstone, R. (Exec. Prod.) (2008), *Kraftwerk and the Electronic Revolution*. [DVD].
   SIDVD541. Sexy Intellectual.
Lynner, D. and Robbley, B. (1976), 'A conversation with Ralf Hutter and Florian Schneider
   of Kraftwerk'. *Synapse*, September/October. http://www.cyndustries.com/synapse/
   synapse.cfm?pc=35&folder=sept1976&pic=11 (last accessed 14 April 2010).
Matten, D. (2009), E-mail communication with the author, 24 and 25 May.
Piltz, A. (1998), 'Interview with Karl Bartos'. *Keyboards*, 9/98, 53.
Reinboth, M. (1991), 'Es wird immer weitergehen . . .: interview with Ralf Hütter'.
   Frontpage. http://kraftwerk.technopop.com.br/magazines_germany_90.php (last
   accessed on 14 April 2010).
Rother, M. (2009), Telephone interview with the author, 25 May.
Schober, I. (1976), 'Kraftwerk: wir sind eine radiostation – interview with Ralf Hütter
   and Florian Schneider', *Musikexpress*, December. http://kraftwerk.technopop.com.br/
   magazines_germany_70.php (last accessed on 14 April 2010).
Toop, D. (1992), *Rap Attack*. St. Andrä-Wördern: Hannibal Verlag.
Ungeheuer, E. (1992) *Wie die Elektronische Musik 'Erfunden' Wurde*. Mainz: Schott Music
   GmbH & Co. KG.

6

Kraftwerk: Playing the Machines

David Pattie

The machines at play

On stage, in 2004–5, they look more staid than ever: ageing executives, perhaps, delivering a PowerPoint at a conference in a regional hotel somewhere. Behind them, the presentation scrolls on: bikes, trains, cars, pills, numbers, text, bars of light and colour – the same, night after night. The band do not play, apparently; they do not even pose. When one of them (the man on the left) sings, he cups his right hand over his cheek, shading his face, as though rather embarrassed by the whole affair. The usual detritus of performance (the mic stands, the cables, the amps) are hidden; aside from the four musicians, standing behind four almost identical consoles, the stage is bare. We have reached an apotheosis of sorts; not the typical kind one might expect in a live event, where the musician's investment in the music is complete, but one in which all the obvious signs of investment have been erased. This is tidy: all clutter discarded, no sweat, no effort. Late in the show, for the first encore, robots replace the musicians; you can spot the change easily – the robots are considerably more animated than the originals (Hutter and Schnieder, 2005).

Those robots have featured in the Kraftwerk touring show for well over 20 years, after their first appearance on the back of the *Computer World* (1981) cover and their incorporation into the tour that followed. The robots were created as, simultaneously, a PR stunt and a deadpan satire on the operations of the music business (Hütter, for example, commented in late 2009 that the robots 'have all this patience with the photographers' [Harrison, 2009, p. 81]). The robots, however, secured their place in the band's live shows because they seemed to confirm something undeniably apparent about Kraftwerk as a band, and about the world that their music seemed to inhabit; a world described in memorably stereotypical terms by Lester Bangs in 1975 as succumbing to the twin influences of the Germans and the machines. There is something in the foregrounding of technology in Kraftwerk's music generally, and in their stage performances in particular, which seems designed to bear Bangs out. On first acquaintance, the kind of performances that the band mount play against a commonly held conception of the role of performance in popular music (see Pattie, 1999; 2007); a conception which holds that performance is an overtly public demonstration of the musician's particular investment in the music. Here the band are, it seems, already distanced from the event; even before the robots appear, they seem only tangentially connected to the performance – it is not automatically apparent that what we see on stage is the outcome of any actions taken by any of the members of the band. Rather, they seem as though they are tending the machines, rather than playing them.

What we have – or, what we seem to have – is a classically postmodern take on the performance event. In rock the musician invested in the music is venerated; in dance the musician is supposed to be a combination, in varying degrees, of craftworker and conduit, between the music and the crowd. Kraftwerk, on the other hand, seem to be disappearing into the event; even the minimal moments of interaction that characterized earlier tours (in particular the encore of 'Pocket Calculator' in 1981, when the band proffered miniature instruments to the crowd to play) have been excised. Now, we have the popular music equivalent of cyborg performance art, as described by Steve Dixon in 2007:

> The shiny new bodies and mythic metamorphoses enacted in metallic performance art celebrate but also forewarn of the gradual disappearance of the human body. Intelligent and conscious machines in the future might take their origins from humans, but they may equally originate from other sentient machines. George Dyson suggests that 'in the game of life and evolution there are three players at the table; human beings, nature and machines. I am firmly on the side of nature. But nature, I suspect, is on the side of the machines.' (p. 332)

And so, it seems, are Kraftwerk. Their performances function as a cyborgian deconstruction of the typical music performance event: in place of the hyper-energized, engaged body more common in rock performance we have the body as adjunct. Instead of the authenticating presence of the actual performer, engaged in making the music we hear, we have the musician as bystander. I have written elsewhere about the role of technology in music performance as a framework for the performer; here the terms are apparently reversed. The four musicians are almost design elements themselves – vertical inserts in a stage picture which otherwise is composed entirely of strong horizontals.

And yet to argue this is perhaps to miss the point: as already noted in the introduction, there is another way of reading this performance – and indeed another way to read the performance history of the group, from its earliest days through to the present. After all, Kraftwerk have always concerned themselves with the quotidian application of technology: electronic instrumentation is not used to conjure up the future, but to illuminate the present. In what follows, I will argue that the performance style the band adopts follows much the same logic. The evolution of Kraftwerk's live performances mirror transformations in the use of technology that have profoundly influenced the development of Western society over the past three decades. In doing so, I will argue below, they conform to the typology of the rock gig as comprised of moments of self-revelation through performance; they also posit an interesting comment on our evolving relationship to technology. It is easy – it is very tempting, indeed – to see Kraftwerk in performance as representatives of a posthuman, cyborgian future; however, as I will show through the rest of this chapter, it would also be a mistake. Under the surface, behind the apparent indifference of the performers and the slickness of the presentation, something more dynamic, and something far more interesting, is going on.

Kraftwerk, cyborgs, posthumans

By the late twentieth century, our time, a mythic time, we are all chimeras, theorized and fabricated hybrids of machine and organism; in short, we are cyborgs. Ths cyborg is our ontology; it gives us our politics. The cyborg is a condensed image of both imagination and material reality, the two joined centres structuring any possibility of historical transformation. (Harraway, 1999, p. 272)

The publication of Donna Harraway's 'A cyborg manifesto: science, technology, and socialist feminism' in 1985 marked, it is fair to say, the beginning of a theoretical trend: it marked the point at which the figure of the cyborg entered the discursive vocabulary of a generation of scholars in the arts, the humanities and the social sciences. Although it is true that something of the irony and ambiguity of Harraway's original manifesto was missed by some of those who incorporated her ideas (see Bell, 2007, for a good discussion of the various malformed versions of Harraway's original thesis), the central concept – that of the cyborg as an extended human, as a creature which functions on the blurred boundary between the biological and the technological or, in some incarnations, between the human and the animal – has proved remarkably tenacious. At a time when the impact of a new form of technology (the first incursion of what we might now call IT) was beginning to spread into mainstream society, and when the world outlined on Kraftwerk's 1981 album *Computer World* was beginning to seem less like an invocation of the future and more like a description of reality, Harraway's manifesto seemed neatly to describe the possibilities inherent in this new, technologized world.

> There are several consequences to taking seriously the imagery of cyborgs as other than our enemies. Our bodies, ourselves; bodies are maps of power and identity. Cyborgs are no exception. A cyborg body is not innocent; it was not born in a garden; it does not seek unitary identity and so generate antagonistic dualisms without end (or until the world ends); it takes irony for granted. One is too few, and two is only one possibility. Intense pleasure in skill, machine skill, ceases to be a sin, but an aspect of embodiment. The machine is not an it to be animated, worshipped, and dominated. The machine is us, our processes, an aspect of our embodiment. We can be responsible for machines; they do not dominate or threaten us. We are responsible for boundaries; we are they. (Harraway, 1991, p. 180)

Harraway's cyborg was only one of a number of new theoretical positions that the new digital world seemed to call into existence. It was one of the earliest examples of a critical trend that sought to account for the new relation between the human and the machine in terms of a fundamental material change in the balance between the animate and the apparently inanimate. Harraway and a generation of feminist theorists talked of the cyborg; other theorists, N. Katherine Hayles for one, talked of the posthuman. In the introduction to *How We Became Posthuman*, Hayles revisited the point of origin (at least in one version of the narrative) of the computer age: the point at which Alan Turing posited a reliable test to determine whether or not a machine was capable of independent thought. For Hayles, this test was now obsolete: it was no longer necessary to do as Turing suggested – to undergo a blind conversational test in which the participant would not be told whether or not he or she was talking to a machine – to arrive at an idea of the level of intelligence machines had attained. We were now, ourselves, the kind of intelligent machine that Turing had envisaged; the real test now happened every time that a human being sat down in front of a computer and switched on. For Hayles,

> [t]he test puts you into a cybernetic circuit that splices your will, desire, and perception into a distributed cognitive system in which represented bodies are joined with enacted bodies through mutating and flexible machine interfaces. As you gaze at the flickering signifiers scrolling down the computer screens, no matter what identifications you assign to the embodied entities that you cannot see, you have already become posthuman. (1999, p. xiv)

Both new categories – the cyborg and the posthuman – posit what is essentially the same relation between humans and technology. They both suggest that this relation is marked by proximity most of all; the new technologies interface with the individual, creating a new, hybrid being which, in the more hysterically apocalyptic scenarios (Fukuyama, 2002, for example), entirely effaces the human – or, on the other hand, opens us to new possibilities by allowing us both a greatly increased set of capabilities and the ability to shape our own identities.

In performance it is probably true to say that the use of technology has tended to follow the second scenario; artists such as Stelarc and performance groups such as Optik, Palindrome and Blast Theory have created work that takes as its inspiration the proximity of technology and the human. Sometimes this work is almost comically obvious and, aside from the frisson provided by the new technology, rather banal; for example, in two experiments – *Project Cyborg 1.0* and *2.0* – the cybernetics professor (and incorrigible self-publicist) Kevin Warwick implanted microchips in his arm which allowed him to, among other things, trigger automatic doors, switch lights on and off, and, in the second experiment, transmit and receive information and instructions from a similar chip, embedded in his wife's arm. Sometimes, as with Blast Theory's *Can You See Me Now?* (2001) and *Uncle Roy All Around You* (2003), the interaction between humanity and technology is much more subtle; participants trace each other, and interact with each other, via mobiles and the net to reach an agreed location. As the game is played, ineluctably, the players are connected across space by the technologies they employ; and at the end of *Uncle Roy* they are asked to continue that connection by committing themselves to each other for a preset time.

In both examples, technology facilitates and structures a new set of relations between the individual, his or her environment and other individuals. In doing so, it creates, it might be argued, new beings; beings who are now defined by their relationship to these new technologies first and foremost. It is not that the human being in these performance events entirely disappears, or is entirely subsumed within, the new media that the events employ; rather, it is that the relation between the human and the machine is rethought – and from this reworking, new ideas of the human emerge.

It is not surprising, in this context, to find Deleuze and Guattari used as a key theoretical touchstone (see, for example, Broadhurst, 2007). Their ideas seem tailor-made for a new area of art that treats the biological human as a machine interacting with other machines. For example, as Broadhurst notes, they replace the idea of desire as a purely psychic or physiological craving, driven by forces inside the individual, with a quasi-mechanical notion of desire as production.

Desire has nothing to do with a natural or spontaneous determination;

there is no desire but assembling, assembled desire. The rationality, the efficiency, of an assemblage does not exist without the passions the assemblage brings into play, with the desires that constitute it as much as it constitutes them. (Deleuze and Guattari, 1988, p. 399)

In the 'assemblage' (to use the term Deleuze and Guattari employ) those parts of the material world (machines, objects, technology) meld with the individual's biology to form an extended body that is no longer uniquely personal. The assemblage, in other words, can only exist at the point at which the boundaries between it and the world outside break down; when it becomes extended – connected to the flows of intensity that surround it. As Gere notes (2002), those who write about the new, digital society have found themselves drawn to this particular notion; the idea that human beings can be thought of as extended bodies, linked rhizomatically in a non-hierarchical network, has been taken as a useful description of the operation of the internet.

It might also be a useful way to describe Kraftwerk; in fact, the idea of the extended human, melded with technology and linked to other extended humans via the series of connections that technology makes possible, seems drawn directly from their music. What is the man-machine if it is not a Deleuzian/Guattarian assemblage? For example, Ralf Hütter in a 1981 interview does sound as though he is describing the human being as assemblage, or the human as cyborg, or the human as posthuman:

We produce sounds with musical machines. Most of the ideas come from our day-to-day experience. We don't look to the moon or to outer space for inspiration. We mostly look at our work and ourselves, things we talk about, things we understand, because we live with them. To us it was quite direct to speak of The Man Machine because that's what we really are. It's the connection and cooperation of men and machines, because sometimes we play our machines, and sometimes they play us. It's like a dialogue: sometimes we switch on certain automatic machines and . . . they play very nice music . . . and we listen. We spend a lot of time listening to our machines, and then we change the programs and reset them. So it's like an exchange of ideas between us two. (Hütter, 1981)

As noted in the introduction, the key feature of quotes like these is the complete ease that they demonstrate with the idea of the relation between technology and the musician. It is of course true that every musician has to establish a baseline of familiarity with an appropriate technology: a piano is an assemblage of moving parts that has to be operated skilfully if it is going to produce something musically pleasing. But there is something more to the quote than this relatively banal truth; it is rather unusual to find a musician ascribing the power of cognition to a musical instrument – far less treating the creation of music as a dialogue between equals, rather than between active musician and passive instrument. Here, to borrow a phrase from Harraway, the machine is not an *it*; the machine is a partner. And when, as they have on tour since the 1980s, the robots appear on stage, it seems as though we have the perfect musical incarnation of a rhizomatic connection between humans and technology. Not so much in the figures of the robots themselves but in the fact that robots, laptops, video streams and musicians play off and around each other in a non-hierarchical network of connections.

However, the robots do not look like the incarnations of a cyborgian future – if anything, they seem to hark back to a mechanical past. They are ungainly; stiffly, awkwardly, they go through a series of movements that suggest, not an easy integration of the digital and the technological, but a creaking robot ballet that seems rather more like a parody of futurism. They look like the incarnation of a line from the *Manifesto of Futurist Mechanical Art*: 'We feel mechanically and we feel made of steel' (qtd. in Dixon, 2007, p. 63) than anything else. Characteristically, the technology that Kraftwerk use to create the music looks forward; the robots, in all their crude glory, look back to a time when a different approach to technology – hardware, rather than software – was thought of as the wave of the future. What is more, the music sequence for the robots (the track is, of course, 'The Robots') is treated differently to the rest of the performance. In 1992, Ralf Hütter pointed out that all the music for each gig was in digital storage and was activated – in effect, played – by the musicians each night, with one notable exception.

> We can make any track longer, according to the gig. Certain things are written, but certain compositions can have a start point and be totally open-ended, with the programming running into a loop function. It can be however we want it. The only thing that's really written from start to finish is 'The Robots', with output from the computer to synchronize the actual robots on stage, so that their movements are all computer-controlled and they are always identical – very robotic. (Sinker, 1992)

An interesting paradox. The robots seem the most obvious sign of the presence of the cyborgian in Kraftwerk's live shows: they bear the faces of the band, they dance to the music in perfect sequence (and the track they dance to is the first on the album *The Man-Machine*), and they are treated by the audience not as an unwelcome intrusion but as old friends. And yet they are the only point in the gig where the seamless integration of man and machine breaks down; where the charge commonly made against Kraftwerk live, that they don't play the music for the audience, is true.

Here, perhaps, we have a characteristically Kraftwerkian moment; what seems like an expression of faith in the cyborgian future is presented, if not satirically, then at least ironically – offered up, and undercut, simultaneously. When asked about the possibility of a fully robotic show, Hütter answered:

> We did it recently in Bonn, Cologne and Paris, at the Musée de la Musique for six months. The robots were a moving exhibit behind glass, but then we were touring in Japan and other places, and we missed them. I think they missed us too. And the audience missed them, so we had to reunite. (qtd. in Witter, 2005)

A characteristically amused, teasing response to a proposition that, given the clichés that have surrounded the band since its early days, one might think would be eagerly accepted. Shortly after, Hütter dismisses the idea of an all-robot show in interesting terms:

> But they're only appropriate for use during 'The Robots'. You can't have them playing the other songs and, if we sent the robots out on the road, it would be a fully mechanised show, which is very different to what we're doing now (mimes fingers playing instrument). It's the man-machine after all. That would be the machine-machine. (qtd. in Witter, 2005)

In other words, the apparent symbol of cyborgian integration – the point in the show where the man-machine might be at its most apparent – has to be ring-fenced, not because it is technically too difficult, but because it doesn't give the correct impression of the band. Going back to an argument previously mentioned, Hütter is very concerned with the '4Realness' of the performances: the shows must give the audience the essence of Kraftwerk – the band must perform themselves, in much the same way as any band does. But the moment when the symbolic nature of the band is most obviously performed, or so it seems, is not a moment that Hütter wants to stand for the performance as a whole. Something else is going on: something that, it might be argued, still represents the man-machine, but in a context that is not quite the same as that suggested by Deleuze and Guattari, Harraway, Hayles and their theoretical followers; a context set not so much by the new technology's impact on the body but rather by its impact on the way that we move, the way that we communicate and the way that we work.

Kraftwerk, networks, mobility

What is specific to our world is the extension and augmentation of the body and mind of human subjects in networks of interaction powered by micro-electronics-based, software-operated, communication technologies. These technologies are increasingly diffused throughout the entire realm of human activity by growing miniaturization [and we may add portability]. (Castells, 2004b, p. 7)

Kraftwerk, it is fair to say, did not initially set out to be a touring band. In their very early days as Organisation, in common with most other bands, they played gigs where and when they could be arranged. As was common at the time, these gigs were part of the emerging art music scene in West Germany – the scene that also supported the fledgling Can, Tangerine Dream, the two Amon Düüls, and the other key experimental rock bands of the time. Organisation played at universities, in art galleries and at other venues where the West German musical avant-garde congregated. When Hütter and Schneider initially formed Kraftwerk, the live shows – this time featuring a number of musicians, most notably Michael Rother and Klaus Dinger (who left Kraftwerk to form Neu! in 1971) – were very much in the style of other bands of the time. Footage of Organisation playing an early version of 'Ruckzuck' in 1970 is not too far removed from the type of performance favoured by other, similar, German bands: perhaps the only indication of the performances to come is the fact that Hütter and Schneider are rather more static than their bandmates.

Roughly coincident with the release of *Ralf and Florian*, however, the stage shows began to evolve. The band at this point, under the influence of Emil Schult, had started to create an image which could sit comfortably with the ethos that was beginning to emerge in their music. *Ralf and Florian*'s front cover, for example, with both musicians looking both studious and quietly amused, photographed in black-and-white against a plain background, looks like an early version of the airbrushed group portrait used for *Trans-Europe Express*. The inside cover shows them seated at their instruments with the distinctive neon signs, one spelling Ralf and the other Florian, on the floor in front of them. These signs became part of the visual signature of the band in performance: footage of Kraftwerk – now a three-piece with the addition of Wolfgang Flür – playing 'Tanzmusik' in 1973 shows their incorporation into the iconography the group were beginning to develop for themselves. Slightly before this, Kraftwerk had played their first show outside of Germany. The gig, in Paris, was reviewed enthusiastically by a French journalist who responded not only to the music, but also to the image projected by the band:

The group is made up of two contemplative intellectuals [Flür had not yet joined the band: Hütter and Schneider used a very early drum machine to provide the rhythms] ... Their music is very smooth, very slack, a kind of long bewitchment, similar to Terry Riley, made by the prolonging and superimposing of multiple rhythms and circular melodies. The public was surprised at first, by the music alone, then when the lights went off and a screen appeared with luminous arabesques projected on to them, the spell was complete. (Bussy, 2005, p. 43)

In this performance, and others like it of the same period, the parameters of the *Gesamtkunstwerk* that Kraftwerk performances would later become are clearly apparent; the close relation between music and visuals, the careful, contemplative musicians and the elegant simplicity of the lighting are all features that become integral to the band's performances in subsequent years.

However, creating the kind of ambience in performance that fitted the band's new image was not a simple thing to do. Kraftwerk have spent most of their creative lives as musicians in the studio and, more than this, in *their* studio – a location which became equally as iconic as the band's music and their image. Kling Klang was not simply a studio: it was a key factor in the development of the music – a combination of rehearsal room, compositional tool, technological playground and, increasingly, instrumental archive (according to Hütter, the band do not dispose of their instruments and equipment once they have become outmoded: they are stored in Kling Klang and are used as the occasion requires it). Other musicians of the time might road-test material, and then take it into the studio (as Pink Floyd did with *Dark Side of the Moon* [1973], for example); or, like Tangerine Dream, they might treat improvisation in the studio and improvisation in performance as part of the same process. Kraftwerk, however, styled themselves as musical workers, and their place of work was Kling Klang.

The crucial role the studio played in the creation of their music gave Kraftwerk some problems when it came to playing live. Aside from anything else, the technology that they used to create their music was not particularly flexible. In the mid 1970s, bands touting synthesizers from territory to territory were vulnerable to local conditions in a way that bands with more conventional instrumentations were not. Touring *Autobahn* in France, for example, the band found that they could be fatally undermined by the French electrical system: the machines and the music, created in Germany on a system that operated at 220 volts at 50 hertz, could not function correctly on a system that ran at 110 volts at 60 hertz.

> I remember well that we played in Paris on 110 volts and all the tempos were out of tune. At 8pm the big factories that plug into the network were making the voltage fluctuate. That's the reality, Peugeot were making our tempos change. The engineers that were travelling with us had to install stabilizers. (Bussy, 2005, p. 67)

Kraftwerk were not the only band of the time to wrestle with the vagaries of live technology (one thinks of Robert Fripp's dryly despairing comment in the sleevenotes of King Crimson's *The Night Watch* [1997]: 'tuning a Mellotron, doesn't'). However, the close integration of all of the elements in a Kraftwerk performance – the reliance on electronic instrumentation, even for percussion, the use of preset elements, the integration of those elements with the rest of the stage show – made the group far more vulnerable than most. No wonder that, unusually for the time, the release of the albums *Trans-Europe Express* (1977) and *The Man-Machine* (1978) were not accompanied by major tours: the logistical problems the band encountered (and also, perhaps, Florian Schneider's reluctance to play live) kept them tied to the studio for most of the later 1970s.

In 1981, after the release of *Computer World*, Kraftwerk undertook an extensive tour. It is probably true to say that a tour at this point in their careers was unavoidable – *The Man-Machine* had been successful, and the new album had been delayed, building expectations for years before its release. At the same time, in some countries (especially the UK and the US), the music scene was now far more accommodating; younger musicians in a variety of genres had either co-opted the group's work, or had been influenced by Kraftwerk to a greater or lesser extent. The technological difficulties the band had encountered previously still remained, however, and they had to be dealt with. The solution that the band arrived at was, in effect, to merge the technologies they used in the studio and the technologies that they used when playing live. Partly this was a common-sensical move, necessary if the band were to be able to transpose the music developed in the studio into the live environment; partly, and unsurprisingly given the band's commitment to the idea of Kraftwerk as *Gesamtkunstwerk*, Hütter described the integration of Kling Klang into the band's live appearances as an extension of the man-machine ethos.

> It took a lot of work to make the Kling Klang Studio transportable, to really stage it, to put it into situation. All the parts are connected, it's a new conception of Kraftwerk: before it was studio plus live, now it's live studio, we play the studio on stage . . . The identity of 'Computer World', the mechanic of instruments and the psychological side of sound and music, are the two concepts that lead to the fact that we don't have Kraftwerk anymore, but Kraftwerk and Kling Klang together. (Perrin, 1981)

However, this changed the dynamic of the man-machine – perhaps only slightly, but none the less significantly. The band were not concerned about the integration of the human body with new, emerging technologies: both man and machine were, in one of the band's favourite phrases, musical workers, operating together to ensure the delivery of technologically complex compositions.

The 1981 tour set the template for Kraftwerk's live work: it solved, as far as was possible at the time, the seemingly intractable problems that touring had posed for the band in previous years. But it is not simply that the new setup allowed Kraftwerk to transfer their music, as far as was possible, to the stage. The organization of the stage, it might be said, made its own overt comment about the relationship between humanity and technology as the twentieth century neared its end. This comment has proved remarkably apposite: arguably, it reflected transformations in the global economy, and in global society, that took another two decades to be fully manifest. The four musicians on stage were arranged in an inverted V formation, with the apex of the V pointing upstage; with one notable exception, they remained in position (the position that they had adopted on previous tours, with Hütter and Schneider flanking the two percussionists Bartos and Flür). In front of the musicians were the instruments they used most frequently – keyboard consoles for Hütter and Schneider (Hütter's console with three keyboards, Schneider's with one), and the twin drum consoles for Flür and Bartos (plus a keyboard for Bartos). Behind them, arrayed around the outer edge of the V, was the paraphernalia of Kling Klang – the limiters, the compressors, the digital delays, the sequencers and the mixers. The studio was put on display: even the lighting – or a significant part of it – spoke more of the workplace than the concert hall. The neon lights that spelled out the names of the band members were joined, in performance, by ultra-violet, red, green, yellow, white and blue striplights which ran up the two arms of the V. The band were costumed as they were on the front cover of *The Man-Machine*, in red shirts and black trousers, with black ties (or, apparently, in black alone for some of the gigs). On stage, the ironic references to Soviet constructivism were rather muted, and the neat shirts and trousers became a rather more aesthetically pleasing version of office wear. The only time during the show when the V formation was broken came during the encores, when the four band members came to the front of the audience, holding small electrical devices (a Stylophone, a drum trigger pad, a rhythm machine and, of course, a small pocket calculator) which were attached to the main set. In a performative moment that managed to be simultaneously ironic and warm, they played, danced and posed, holding the devices out so members of the audience could trigger the sounds for themselves.

In successive tours (the tour that followed the release of *The Mix* in 1991 and the tours the band undertook in the late 1990s/early 2000s), the stage evolved: the V-shape became a near-straight line, the video screens faced the audience directly (before joining up to create a video wall behind the musicians) and, most notably, the machines that formed the outer wall of the V in 1981 were replaced by laptops, simple keyboards and streamlined studio consoles, all small enough to rest on a podium in front of the musicians. However, the aesthetic remained the same: not only did the same footage appear on the screens (the black-and-white footage of models for 'The Model', the train lines for 'Trans-Europe Express'), but the stage itself was designed along the clean, economic lines first realized successfully in 1981. It is tempting to conclude that the band stayed with the basic aesthetic not only because it gave them a template that they could vary from tour to tour but also because it allowed them to occupy two places at once: to be in the studio on stage. Such a solution, though, changed the nature of the live event. Rather than being, as it is for most bands and musicians, a chance to give their audience an experience that exists outside of quotidian time – an experience which, in the mythology of popular music, stands against the routines of the everyday world – Kraftwerk made a performance out of their working environment, and they did so at a time when the working world was itself beginning to change.

In 1975, Hütter described one of the underlying dynamics that shaped the band's music. Noting the prevalence of images of movement in the band's recent material, he commented, 'The idea is to capture non-static phenomenon because music itself is a non-static phenomenon. It deals with time and movement in time. It can never be the same' (qtd. in Smaisys, 1975).

Anyone familiar with Kraftwerk's music will recognize this description: music as flow, as an exercise in endless momentum – the 'Musique Non-Stop', towards which much of the band's output tends. The comment, however, chimes interestingly with a later attempt to envision the relation between humanity and technology. In 1996, the sociologist Manuel Castells argued (in the seminal work *The Rise of the Network Society*) that the impact of information technologies was at its most apparent not at the physical level but in the way that they re-organized the quotidian experience of space and time. For Castells, the idea of specific locations being related to each other by structures of economic and political power and dependence had been replaced by routes through which information passed through the global economy (Castells termed this new spatial organization 'the space of flows' [2000, p. 405]). This new means of organizing space had an impact on the social perception of time: a series of sequential events, with traceable chains of capitalist cause and effect, was replaced by 'Timeless time' (p. 460). Castells described this as the experience that technology provided, of living in an endless present:

> The dominant trend in our society displays the historical revenge of space, constructing temporality in different, even contradictory logics according to spatial dynamics. The space of flows . . . dissolves time by disordering the sequence of events and making them simultaneous, thus installing society in eternal ephemerality. (p. 497)

Such a radical restructuring of space and time finds an echo in the culture of this new society:

[It] can be argued that the manipulation of time is the recurrent theme of new cultural expressions. A manipulation obsessed with the binary reference to instantaneity and eternity: me and the universe, the self and the Net. Such reconciliation, actually fusing the biological individual into the cosmological whole, can only be achieved under the condition of the merger of all times . . . Timelessness is the recurrent theme of our age's cultural expressions, be it in the sudden flashes of video clips or in the eternal echoes of electronic spiritualism. (pp. 493–4)

The collapsing of time, in a world now governed by flows of information through a new, abstracted space: if there is an image which seems to fit the aesthetic developed on stage by Kraftwerk since 1981 then surely it is this. The juxtaposition of past (the black-and-white footage of trains, autobahns and models) and future (soberly dressed workers, tending the technology responsible for the radical transformation of society – and doing so at the point at which that transformation begins to happen) is, it might seem, a paradigmatic example of the timelessness of the network society.

And yet, as so often with Kraftwerk, there is more to the image than this. Castells's model of the new society has been critiqued, most notably (certainly for the purposes of this argument) by John Urry. Urry makes the point that Castells is too quick to see the experience of the network society as necessarily fragmented and isolating (as in the previous quote, 'me and the universe, the self and the Net.'). For Urry, the society ushered in by the new technologies does depend on the idea of mobility, enshrined as a fundamental principle of social organization, but, Urry argues, it would be wrong to see the members of this society purely as isolated nomads, endlessly in transit. Rather, the network creates a new model of social interaction:

Specific others are not so simply 'there'; or rather they are or may be there but mainly through the mediation of very many virtual objects distributed in relatively far-flung networks. There are various consequences. First, there is increasingly 'connected presence' where small gestures or signs of attention are significant in indicating that others are there but at a distance. Second, family and friendship becomes networked rather like much economic life; network membership becomes crucial. Indeed the apparently different domains of work, family and social life becoming [sic] more networked, more similar to each other, more self-organised and more interdependent. (Urry, 2007, pp. 212–13)

When I watch footage of Kraftwerk in performance (and when I finally saw the band live, at the Manchester Velodrome in 2009), this is the model that comes to mind first: the separate but connected community, linked together by the technologies that shape not only the music, but also their interaction as musicians. The four band members, in whichever combination they occur, are part of an environment on stage that blends a number of locations: it is a performance space, it is a workplace, it is a location which facilitates a particular type of social interaction (the 'small gestures and signs of attention' that indicate the presence of others, but 'at a distance'). The robots might gesture (literally might gesture – in an obvious, unmissable, and hence rather ironic, way) *towards* the cyborg or the posthuman, as they occur both in Harraway and Hayles, and in popular culture; but the performance as a whole is configured as a network – the kind of integrated but distant communicative framework created by our interaction with the technologies that we have shaped, and which shape us in their turn.

Playing the machines

To return to the opening image, perhaps the suggestion it contains – that the band in the early years of the decade appear, at least momentarily, as musical middle-management, keying in the changes in this year's version of last year's presentation – contains a kernel of truth. For Kraftwerk, the stage is a place of work; for over two decades the band has made great play of the fact that Kling Klang travels with them when they tour. However, it is not the whole story: the Kraftwerk live show, from the release of *Computer World* onwards, prefigures wider changes in the configuration of the social world (at least in those parts of the world wired up to the information network). In an insightful article on the use of laptops in contemporary music, Nick Prior ties the mobility the laptop offers to the mobility promised by the kind of information networks Castells and Urry identify:

> Very much a device that fits the descriptions of contemporary society in these terms, the laptop is one of a number of nomadic machines of the digital age. Allied with prospects of unfettered International travel and promulgations of a flexible capitalism traversing the globe in networked circuits, the laptop is the image of the quick, mobile and efficient device. In a perspective of relationality, it is yet another node in a network of hubs, flows and networks, representing a new technological paradigm organized around powerful but flexible information technologies and information processing devices. From the perspective of spatiality it is emblematic of socio-technical practices inherent in a new urban metabolism. (Prior, 2008, pp. 915–16)

Useful as the article is, however, Prior misses a crucial part of the development of what might be termed 'nomadic music machines'. He notes at one point that '[gone] are the days when bands such as Tangerine Dream and Kraftwerk resorted to taking their recording studios on the road with them to recreate the sounds of their recorded sounds' (p. 916). Musically, this isn't quite true: Tangerine Dream did tour with a very large (and for the time extremely impressive) amount of technology, but they did not bring their studio with them. Kraftwerk did, and their studio was already part of the iconography of the band – it was the place where these musical workers did their work. Since 1981, the band have gradually transformed Kling Klang into the kind of 'quick, mobile and efficient device' that Prior describes. Here, performatively at least, Kraftwerk were ahead of the curve: rather than creating performance events that hymn the cyborg, they created a performance environment which prefigured the integration of information technology into the world of work, the social world and, gradually, the cultural world. Prior misses the point that the laptop is not only a compositional tool which seems to promise a nomadic freedom in the new 'space of flows' we all negotiate in the network society. It is also a place of work; I type this on my laptop – and as I do, I am both liberated (I can take my work with me anywhere) and constrained (my work can come with me anywhere).

At the end of shows on the 2004 tour, Kraftwerk returned to the stage for two encores. They returned, dressed in exaggerated cycling costume: skintight, with strips of luminescent green running vertically and horizontally across the material. The group, perhaps, had done their work for the day; now the encores had come, they could play (in much the same way as the encore of 'Pocket Calculator' offered an overtly playful end to the 1981 shows). The costumes suited the first encore – 'Aerodynamik' from *Tour de France Soundtracks* – perfectly; and for the second encore ('Musique Non-Stop'), each member of the band performed a short solo, before bowing and exiting one by one. They have worked, and then they have played, but through the course of the gig they also played where they worked, and worked where they played. They have not proved themselves avatars of the posthuman; they have not revealed themselves as cyborgs. They have performed in a place with which we are all (at least those of us in the network society) familiar: a space of flows, where the relation between previously discrete areas of activity has fundamentally changed – where the man-machine described by Hütter and Schneider in interview after interview occupies not only the stage, but also the auditorium.

References

Bell, D. (2007), *Cyberculture Theorists*. London: Routledge.

Broadhurst, S. (2007), *Digital Practices: Aesthetic and Neuroesthetic Approaches to Performance and Technology*. Basingstoke: Palgrave.

Bussy, P. (2005), *Kraftwerk: Man, Machine and Music*. (3rd edn). London: SAF.

Castells, M. (2000), *The Rise of the Network Society*. Oxford: Blackwells.

—— (ed.) (2004a), *The Network Society*. Cheltenham: Edward Elgar.

—— (2004b), 'Internationalism, networks, and the network society: a theoretical blueprint', in M. Castells (ed.), *The Network Society*. Cheltenham: Edward Elgar, pp. 3–48.

Deleuze, G. and Guattari, F. (1988), *A Thousand Plateaus: Capitalism and Schizophrenia*. London: Athlone Press.

Dixon, S. (2007), *Digital Performance: A History of New Media in Theatre, Dance, Performance Art and Installation*. Cambridge, MA: MIT Press.

Fripp, R. (1997), 'Liner notes'. *The Night Watch*. Discipline.

Fukuyama, F. (2002), *Our Posthuman Future: Consequences of the Biotechnology Revolution*. London: Profile.

Gere, C. (2002), *Digital Culture*. London: Reaktion Books.

Harraway, D. (1985/1999), 'A cyborg manifesto', in S. During (ed.) *The Cultural Studies Reader*. London: Routledge.

—— (1991), *Simians, Cyborgs and Women: The Reinvention of Nature*. London: Routledge.

Harrison, I. (2009), 'Back to the future: interview – Ralf Hütter'. *Mojo*, 192, November, 72–84.

Hayles, N. K. (1999), *How We Became Posthuman*. Chicago: University of Chicago Press.

Hütter, R. (1981), 'Interview', *Beacon Radio, Birmingham, UK* [not Manchester], 14 June. http://kraftwerk.technopop.com.br/interview_122.php (last accessed on 21 March 2010).

Hütter, R. and Schneider, F. (Prods/Dirs) (2005), *Kraftwerk: Minimum–Maximum*. [DVD]. 336 2949. Kling Klang/EMI.

Pattie, D. (1999), '4 Real: authenticity, performance and rock music'. *Enculturation*, 2, (2), Spring. http://enculturation.gmu.edu/2_2/pattie.html (last accessed 26 March 2010).

—— (2007), *Rock Music and Performance*, London: Palgrave.

Perrin, J.-E. (1981), 'Komputer: interview – Ralf Hütter'. *Rock & Folk*, no. 178, November. http://kraftwerk.technopop.com.br/interview_112.php (last accessed 26 March 2010).

Prior, N. (2008), 'OK computer: mobility, software and the laptop musician'. *Information, Communication and Society*, 11, (7), October, 912–32.

Sinker, M. (1992), 'Arts and krafts: interview – Ralf Hütter'. *Music Technology*. December. 41–4. http://kraftwerk.technopop.com.br/interview_40.php (last accessed 26 March 2010).

Smaisys, P. (1975), 'Interview: Ralf Hütter & Florian Schneider'. *Triad*. June. http://pages. ripco.net/~saxmania/kraft.html (last accessed 14 April 2010).

Urry, J. (2007), *Mobilities*. Cambridge: Polity.

Witter, S. (2005), 'Paranoid androids?: interview – Ralf Hütter'. *Mojo*, August, 46–52. http://kraftwerk.technopop.com.br/interview_115.php (last accessed 27 March 2010) .

II

Influences and Legacies

7

Europe Non-Stop: West Germany, Britain and the Rise of Synthpop, 1975–81

Sean Albiez

In histories of popular electronic music, Kraftwerk are rightly identified as key innovators and 'godfathers' of several electronic music genres that developed in the late 1970s and early 1980s; techno in Detroit, electro/hip-hop in New York and other American urban centres, the European electronic body of music of D.A.F and Liaisons Dangereuses, and electronic dance music that has developed from these forms since the late 1980s. However, in the context of British synthpop/rock in the post-punk era, a precursor to and important influence on many of these styles, there was a more complex relationship with West German music that moved beyond Kraftwerk. In the 1975–81 period Neu!, La Düsseldorf, Harmonia, Cluster, solo releases by Michael Rother and the production work of Conny Plank inspired British synthpop/rock artists to embrace new musical vistas that led to the eventual emergence of synthpop. Between West German and British musicians a trans-European *sonoscape*[1] was forged that explored experimental electronic sound within the context of a radical reinvention of Anglo-American rock music. As a result, the British synthpop/rock of Ultravox, Gary Numan and Simple Minds, and the closely ensuing synthpop of, for example, Depeche Mode and Soft Cell, saw musicians averting their gaze from the musical and cultural iconography of the United States in the embrace of a new European aesthetic. Of these artists, Numan and Depeche Mode played an important role in inspiring later electronic popular music – a role often solely placed at the door of Kraftwerk's Kling Klang studio.

Fuelling this reorientation of musical aspiration was a desire to experiment and innovate in the wake of the reductive and banal musical template of punk. It was also fed by 1970s cultural arbiter David Bowie championing Kraftwerk, Neu!, Harmonia, Cluster and La Düsseldorf, and the resultant interest in the British music press in these bands. Bowie's 1976–79 relocation to Berlin also helped inspire a retro-Germanophilia in post-punk club scenes where Weimar-era 'Berlin decadence' 'became a kind of byword' (Rimmer, 2003, p. 40). Additionally, the anti-Americanism of British punk (Deer, 2004, p. 169) underpinned a contemporary resistance to US rock. Alongside sustaining the pop/art innovations of Bowie, Eno and Roxy Music, and an ambiguous interest in Germany's Nazi past (Thompson, 2002, pp. 41–2), British post-punk musicians moved to embrace a European aesthetic in their music. For many it was Krautrock,[2] mediated through the work of Bowie, Eno and Plank that provided direct or indirect creative sustenance.

This study will highlight the importance of Neu!, Cluster, Harmonia and La Düsseldorf who, alongside Kraftwerk, had a major influence on British synthpop/rock bands. It will demonstrate there was a network of influence and collaboration (actual and virtual) between Michael Rother (Kraftwerk, Neu! and Harmonia), Klaus Dinger (Kraftwerk, Neu! and La Düsseldorf), the musicians Dieter Moebius and Hans-Joachim Roedelius (Cluster and Harmonia), the producer Conny Plank, David Bowie and Brian Eno, and British synthpop/rock musicians. This trans-European network had *synergetic* and *memetic* qualities: *synergetic* as there was a concurrent musical cross-pollination leading to the development of shared musical tropes that problematizes notions of origin and influence; *memetic* as this network, supported by music press and other media coverage, enabled the direct and indirect transmission of thematic ideas and musical techniques – or memes (Dawkins, 1976, p. 192).[3] The aim of this chapter is not to diminish Kraftwerk's importance, but to place them in a more nuanced and balanced national and transnational context than their canonized status usually allows.

The (re)birth of Krautrock

Kraftwerk's iconic status has meant they have rarely faded from the consciousness of music fans and critics over the last four decades. However, from the mid 1990s there developed a burgeoning interest in other Krautrock artists who had become obscure since the 1970s. This revival was partly a result of Julian Cope's (1995) passionately written but factually suspect *Krautrocksampler*, and also due to the British and American music press taking a positive interest in music of this period (McCready, 1996; O'Hearn, 1997; Gill, 1997a). It was also prompted through Sonic Youth, Stereolab and Tortoise, among others, acknowledging Neu! as a key influence, the re-release of many Krautrock albums in the 1990s (Reynolds, 1995) and the growing online accessibility to information about music from this period. What seemed to have been forgotten in this 'excavation' was that British synthpop/rock bands of the late 1970s and early 1980s got there first and, as will be demonstrated later, continually referenced Krautrock as a key inspiration.

Interestingly, the largely positive assessment of Krautrock in the mid 1990s was somewhat at odds with early British music press reports of the 1970s. For example, Michael Watts praised West German rock music in his *Melody Maker* 'Deutsch rock' article (1972), singling out Can, Amon Düül II, Guru Guru, Tangerine Dream and Kraftwerk who he suggested were 'more adventurous than the majority of their Anglo-American counterparts and virtually all the other Europeans'. On Kraftwerk, he proposed that 'they've got the most "mechanical" energized sound I've ever heard in places' (p. 25). Ian McDonald's three-part 'Germany calling' *New Musical Express* (*NME*) series (1972a; 1972b; 1972c) suggested West German rock music rejected 'all the traditions behind the Anglo-American front (i.e. the conceptual and/ or harmonic frameworks of blues, folk, jazz or classical pastiche)' and built 'upon extremely simple formats, a superstructure of open-ended improvisa-tion' (1972a, p. 27). However, he was unconvinced by much of the music he encountered. On Kraftwerk he wrote, '[f]or me, the music is hard without convincing structure, heartless with no redeeming dignity, and ultimately a numbing bore'. Nevertheless, Neu! are described as similar to Kraftwerk but 'nearer to the emotional wellspring of Teutonic emotional expression . . . [they] project a warmth and imagination which, theoretically, just shouldn't be there' (McDonald, 1972b, p. 36). The title of McDonald's series, 'Germany calling', a barbed reference to English-language World War II Nazi propa-ganda broadcasts, tapped into British anti-German attitudes of the time that often informed the critical stance taken by music journalists.

Kraftwerk's press coverage later in the 1970s was at times equally negative. In September 1975, the *NME* reprint of Lester Bangs's *Creem* magazine article 'Kraftwerkfeature or how I learned to stop worrying and love the balm' was retitled 'Kraftwerk: the final solution to the music problem'. The unambigu-ously offensive feature appeared with an accompanying photomontage that included Kraftwerk surrounded by what appear to be images of Nazi soldiers and musicians from one of the Nuremberg rallies (Bangs, 1975b, pp. 20–1). Miles (1976) offensively derided their music, suggesting, 'They sound so detached, the kind of guys who could blow up the planet just to hear the noise it made'. However, by 1977–78, and largely due to Bowie's and Eno's patronage, Kraftwerk, Neu!, Cluster, Harmonia and La Düsseldorf were regularly referenced in the British music press, as Miles (1978) intimates: 'Unfortunately, this piece is not about Germans. It's about Ultravox. However, it does take place in Germany. Will that do?' This aside indicates the fash-ionable ubiquity of Krautrock in the *NME* and the other influential weekly British music papers at the time; through this coverage larger numbers of British music fans and musicians began to encounter this music.

So what characterized the music represented by these bands and why was it so influential for the British synthpop/rock artists? As McDonald and Watts suggest, at the tail end of the 1960s experimental rock musicians in West

Germany forged new forms of pop/rock based on studio experimentation that manipulated sound through electronic recording technologies, mixing desks, sound processors and tape editing. A new 'indigenous' musical vocabulary developed that embraced cyber-mysticism, 'freakout' improvisations, space-age electronic sound collages, ethnic and makeshift instruments, and fresh compositional and recording methods – often splicing together tracks from long-form home-studio jams. Though there were many bands working in this field, the most high-profile and successful in the UK were Tangerine Dream, Can, Kraftwerk, Faust and Neu!. Despite the lack of any real coherence across the music that could suggest a distinct scene or sound, Faust perhaps spoke for all when they stated:

> Unlike rock musicians in other countries, this new breed of German musicians is not interested in imitating what's gone before them. They're looking for new sounds and new forms of expression. Their music is no hand-me-down Beatles or Stones or the white man's idea of R&B. It's their own, building as much on the immense tradition of German music as on the Anglo-Saxon-dominated traditions of current pop. (Faust press release qtd. in DeRogatis, 1996, p. 125)

Though the West German critique of rock challenged and appeared to reverse the usual flows of the Anglo-American musical hegemony, Walker (1978) suggests there were clear precursors and influences in this music:

> [I]nspiration for this music can literally be found everywhere – Bach ... Stockhausen, John Cage and Harry Partch; the electronic experimentation of Edgar Varese; the haunting film scores of Bernard Herrmann; the jazz of Ellington, Coltrane and Parker; traditional forms of all kinds (most predominantly Celtic, Gregorian, Indian, Tibetan, Moroccan and Japanese) and of course the acid-crazed American rock bands of the late '60s.

The musicians central to this study display these musical memes, as well as others drawn from, for example, late 1960s Pink Floyd. However, they later forged innovative music with a distinct identity from these sources. It is important to briefly outline the characteristics of the music of Kraftwerk, Neu!, Cluster, Harmonia and La Düsseldorf to indicate what made the area of Krautrock represented by these bands distinctive and attractive to Bowie, Eno and British synthpop/rock musicians.

The use of the term 'electronic music' to describe these bands is both apt and misleading. It is apt as they all attempted to push music production into new creative territory by exploring experimental approaches to the technologies of sound production, recording, processing and editing – often with the help of influential West German producer Conny Plank. However, the term is potentially misleading as sound sources were diverse. Synthesizers, usually synonymous with the term electronic music, are used only sparingly, if at all, until later in the 1970s. Even then, Kraftwerk were alone among these bands in forging a fully synthesized electronic sound. The bands as a whole initially utilized rock, classical and more esoteric ethnic instruments, electronic organs and keyboards, rhythm machines, pianos, mixers, tape recorders and effects units. Roedelius in reference to Cluster/Harmonia's Forst studio retreat suggests that '[in] some ways the cheap gear was a hidden blessing for us . . . it forced us to improvise and not polish the rough edges off the music. We wanted that unpredictable sound' (qtd. in Iliffe, 2003, p. 40). This kind of unpredictability was discarded by Kraftwerk after *Autobahn* (1974) in place of a highly disciplined sound. However, in Kling Klang, improvisation, experimentation and conceptual thinking still lay at the heart of Kraftwerk's creative process.

Kraftwerk, with Ralf Hütter and Florian Schneider as core band members,[4] initially had a good deal in common in conceptual and musical terms with their former bandmates Neu!, and both shared Conny Plank as producer on their early albums. There are also musical and sonic similarities between *Kraftwerk* (1970), *Kraftwerk 2* (1972) and *Ralf and Florian* (1973), Cluster's *Zuckerzeit* (1974) and *Sowiesoso* (1976), and Harmonia's *Musik von Harmonia* (1974). All are largely *aphonic* and comprised of music with repetitive patterns, looping minimalist phrases and heavily processed sound constructed through relatively primitive studio equipment, and all eschew instrumental virtuosity and traditional song structures.

However, *Autobahn* was a watershed; the band split from Plank and began to produce song-based vocal/vocoded music. Kraftwerk's sound became entirely created through analogue synthesizers, electronic drums and rhythm machines, sequencers, vocoders and 'pre-sampler' samples of recorded sound until after their 1981 *Computer World*, which actually used no computers in its production (confirmed by Hütter in Dalton, 2009, p. 71). This set them apart from Neu!, Cluster, Harmonia and La Düsseldorf who continued to combine electronic studio techniques, synthesizers, live and electronic drums, guitars, organs, pianos and ethnic instrumentation (such as Harmonia's use of a Japanese Nagoya harp and Neu!'s use of a 'Japan banjo', zither and accordion). This could explain why for Bowie and Eno, and British synthpop/rock artists such as Ultravox, Gary Numan and Simple Minds, other West German artists appeared to provide more obvious musical inspiration. Kraftwerk's music both enthused and alienated these musicians due to its technologically pristine and futuristic sound. Until synthesizers and sequencers became easily available, few could understand or approximate Kraftwerk's production techniques. Their cultivation of techno-myths and secrecy around their compositional and performance methods initially meant they were more abstract and conceptual in their influence than is usually assumed. Though the original line-up of the Human League achieved a Kraftwerk-like synthesizer-based sound in the late 1970s, it was not until 1980 that a wider range of artists such as the second incarnation of the Human League, Depeche Mode and John Foxx followed suit in creating synthpop that largely broke from the rock instrumentation still deployed in the synthpop/rock of Ultravox, Numan and Simple Minds. Apart from Orchestral Manoeuvres In The Dark (OMD) (see Witts in this collection), they mostly forged a sound containing only traces of Kraftwerk, rather than copying their music in a wholesale manner. Arguably, Kraftwerk's influence is therefore more identifiable in the appropriation of the man-machine trope and related cyborgian and technological themes/memes by British synthpop/rock and synthpop that often focused obsessively on machines and technology – sometimes underpinned by machine-like vocal delivery (e.g. Gary Numan and John Foxx).[5] Song titles provide evidence of the memetic influence of Kraftwerk across this music (e.g. Ultravox's 'I Want to Be a Machine', Numan's 'The Machman' and 'Are 'Friends' Electric?' and OMD's 'Genetic Engineering' and 'ABC Auto-Industry'). Former Kraftwerk percussionist Karl Bartos suggests the band's interest in cyborgian themes was driven by press coverage of the band, stating:

> The media . . . is like a mirror, and if you read the *NME* or . . . a newspaper they tell you what you are – people . . . kept telling us 'they are like robots' . . . 'they are machines'. So we thought if they consider us as machines lets make songs about the connection between man and machine. (qtd. in Bendjelloul, 2001)

Therefore the memes encompassed by Kraftwerk's man-machine trope proved attractive to British musicians, though they mostly avoided a *mimetic* appropriation of Kraftwerk's musical innovations – either through technical inability or through a desire to strike out in their own musical direction.

Central to Kraftwerk's *modus operandi* was the notion that they were a *Gesamtkunstwerk* that explained the homologous thematic relationship of their music, performance and related visual iconography. This particularly influenced Numan who on Tubeway Army's *Replicas* (1979), and solo albums *The Pleasure Principle* (1979) and *Telekon* (1980), created a similar homologous pop-*Gesamtkunstwerk*. However, he typically described this in simpler terms than Kraftwerk, suggesting, 'To me a career is just like a machine. All the pieces have to fit together perfectly or else the machine will tear itself apart' (Numan, 1998, p. 50).

Neu!, like Kraftwerk, were geographically and musically removed in Düsseldorf from the 'pastoral trip' (Keenan, 2009) of West German kosmische music (represented by, for example, Klaus Schulze and Popol Vuh). On leaving Kraftwerk in 1971, they initially created a modernist and disciplined driving sound that pre-empted the trance-like turn in Kraftwerk's music from *Autobahn* onwards. They initially used only rock instrumentation on *Neu!* (1972) and *Neu!2* (1973), but for *Neu!75* (1975) they expanded their sound with piano, synthesizer and other 'electronics'. Plank acted as producer and engineer on these albums that have an electronic 'feel' due to the heavy sound processing in the production work. Kopf (1999) describes Rother and Dinger's music as

> a form of Unterwegs [meaning en route, in motion] music remarkable for the urgency of its desire to keep moving. Neu! music is not so much a matter of musical composition – it's a competition of velocities. Powered by a rhythmic tic clawing the asphalt – the basis of all motorik disco to follow – yearning, yawning guitar noises race against each other, some accelerating ahead, others receding in the distance. And every now and then a menacing bass rumble hurtles past in the outside lane. (p. 50)

However, Kopf is only describing an element of Neu!'s output; 'Weissensee' and 'Im Glück' from *Neu!75* have a proto-ambient stillness that this portrayal does not allow for. Although there is a *motorik* quality to much of Neu!'s music, their 'dichotomik' speed and stillness would come to characterize much of the music they influenced (not least Bowie's *Low* [1977] and *"Heroes"* [1977]).

Unlike Neu! and Kraftwerk, Cluster were not inhabitants of Düsseldorf. Moebius and Roedelius formed Kluster (alongside Conrad Schnitzler) at the Zodiak Free Arts Lab in Berlin in 1969, and contributed to the early development of the Kosmische Musik scene. Kluster's music was an improvised, cacophonous and jarring industrial sound, developed across two 1971 albums, *Klopfzeichen* and *Zwei-Osterei* (again engineered by Plank). On Schnitzler's departure, Moebius and Roedelius became Cluster, releasing *Cluster* (1971) with Plank as a full band member, and *Cluster II* (1972). The music retained the disorienting urban-industrial and proto-ambient feel of the Kluster releases. Rather than soundtracking the utopianism of 1960s countercultural idealism, Kluster/Cluster initially seemed to be performing the paranoia and violence of the repressive West German political landscape of the early 1970s (Iliffe, 2003, pp. 29–31).

In 1973, Cluster relocated to a rural retreat at Forst in Weserbergland, Lower Saxony, and built a studio that became a laboratory for musical experimentation, much like Kling Klang. Neu!'s Michael Rother soon joined them to pursue the prospect of Cluster and Neu! forming a live performance unit. Though this did not work out, Rother decided to stay on. He produced the Cluster album *Zuckerzeit*, and under his influence Cluster's music became more minimalist, melodic and accessible, while retaining an experimental edge. Iliffe (2003) suggests that 'Rother's chief import . . . was rhythm. That and some intriguing musical toys to play with: primitive first-generation drum boxes plus an early unstable sequencer' (p. 41). He also suggests that *Zuckerzeit* is

> groundbreaking for many reasons. It doesn't flow out of the Mississippi Delta or the Mersey. Nor does it evoke Berlin's urban claustrophobia or replicate the *autobahn* speed rush. *Zuckerzeit* is pure electronic music . . . But there's a sense of grass, open air, rusty generators powering its jump starting grooves, of putting down new roots in the alluvial soil of Weserbergland. (p. 44)

Out of this collaboration Moebius, Roedelius and Rother formed Harmonia at Forst, with their first album, *Musik von Harmonia*, seeming to be a Neu!/Cluster hybrid. Part urban, part rural; machinic and proto-ambient; improvised and disciplined. The later album *Deluxe* existed somewhere between *Autobahn*, *Neu!75* and Cluster's *Sowiesoso*.

La Düsseldorf, who proved influential for Bowie, Ultravox and Simple Minds in particular, in effect formed on side two of *Neu!75* where Hans Lampe and Thomas Dinger joined Rother and Klaus Dinger in creating a more intensive *motorik* energy with a proto-punk attitude. With the break-up of Neu! both Dingers and Lampe, initially with Plank, extended the repetitive aspects of the Neu! sound. Their music (on *La Düsseldorf* [1976]; *Viva* [1978]; *Individuellos* [1980]) embraced Abba-esque chord progressions, *Schlager*-like melodies, football chants, swirling synthesizer washes, *motorik* guitar thrash, samples and sound collages. Their music was Düsseldorfian in name, theme and *motorik* in the extreme.

The areas of Krautrock outlined above played a crucial role for British pop/rock musicians drawn to electronic music experimentation from the mid 1970s. In simple terms it was the innovative electronic production sound, compositional minimalism and the machinic rhythms of this music that proved most significant for Bowie, Eno, Ultravox and eventually Numan and Simple Minds. From 1975–81, the flows of musical exchange between British and West German electronic popular music was complex. However, it is clear that through the mediation of Plank, Eno, Bowie and British DJ Rusty Egan, avant-garde West German experimentation became hugely influential in areas of British popular music at the end of the 1970s, resulting in the rise of synthpop in 1980. What is also clear is that Kraftwerk were only a component part of this wider network of musical flows and influence.

The British–West German sonoscape

The musicians central to this study, by collaborating and referencing each other's work, created a shared repository of musical techniques, sounds and musical resources that operated synergistically and memetically across the already identified sonoscape. Rother acknowledges this, stating that

> [e]verybody in Harmonia was really fond of the first [Eno] Roxy Music albums, but we didn't want to draw from those for our own music . . . Brian's later albums (*Another Green World, Before & After Science* etc.) I liked a lot. But I always had the rule that my own work shouldn't possibly be influenced . . . But of course an exertion of influence never can be ruled out, even if it is not desired . . . Fact of the matter is that nobody lives by himself on an island and creates his music out of a vacuum. And this applies to all of us. (qtd. in Hargus, 1998)

It is equally important to note that Eno, when creating the albums mentioned, had in turn been influenced by Cluster and Rother. Sheppard (2008) asserts that Eno's *Another Green World* (1975) drew heavily from Cluster's electronic rhythms and, in 1975,

> [a]n import copy of Cluster's *Zuckerzeit* LP had been on Eno's turntable consistently all summer; its most palpable influence on his new music was in its use of drum machines . . . Eno would mimic and then expand upon the electronic rhythm processes pioneered by Cluster producer Michael Rother and studio engineer Conny Plank, feeding drum machines through echo, delay and reverb units to create eccentric polyrhythms. (pp. 200–1)

There is a therefore circularity of influence and counter-influence that is remarkable in this period which includes, but moves beyond, Kraftwerk. The West German and British music under consideration in this study was constructed both wittingly and unwittingly by artists working in the shadow and light of each other's works. The shared repository of memetic texts, ideas, techniques, references and touchstones became trans-locational foundations upon which musical creativity synergistically thrived. It is important to further discuss the key protagonists who had important nodal and mediating roles underpinning the network of influence in this trans-European sonoscape.

Conny Plank

As has already become apparent, a key figure at the hub of experimental musical practice tangibly connecting West German and British musicians was Konrad (Conny) Plank. He acted as a producer, musician, engineer and facilitator with Cluster, Kraftwerk, Neu!, La Düsseldorf, D.A.F. and Ultravox among many others. While working as a studio engineer at the Westdeutscher Rundfunk (WDR) electronic music studios in Cologne with Karlheinz Stockhausen and Mauricio Kagel in the 1960s, he would experiment after hours with classical musicians constructing live electronic improvised compositions. Plank said in 1987 that in the late 1960s he, like members of Kraftwerk, Cluster and Neu!,

> listened to Koenig, Stockhausen, Varese. I used to work with these people in '67, '68, and '69. Mauricio Kagel gave me a lot of ideas about sounds. In those recordings I worked with very academic musicians being very precise doing these sounds, and to me it seemed lifeless, and dry. I then tried to find people that looked in a different way to these materials, that tried to improvise with these dirty sounds, these electronic sounds – to have a feeling that a jazz musician has to his instrument. (Diliberto, 1987)

He therefore shared with Kraftwerk, Cluster and Eno a grounding in modernist electronic and experimental music, but was also committed to relocating these techniques to the pop/rock context. Until his death in 1987, Plank played a pivotal role in West Germany by providing a studio environment informed by innovations in academic electronic music, but that welcomed technological play and had no professionalized production-house style (unlike many other West German and British studios). His work and technological approach would prove to be highly influential. For example, producer-auteur Martin Hannett's work with Joy Division on *Unknown Pleasures* (1979) was directly informed by Plank's production work with Neu! and La Düsseldorf (Sharp, 2007, p. 107).

Brian Eno

In considering the wider influence of West German music in this period, it is important to consider the chief aural theoretician of the sonoscape, Brian Eno. As collaborator and facilitator, he formulated a progressive intellectuality that spoke through and for many British and West German electronic artists. Tamm (1995) suggests that Eno's key innovation in the 1970s was to sideline musical notation as a criterion for aesthetic or compositional judgement. Instead, he concentrated on

> aspects of musical style which are extremely important in popular music, but which are difficult or impossible to notate, such as overall 'sound' (or what are known as 'production values'), timbre, vocal quality and nuance, and ornamentation. (p. 9)

Eno highlighted the importance of focusing on timbre and sonic texture in composition, and by emphasizing these para-musical features he developed a new conceptual arena for popular/art music experimentation. Crucially, he often identified himself as a non-musician to emphasize his interest in *sonicality*, rather than musicality. In the late 1970s, Eno stimulated 'countless young artists to liberate themselves from the musical conventions in which they had been raised, and to follow no dogma – including Kraftwerk's techno-rock gospel – blindly' (Doerschuk qtd. in Tamm, 1995, p. 170). Aikin (1981) agreed, asserting, 'The real rewards of Eno's influence are bound to go not to those who ape his innovations in composition and sound processing, but to those who are willing to apply his insights so as to discover the sources of their own creativity' (p. 216). Eno's contribution to the sonic reinvention of rock music is of particular importance for British synthpop/rock, but drew from his collaborations with West German artists. Though his work with Bowie, Ultravox, Devo and Talking Heads is better known, until recently his work with Cluster, Harmonia and Plank in the 1970s has been more obscure. Eno in 1997 explained his attraction to Krautrock, identifying Neu!'s disciplined, uncompromising and consciously experimental music, and Kraftwerk's natural minimalism and restraint as key attractions. He also stated that

> a lot of the German bands had that commune thing, and a lot of them, like Can, owned their own stuff and stayed outside the business in a way I also liked – there was a sense of them taking a musical position which was the obvious outcome of a philosophical, political and social statement. I've always wanted music to be bound up with all those things. (Gill, 1997b)

Eno sought out Harmonia at a gig in Hamburg in 1974, spontaneously jammed with them on stage, and was afterwards invited to work with them at their Forst studio. He did so in late summer, 1976, recording sessions with Roedelius, Moebius and Rother that were not initially intended for release. A representative selection from these sessions became available on Harmonia & Eno '76's *Tracks and Traces* (2009), which expanded on the more limited Harmonia '76 version compiled by Roedelius in 1997 (Neate, 2009). After Rother left Harmonia to concentrate on his solo albums (*Flammende Herzen* [1977], *Sterntaler* [1978] and *Katzenmusik* [1979] that were influential in their own right for Simple Minds and Ultravox), Eno returned to work with Moebius and Roedelius on 1977's *Cluster and Eno*, and 1978's *After the Heat*. These sessions also enabled Eno to work closely with Plank, who he described as 'inspired; he thought that the job of being an engineer was highly creative, so he was very much a contributor to the things that came out of . . . [his] studio' (Sheppard, 2008, p. 60).

Eno enjoyed the working methods employed in these collaborations, saying that

[o]ne nice aspect . . . was that everybody had just about the same sense of how long you should stay in the same place . . . With Cluster, we could stay in the same place for 25 minutes or so, really get into the details of a piece, start to feel it as a landscape, not as just a moment in the music, but as a place. (Gill, 1997b)

Compositional and studio improvisation were at the heart of his work with Cluster and Harmonia, and the idea this music suggested a 'landscape' chimes with Eno's emerging interests in aphonic instrumental and environmental music. While working with Cluster at Plank's studio, Eno began work with Plank's assistance on his album *Ambient 1: Music for Airports* (1978). It is here that many of his ideas around environmental music concretized in the first unambiguous adoption of the label 'ambient',[6] and there is no doubt that the development of this music had been inflected by his collaborations with Harmonia, Cluster and Plank.

Eno's contemporary influence on British synthpop/rock musicians is clear, though often it is his music and his use of synthesizers, not his conceptualism, that caught their imagination. For example, Numan (on *Telekon* [1980] and *Dance* [1981]) musically referenced Eno – and therefore indirectly all of those who had worked with him in the mid 1970s. This does not necessarily mean Numan deployed Eno's intellectual innovations around musical systems, cybernetics and 'oblique strategies' (his aphoristic aids to composition and studio production). In fact, Numan was suspicious of Eno's ideas but was intrigued by the outcomes of this intellectual play (Numan, 1998, p. 48). On *Dance* Numan explored some of Eno's textures and timbres; Eno's 'Sky Saw' from *Another Green World* is a direct ancestor (fretless bass, heavily synthesizer-processed guitar, vocal delivery) of Numan's 'She's Got Claws' and 'A Subway Called "You"'; Eno's 'Over Fire Island' a precursor of Numan's 'Slowcar to China'. Other synthpop/rock artists such as Ultravox and Simple Minds would also look to Eno's instrumental and environmental ambient music for inspiration.

David Bowie

In his previously mentioned albums *Low* and *"Heroes"*, and *Lodger* (1979), Bowie brought some of the techniques and sounds of Krautrock experimentation into the mainstream currents of Anglo-American popular music. From the mid 1970s he expressed admiration for this music:

I was a big fan of Kraftwerk, Cluster and Harmonia, and I thought the first Neu! album, in particular, was just gigantically wonderful . . . Looking at that against punk, I had absolutely no doubts where the future of music was going, and for me it was coming out of Germany at that time. I also liked ... Can [and] Edgar Froese['s], *Epsilon In Malaysian Pale* ... In a way, it was great that I found those bands, because I didn't feel any of the essence of punk at all in that period, I just totally by-passed it. (Gill, 1997a)

Bowie's unsuccessful attempts to team up with Kraftwerk and Rother[7] when he relocated from the US to Europe did not prevent these albums from owing a great deal to Krautrock. Though they actually represent 'the hybridization of R&B and electronics' (Bowie, 2001) that Bowie had begun on *Station to Station* (1976), Neu!'s 'Hero' partly inspired Bowie's '"Heroes"', 'V-2 Schneider' was an ambiguous homage to Kraftwerk and *Lodger*'s 'Red Sails' seemingly a direct tribute to Harmonia's 'Monza (Rauf und Runter)' from *De Luxe* (1975). Likewise, Iggy Pop viewed his 'Berlin' collaborations with Bowie (*The Idiot* [1977], *Lust for Life* [1977]) as a fusion of James Brown and Kraftwerk. Importantly Eno's collaborative work on the most experimental aspects of Bowie's 'Berlin' albums constructed an indirect but distinct creative connection with Neu!, Cluster and Harmonia through his work with Rother, Moebius and Roedelius.

For Bowie, though Kraftwerk were a creative inspiration due to a 'singular determination to stand apart from stereotypical American chord sequences and their wholehearted embrace of a European sensibility', he felt their music had 'little place in my scheme'. Bowie suggests that 'theirs was a controlled, robotic, extremely measured series of compositions, almost a parody of minimalism', whereas his music 'tended to expressionist mood pieces, the protagonist ... abandoning himself to the zeitgeist ... with little or no control over his life. The music was spontaneous for the most part ... we were poles apart' (2001). However, *Neu!75* in its segregated organization (quiet, meditative A-side followed by a loud and hysterical B-side) proved a more obvious touchstone, providing a split-sided model for *Low* and *"Heroes"*. Harmonia's Cluster/Neu! split personality was also a key point of reference. Though Bowie clearly admired Kraftwerk's music, his own music drew more widely from Krautrock, and Kraftwerk were only one among several sources of creative inspiration.

In 1976, Bowie was drawn to Berlin and its geographical isolation as a Cold War no-man's land where he could clean up (not always successfully) and become relatively anonymous. However, rather than becoming a recluse, he actually travelled widely in this period. Several recording and mixing sessions for his and Iggy Pop's 'Berlin' albums took place in France, Munich, Switzerland and New York. He toured the UK, US and Canada with Pop in 1977, and in addition for his own 1978 tour added several other European countries, Australia and Japan. Despite this restlessness, being physically located in Berlin for part of the 1976–79 period was significant for these albums. Hansa Tonstudios where mixing sessions for *Low* and recording and mixing sessions for *"Heroes"* took place were adjacent to the Berlin Wall. This backdrop partly provided the *mise-en-scène* of Bowie's work that enacted the psycho-geography of Berlin (most specifically in 'Weeping Wall', 'Art Decade', '"Heroes"' and 'Neuköln'). Connell and Gibson (2003) suggest Hansa proved popular for Bowie as it 'represented a location, with a political and cultural style, that somehow combined pre-war hedonism with post-war geopolitical tensions' (p. 105). The 'touristic gaze' (Urry, 1990) of Bowie's 'Berlin' albums are in part snapshots and souvenirs of a brief dalliance with West German music and a 'muddled' interest (to put it kindly) in twentieth-century German history and culture (see Witts in this collection). The albums acted as a crucial conduit through which travelled Krautrock and pre-war hedonistic and post-war geopolitical German myths and memes that fascinated British fans and musicians.

Rusty Egan

If Eno and Bowie had initially alerted British audiences to the West German musicians covered in this study, a key figure in bringing the music to the attention of club-goers, musicians and eventually the music press was Rusty Egan. Though British Radio 1 DJ John Peel had played tracks by Neu! and other Krautrock acts as early as 1971 (if not earlier) (Cope, 1995 p. 42), Egan appears to have introduced this music to a more receptive crowd ready to embrace the new European electronic sounds. Egan drummed with a number of punk and post-punk bands (including the Rich Kids and the Skids), but is now perhaps best remembered as an influential club promoter and DJ, beginning his career at the Soho club Billy's 'Bowie Nights' in 1978. Bowie, Roxy Music and Kraftwerk loomed large on his playlist, but after altercations with the club's owners (Rimmer, 2003, p. 37), he decided to pursue his Bowie-inspired German musical interests and travelled to Berlin and Düsseldorf. Rimmer suggests Egan was highly influenced by the Berlin clubbing scene and the music he encountered, and by an unplanned meeting with Kraftwerk in Düsseldorf with whom he kept in contact. On his return to the UK in 1979, he began to play tracks by the Human League and the Normal, the industrial sounds of Cabaret Voltaire and Throbbing Gristle, tracks by Magazine, Simple Minds and Ultravox, and La Düsseldorf and Cluster & Eno. His playlist had taken on a strong European and international dimension and, as Rimmer indicates:

> Egan . . . turned his back on the authenticist Anglo-American rock tra-
> dition . . . he culled sounds from Germany (Kraftwerk, La Düsseldorf,
> Gina X, Giorgio Moroder, Nina Hagen), Belgium (Telex), Japan (Yellow
> Magic Orchestra) and Switzerland (Yello) . . . Egan's playlist thus rep-
> resented an assortment of different musical trajectories that could only

have intersected on one dancefloor at this particular point in history. The only thing they had in common was the still relatively new and surprising sound of the synthesizer. (p. 88)

The audience exposed to Egan's DJing at the London club Blitz, and by 1981 at Club for Heroes, included a mixture of aspiring and influential musicians, style and music journalists, art students, fashion designers, record producers and record label entrepreneurs (Ure, 2004, pp. 59–60). In 1981 he indicated he had added more esoteric Cluster and Plank releases to his playlist:

'Electro-disco' is the label that's been slapped on it. Among the most requested items are such unusual fare as 'Self Portrait' by Rodelius [sic], 'News' by Mobius and Conny Planck [sic] as well as sundry other tracks by La Düsseldorf and, the founding fathers of the whole style, Kraftwerk. (Stand, 1981 p. 38)

Egan's close friend and fellow Rich Kid Midge Ure was also enamoured with La Düsseldorf and Neu! In 1978 he began accumulating synthesizers, and worked with Egan on dance-based electronic music projects (Ure, 2004, pp. 52–60). With Dave Formula, Barry Adamson and John McGeoch from Magazine, Billy Currie from Ultravox, and Egan's club-promoting partner Steve Strange on vocals, they formed Visage who became the musical front for the Blitz scene. Ure later joined and fronted the second incarnation of Ultravox, who provided another crucial link between British and West German artists.

The birth of synthpop/rock: Ultravox(!), Gary Numan and Simple Minds

There is little space here to undertake a thorough mapping of the impact of Krautrock on British pop/rock music in the 1977–81 period, therefore I will briefly consider the important influence of this music on the transitional synthpop/rock of Ultravox, Numan and Simple Minds that led to the subsequent rise of synthpop in 1980.

As has been established, Eno and Plank undertook crucial collaborative and mediating roles that nurtured the new electronic music emerging across the trans-European sonoscape in the 1970s. Both also separately undertook co-production roles with the British band Ultravox. The band, headed by John Foxx from 1976–79, drew heavily on art-rock influences, and comparisons were drawn at the time to Roxy Music, the Velvet Underground, Sparks, the New York Dolls and Bowie. Reynolds (2005) suggests that

[w]hat made Ultravox crucial precursors of the1980s synthpop/rock explosion was their European aura and . . . John Foxx's frigid imagery

of dehumanization and decadence. The group's style was based on rejecting rock's standard 'Americanisms'; Billy Currie, their keyboardist, was a classically trained viola player and determinedly avoided blues scales. (p. 325)

Foxx regarded Eno's *Another Green World* as 'the start of something New, British and Electronic – another New Form of Life' (Sheppard, 2008, p. 234), and asked Eno to co-produce their first album, *Ultravox!*, in 1976. The band enjoyed the experimental systems and oblique strategies fostered by Eno, though drummer Warren Cann was disappointed at his lack of technical prowess, saying, 'We had been under the impression, due to Brian's image from Roxy [Music] that he was a real "technical type" . . . we were hungry to learn how to push the boundaries of the studio environment' (Wårstad, 1997). It soon became apparent Eno was not a hands-on producer. Additionally, Ultravox were working within short song forms and resisted Eno's Cageian indeterminacy that emphasized process over outcome (Sheppard, 2008, p. 235).

At the end of 1977, Ultravox released their second album, *Ha!-Ha!-Ha!*, that ended with the electronic 'Hiroshima Mon Amour', sounding like Kraftwerk with Bowie on saxophone. They were keen at the time to ally themselves with the new Europeanism propagated by these artists, and the new electronic aesthetic of Krautrock. While recording their synthesizer-heavy third album, *Systems of Romance*, at Plank's studio in 1978, Foxx stated, 'We feel European. The sort of background and melodies we tend to come out with just seemed to be sort of Germanic even before we came here' (Miles, 1978). Foxx also suggested that the choice of Plank as co-producer was partly due to their interest in Neu!, *et al.*, and

> because there was nowhere in England that really had the experience to handle the things that we wanted to do . . . We wanted to find some place where we could try things out without being under the pressure of studio time . . . Also, because Connie [*sic*] has worked in the past with the German electronic bands he has the experience and the facilities. (Miles, 1978)

Plank as co-producer enabled Ultravox to 'push the boundaries of the studio environment' in a way Eno had not. He also introduced them to the solo work of Rother that would later influence their sound. However, poor sales followed and Foxx became disillusioned with the band and left to pursue more minimalist electronic pop music in 1979, releasing his influential synthpop album *Metamatic* in 1980. Disheartened Ultravox synthesist, violinist and keyboard player Billy Currie began work on the Visage project with Rusty Egan and Midge Ure, and recorded and toured with Gary Numan who continually cited Ultravox as his key recent inspiration (Morley, 1980). The new Ultravox with Midge Ure as vocalist continued to work with Plank on their albums *Vienna* (1980) and *Rage in Eden* (1981), drawing further influence from Neu! and La Düsseldorf, and began to introduce Eno-like ambient experimentation into their music. However, before the re-emergence and commercial success of the new formation in 1980, Gary Numan had already opened the synthpop floodgates.

In 1979, Numan became a hugely successful avatar for all that had gone before in the then emerging British popular electronic music and Krautrock contexts of recent years. He synthesized the musical and thematic memes transmitted across the trans-European sonoscape and translated them into a form that made him an international pop star. With the Tubeway Army album *Replicas* (1979) and single 'Are 'Friends' Electric?', followed by his solo album *The Pleasure Principle* (1979) and the single 'Cars', Numan formulated a sound informed by Bowie, Eno, Kraftwerk, Neu! (Savage, 1979, p. 100) and Ultravox, but was his own. He pushed synthesizers to the forefront of his music with simplicity and confidence, and did so with a rock – drum, guitar and bass – rhythm section that provided a punch missing from the pure electronic sound of Kraftwerk. He unashamedly adopted and emphasized synthesizer textures that flew in the face of the Anglo-American rock hegemony. Moore (2001) also suggests 'the pitch material' of 'Are 'Friends' Electric?' and 'Cars' 'does not have a pentatonic basis' that therefore sets these songs 'apart from styles of rock that consciously owe their origins to rhythm'n'blues' (p. 153). Although Numan's sound was intensely musically minimalist and self-avowedly eschewed instrumental virtuosity, Reynolds (2005, p. 323) states that 'his music *rocked*, and even when it didn't it possessed an almost symphonic grandeur'.

Though commercially successful, Numan faced much critical disdain. Bowie and Eno both criticized him, perhaps feeling the wind had been taken from their sails by a young (21-year-old) pretender (Numan, 1998, pp. 100–1). Recently Kraftwerk's Karl Bartos[8] suggested Numan misappropriated Kraftwerk's stage persona and look, though Kraftwerk adopted their all-black stage clothing after Numan had 'pioneered' it. Others resorted to opprobrium; Frith (1984/1988) suggested Numan was a 'creep', and Shaar-Murray (1980) complained, 'His mannered whine drives me completely up the wall'.

However, I would argue that rather than having a simple mimetic relationship to his influences, Numan's fusion of the memes that he had absorbed allowed him to produce an individual and populist version of the intellectually driven pop/art music of Bowie, Eno, Kraftwerk and their compatriots. Numan's creative voice may have spoken through musical and thematic languages that were 'already populated with the social intentions of others' (Bakhtin qtd. in Toynbee, 2000, p. 46) but he compelled them to serve his own intentions in an innovative manner. Likewise, Numan's dystopian science-fiction fantasy narrative that underpinned his music at the time was inspired by Philip K. Dick, George Orwell, J. G. Ballard, Isaac Asimov, Fred Saberhagen and William S. Burroughs (Numan, 1998, p. 36) but again was his own. Numan made no secret of his influences at the time, and later suggested he merely created a new hybrid sound with no claims to originality (p. 50).

The fit Numan forged between the synthesizer, science fiction, futurism and posthuman technological themes/memes enabled him to create a homologous musical package that lay behind his mass appeal. Although Kraftwerk similarly addressed these themes, they did so with an amount of intellectual irony, with Rhine-Ruhr and German references and sub-texts, and a conceptualism that was not as immediately appealing to British pop fans as the fantasy dystopian world conjured by Numan. His substantial record sales convinced the British music industry of the commercial viability of electronic popular music, and from 1980–82 British pop music became dominated by synthpop.

In Scotland, Simple Minds looked to Ultravox and Numan and began to forge music that likewise drew from Krautrock. Their first album release, 1979's *Life in a Day*, has close similarities and made similar musical references to Ultravox's first two album releases two years earlier; but missing from the album is any sense of the European experimentalism that had enthused Ultravox, Numan and other contemporary artists. However, the release of *Real to Real Cacophony* later in 1979 demonstrated that the band had begun to listen intently to Krautrock. Guitarist Charlie Burchill suggests that after listening to Can, 'we discovered La Düsseldorf, Neu!, Michael Rother, Cluster. It seemed as if all the best music in those days came from Germany' (qtd. in Bos, 1984, p. 17). Keyboardist Mick McNeil (2005) suggested that he felt the relentlessness of La Düsseldorf, the colour and almost classical melody of Kraftwerk and Rother's *Katzenmusik* were his key influences at the time. Singer Jim Kerr concurred, stating:

> We used to hitch-hike in Europe . . . before joining the group. We liked groups like Neu[!], [La] Düsseldorf and Can, all of whom are influenced by the Velvet Underground . . . We've always found them more innovative . . . The Europeans have got a much better suss for keyboards and sounds. (qtd. in Sweeting, 1988, p. 50)

Real to Real Cacophony (1979) was almost entirely constructed through studio composition and experimentation, and appeared to be a form of musical catharsis, purging one set of obvious influences while exploring new possibilities exhibited in Krautrock. By *Empires and Dance* (1980) the band adopted a more synthesizer-heavy dance-trance that drew more directly from the *motorik* repetition of Neu!, Kraftwerk and La Düsseldorf. Kerr noted that 'Neu! . . . repeat a riff forever . . . When you use repetition you have to continue for a long time, otherwise it's not effective. Some riffs don't start to work until they've been repeated for four minutes' (Bos, 1984, p. 61). Through their Krautrock-influenced repetitive, groove-based, electronic trance-rock, Simple Minds created what Rimmer (1982) termed 'ambient dance music' (p. 12). Alongside their song-based material they began to explore soundscapes through instrumental and environmental music. This was not ambient in Eno's terms (i.e. contemplative, background, non-developmental, cyclic, pulses rather than rhythms) (Tamm, 1995, p. 132). From *Real to Real Cacophony* until 1982's *New Gold Dream*, they created examples of aphonic music that called direct attention to itself – 'Veldt', 'Theme for Great Cities' and 'Sound in 70 Cities' all evoke the environments of their titles. Aphonic music is also a feature of the work of other synthpop/rock and synthpop bands, as in OMD's 'Architecture and Morality' and 'Dazzle Ships, pt.1–3', and Ultravox's 'Alles Klar', who appeared to follow the lead of Krautrock bands in exploring such music.

Simple Minds' interest in travel also had a European dimension. Kerr stated at the time, 'the band is often associated with travel, but that point of view is too limited. It is much more: not travel, but *movement*. It's in the music as well: repetition, that's pure movement' (qtd. in Bos, 1984, p. 34). *Empires and Dance* (1980) also adopted European memes partly derived from Kraftwerk's 'Europe Endless'.[9] During Simple Minds' first European tour Kerr 'felt close to a common European culture. I didn't look at it as Holland and Germany and France, to me it was a whole' (qtd. in Bos, p. 57). On *Sons and Fascination/Sister Feelings Call* (1981), the band chose Steve Hillage as producer as they felt

> through him we might be able to get in touch with the continental music of the seventies . . . Not only had he played with Gong, he was also a fan of the scene around Conny Plank . . . the first thing he played us was [Eno, Moebius and Roedelius's] *After the Heat*. (Kerr qtd. in Bos, p. 82)

Conclusion

As this study has indicated, though Kraftwerk were a key inspiration for British rock and synthpop artists from the mid 1970s to early 1980s, these artists also drew more widely from Krautrock in this period than is usually appreciated. In doing so, they created a trans-European sonoscape that became a complex network of influence and counter-influence that eventually extended across the Atlantic. In the development of electro and techno in the US in the early 1980s, Numan for one is perhaps unfairly overlooked as a key innovator in the rush to attribute the primary influence to Kraftwerk. Electro pioneer Afrika Bambaataa supports this by stating:

Gary Numan. Man he was dope. So important to us . . . When we heard that single, 'Are 'Friends' Electric?', it was like the aliens had landed in the Bronx . . . We were just throwing shapes to this tune, man . . . More than Kraftwerk, Numan was the inspiration. He's a hero. Without him, there'd be no electro. (qtd. in James, 2002, p. 62)

In 2001, techno pioneer Juan Atkins provided further evidence for this claim by suggesting that the only artist he was interested in remixing was Numan (Taylor, 2001).[10] Sicko (1999) indicates that Ultravox, Numan and Visage were influential in Detroit's proto-techno clubs. Ultravox's 'Mr. X' was a template for Cybotron's 'Alleys of Your Mind', and Visage's 'Frequency 7' was a seminal dance track. Depeche Mode were also held in reverence by Detroit techno musicians Derrick May and Kevin Saunderson, and acknowledged as influences by house music innovators Todd Terry and Frankie Knuckles (McReady, 1989). Other British electronic bands, such as Nitzer Ebb, Section 25 and New Order, played an influential role, and May identifies Cabaret Voltaire as influential for many early Detroit techno DJs (Hollings, 2002). This evidence would suggest that like the mistaken assumption that Kraftwerk were the only important West German influence on British electronic popular music in the late 1970s, the innovations of British artists are also important to acknowledge in the development of electro, techno and house. As such it is time for a more historically accurate understanding of the transformation of the trans-European sonoscape into a more complex trans-Atlantic network of musical and cultural flows.

The author would like to thank Mick McNeil
and Davy McConnell.

Notes

1. After Appadurai (1993) who argued global conditions are characterized by dynamic flows across 'scapes' – the *sonoscape* is a metaphoric musical network through which the musicians in this study exchanged overlapping musical and thematic ideas or memes.

2. Krautrock, a xenophobic nomenclature Ralf Hütter has described as 'an insult' (qtd. in Dalton, 2009, p. 68), is used in this study for want of a better term as it has gained wide currency.

3. The use of 'memes' and 'memetic' in this study is an attempt to indicate the flow of influence between the musicians studied was not *mimetic*. It is better understood as memetic – themes, ideas and musical strategies were transmitted across the sonoscape through complex interchange.

4. Though Hütter and Schneider were the core of Kraftwerk until 2009, Karl Bartos has compositional credits on *The Man-Machine, Computer World* and *Electric Café*, and

Wolfgang Flür was involved in designing and constructing the Kling Klang studio in the late 1970s (Bendjelloul, 2001).

5. For a more detailed study of the sonic qualities and thematic connections of the music discussed in this study see Albiez (2003).

6. Eno's term 'ambient music' referred to 'music that surrounded the listener with a sense of spaciousness and depth, encompassing one on all sides rather than coming *at* the listener. It blended with the sounds of the environment, and seemed to invite one to listen musically to the environment itself' (Tamm, 1995, pp. 131–2).

7. Kraftwerk intended to collaborate with Bowie but nothing came to fruition after initial meetings. In 1976 they stated, 'We are going to record with Bowie. He will come to Düsseldorf pretty soon for that. We still don't know what we're gonna do together, it's mostly an encounter . . .' (Alessandrini, 1976). Rother did not turn Bowie down as Bowie believed – both were duped by somebody in Bowie's management into believing the other had changed their mind about recording together (Young, 2001; Davies, 2006).

8. Quoted in Johnstone (2008).

9. In 2009, Hütter stated that the themes and images of *Trans-Europe Express* represented 'our cultural identity as Europeans, with the spirit of European culture' (Dalton, 2009, p. 69). This parallels the Europeanism expressed by Simple Minds, John Foxx and others in British synthpop/rock.

10. See Albiez (2005) for a detailed study of British synthpop/rock's influence, alongside Kraftwerk, in early electro and techno.

References

Aikin, J. (1981), 'Brian Eno', in G. Armbruster (ed.) (1982), *The Art of Electronic Music*. New York: William Morrow.

Albiez, S. (2003), 'Sounds of future past: from Neu! to Numan', in T. Phleps and R. von Appen (eds), in *POP SOUNDS: Klangtexturen in der Pop – und Rockmusik*. Bielefelder: Transcript-Verlag.

—— (2005), 'Post soul futurama: African American cultural politics and early Detroit techno'. *European Journal of American Culture*, 24, (2), 131–52.

Alessandrini, P. (1976), 'Haute tension: Kraftwerk'. *Rock & Folk*. November, 54–7. http://www.thing.de/delektro/interviews/eng/kraftwerk/kw11-76.html (last accessed 14 April 2010).

Appadurai, A. (1996), *Modernity at Large: Cultural Dimensions of Globalisation*. Minneapolis: University of Minnesota Press.

Bangs, L. (1975a/1996), 'Kraftwerkfeature or how I learned to stop worrying and love the balm', in *Psychotic Reactions and Carburetor Dung*. London: Serpent's Tail, pp. 154–64.

—— (1975b), 'Kraftwerk: the final solution to the music problem'. *New Musical Express*, 9 September, 20–1.

Bendjelloul, M. (Dir.) (2001), *Kraftwerk Documentary [Part 2]*. Pop i fokus [Swedish Television]. http://www.youtube.com/watch?v=OwHBdcWn6EQ&feature=related (last accessed 14 April 2010).

Bos, A. (1984), *Simple Minds: The Race is the Prize*. London: Virgin Books.

Bowie, D. (2001), 'Uncut interview: David Bowie on Berlin – the real "uncut" version'. http://www.bowiewonderworld.com/features/dbuncut.htm (last accessed 14 April 2010).

Connell, J. and Gibson, C. (2003), *Sound Tracks: Popular Music, Identity and Place*. London: Routledge.

Cope, J. (1995), *Krautrocksampler: One Head's Guide to the Great Kosmische Musik – 1968 onwards*. London: Head Heritage.

Dalton, S. (2009), 'Album by album: Kraftwerk'. *Uncut*. Take 149, October, 68–71.

Davies, C. (Dir.) (2006), *David Bowie: Under Review 1976–1979: The Berlin Trilogy*. [DVD]. SIDVD512. Sexy Intellectual.

Dawkins, R. (1976/2006), *The Selfish Gene*. (3rd revised edn). Oxford: Oxford University Press.

Deer, P. (2004), 'The dogs of war: myths of British anti-Americanism', in A. Ross and K. Ross (eds), *Anti-Americanism*. New York: New York University Press, pp. 158–78.

DeRogatis, J. (1996), *Kaleidoscope Eyes: Psychedelic Music from the 1960s to the 1990s*. London: Fourth Estate.

Diliberto, J. (1987), 'Man vs. machine: Conny Plank'. *Electronic Musician*, February. http://emusician.com/em_spotlight/interview_conny_plank/ (last accessed 14 April 2010).

Frith, S. (1984/1988), 'All wrapped up', in *Music for Pleasure*. Oxford: Polity Press, pp. 192–3.

Gill, A. (1997a), 'Krautrock'. *Mojo*, April. http://www.rocksbackpages.com/article. html?ArticleID=6371 (last accessed 14 April 2010).

—— (1997b), 'Eno: for the British musical maverick, Germany successfully reinvented rock's wheel'. *Mojo*, April. http://music.hyperreal.org/artists/brian_eno/interviews/ mojo97a.html (last accessed 14 April 2010).

Hargus, B. (1998), 'Michael Rother interview', *Perfect Sound Forever*, March. http://www. furious.com/perfect/Michaelrother.html (last accessed 14 April 2010).

Hollings, K. (2002), 'Cabaret Voltaire'. *The Wire*, 215, January. http://www.thewire.co.uk/ articles/212/print (last accessed 14 April 2010).

Iliffe, S. (2003), *Roedelius: Painting With Sound*. London: Meridian Music Guides.

James, M. (2002), *Fatboy Slim: Funk Soul Brother*. London: Sanctuary.

Johnstone, R. (Exec. Prod.) (2008), *Kraftwerk and the Electronic Revolution*. [DVD]. SIDVD541. Sexy Intellectual.

Keenan, D. (2009), 'The primer: kosmische music'. *The Wire*, 308. October, 44–51.

Kopf, B. (1999), 'White line fever', *The Wire*, 184, June, 48–51.

McCready, J. (1989), 'Modus operandum: Depeche Mode in Detroit'. *The Face*, February. http://www.rocksbackpages.com/article.html?ArticleID=681&SearchText=depeche+ mode (last accessed 14 April 2010).

—— (1996), 'Welcome to the machine'. *The Face*, 98, November. http://www. rocksbackpages.com/article.html?ArticleID=5948&SearchText=welcome+to+the+mac hine (last accessed 14 April 2010).

McDonald, I. (1972a), 'Germany calling: part one'. *NME*, 9 December, 26–7.

—— (1972b), 'Germany calling: part two'. *NME*, 16 December, 34–6.

—— (1972c), 'Germany calling: part three'. *NME*, 23 December, 34.

McNeil, M. (2005), E-mail communication with the author, February 2005.

Miles (1976), 'Kraftwerk: Exceller-8, Radio-Activity'. *NME*, 31 January. http://www.rocksbackpages.com/article.html?ArticleID=10210&SearchText=kraftwerk (last accessed 14 April 2010).

—— (1978), 'Ultravox: vee hav vays of makink you experiment'. *NME*, 2 September. http://www.rocksbackpages.com/article.html?ArticleID=12687&SearchText=ultravox (last accessed 14 April 2010).

Moore, A. F. (2001), *Rock: the Primary Text: Developing a Musicology of Rock*. Aldershot: Ashgate.

Morley, P. (1980), 'Forever and ever Ultravox'. *NME*, 13 September. http://www.rocksbackpages.com/article.html?ArticleID=11154&SearchText=ultravox (last accessed 14 April 2010).

Neate, W. (2009), 'Krautrock deluxe: Michael Rother (part 2)'. *Blurt*, 18 September. http://www.blurt-online.com/features/view/454/ (last accessed 18 April 2010).

Numan, G. (1998), *Praying to the Aliens: An Autobiography* (*with Steve Malins*). London: Andre Deutsch.

O'Hearn, P. (1997), 'A taste of Krautrock'. *Perfect Sound Forever*. http://www.furious.com/perfect/atasteofkrautrock.html (last accessed 14 April 2010).

Reynolds, S. (1995), 'Surfer silver'. *Melody Maker*, 25 February, 37.

—— (2005), *Rip it Up and Start Again: Post-punk 1978–1984*. London: Faber & Faber.

Rimmer, D. (1982), 'Jim Kerr's glittering dream'. *Smash Hits*, 4, (19), 16–29 September, 12–13.

—— (2003), *New Romantics: The Look*. London: Omnibus.

Savage, J. (1979/1996), 'Gary Numan: in every dream car, a heart-throb'. *Melody Maker*, 20 October 1979. in *Time Travel: from the Sex Pistols to Nirvana: Pop, Media and Sexuality, 1977–96*. London: Chatto & Windus, pp. 96–109.

Shaar-Murray, C. (1980), 'Gary Numan: Telekon'. *NME*, 6 September. http://www.rocksbackpages.com/article.html?ArticleID=12307 (last accessed 30 July 2010).

Sharp, C. (2007), *Who Killed Martin Hannett?: The Story of Factory Records' Musical Magician*. London: Aurum Press.

Sheppard, D. (2008), *On Some Faraway Beach: The Life and Times of Brian Eno*. London: Orion Books.

Sicko, D. (1999), *Techno Rebels: The Renegades of Electronic Funk*. New York: Billboard.

Stand, M. (1981), 'Night moves', *Smash Hits*, 3, (15), 23 July–5 August, 38.

Sweeting, A. (1988), *Simple Minds*. London: Sidgwick & Jackson.

Tamm, E. (1995), *Brian Eno: His Music and the Vertical Color of Sound*. New York: Da Capo Press.

Taylor, K. (2001), 'Juan Atkins may be the godfather of techno, but he's still da man'. http://www.virginmegamagazine.com/default.asp?aid=75B (last accessed 5 August 2003).

Thompson, D. (2002), *The Dark Reign of Gothic Rock*. London: Helter Skelter.

Toynbee, J. (2000), *Making Popular Music: Musicians, Creativity and Institutions*. London: Arnold.

Ure, M. (2004), *If I Was: The Autobiography*. London: Virgin Books.

Urry, J. (1990), *The Tourist Gaze: Leisure and Travel in Contemporary Societies*. London: Sage Publications.

Walker, J. (1978), 'Techno-rock: six Teutons and what do you get – a programmed sequencer and the doppler effect'. *Waxpaper*, 15 September. http://www.rocksbackpages.com/article.html?ArticleID=12111&SearchText=moroder (last accessed 17 March 2010).

Wårstad, J. (1997), 'Ultravox: the story – Warren Cann interview'. http://www.ultravox.org.uk/images-history/Ultravox-History_Screen_v1.0.pdf (last accessed 17 March 2010).

Watts, M. (1972), 'Deutsch rock'. *Melody Maker*, 15 April, 25.

Young, R. (2001), 'Langer atem: Junkmedia speaks with Michael Rother of Neu!'. September. http://www.junkmedia.org/index.php/junk/5/index.php?i=37 (last accessed 17 March 2010).

8

Vorsprung durch Technik – Kraftwerk and the British Fixation with Germany

Richard Witts

We were pretty sure that we weren't raised in Liverpool. Our generation had to come up with a counterpoint to that . . . Kraftwerk was willing to relate to the past of German identity.
(*Karl Bartos – Kraftwerk, 1975–91*)[1]

I can think of no people more fragmented than the Germans. Craftsmen you see, but no humans, thinkers, but no humans.
(*Hölderlin's* Hyperion, qtd. in Del Caro, 1991, p. 55)

Kraftwerk first came to Britain in September 1975. The quartet toured for three weeks to promote their *Autobahn (1974)* album. They went *fahr'n fahr'n fahr'n* up and down the M1 and the A34 to visit seventeen venues of varied suitability. On the 11th of September, the band played at the spacious Empire Theatre in Liverpool. Most of its 2,400 seats remained empty as roughly a tenth of this capacity turned up to see what the music newspaper *Record Mirror* had called 'the Krautrock novelty act' (Anon., 1975, p. 15)

John Hawkins of Merseyside reggae/punk band Activity Minimal was one of the three hundred or so in attendance. He recalls:

The first surprise for me was in the foyer. There was a very large blown-up photograph, mounted on cardboard, of the band with short, tidy hair. I think it was probably the photo that became the cover of *Trans-Europe Express*. All of the bands that me and my mates associated with Kraftwerk were basically hippy-looking – Tangerine Dream, Pink Floyd, Peter Gabriel's Genesis, and so on. My perception was that they too must be a progressive, long-haired band. After all, the 'Autobahn' single was twenty minutes long. But when they came on stage they really did look like businessmen.

The next surprise was that the auditorium was virtually empty. It was a very odd atmosphere, as the Empire was a huge venue and it seemed even bigger unfilled. It must have been strange for the band. I recognized faces from the Stadium. The Liverpool Stadium was a former boxing ring that had become the main venue for up-and-coming bands, run by Roger Eagle who later owned the club *Eric's*. So, it was basically the Stadium regulars in an empty theatre. (Hawkins, 2009)

Four nights later Kraftwerk played at Manchester's large Free Trade Hall. Tim Lyons, singer of the band the Things, recalls being part of a very small audience, 'maybe even less than Liverpool'. He had placed Kraftwerk in the context of the 'Krautrock' alternative German rock group genre of the early 1970s. He considers it

strange now to see how accessible this scene was to us. I first came across a poster for Can's *Future Days* LP in 1973 at Rare Records shop, bought the album, and within a couple of weeks I saw them at the Stoneground! Better than boring progressive rock.

But Kraftwerk was striking in its difference:

They made the most of those black shirts and trousers. Along with their names on neon signs there were lots of neon lights, and hand and arm movements,[2] more so than later visits [to Manchester]. I felt that Kraftwerk had a 'punk' aspect, too, in that it was more to do with creativity and style than musical ability. I also thought that there was a kind of folky element. I once compared Kraftwerk to the Incredible String Band! (Lyons, 2009)

Local press reviews of this tour add to the impression that a small but intrigued public considered Kraftwerk to be a fresh and entrancingly eccentric development of – or corollary to – the Krautrock genre. Yet, a year later the mediated views drew on less approving images of Germany. For example, Miles (1976) reviewed the *Radio-Activity* (1975) tour in the *NME* under the title 'This is what your fathers fought to save you from . . .' He claimed that the 'electronic melodies flowed as slowly as a piece of garbage floating down the polluted Rhine' and commented sarcastically on 'this '40s decadent look'; Edmonds (1976a) wrote of Kraftwerk's 'fascist drone'.

What seems to have encouraged such a critical turn was a vogue for the music of Kraftwerk led by the British singer David Bowie in early 1976. Enthused by *Autobahn*, Bowie had invited the band to support him on his

1976 *Station to Station* tour of North America and Europe, though Kraftwerk declined. He told Edmonds (1976b), 'I think that there are two bands now who come close to a neo-Nazi kind of thing – Roxy Music and Kraftwerk'. In recent months Bowie had made comments in support of political dictatorships, culminating in a declaration to a Swedish journalist that Britain would benefit from the rule of a fascist leader.[3] He alleged elsewhere that he was writing a musical about the Nazi propaganda minister Goebbels, and declared that he was in training to play the Nazi colonel Radl in the forthcoming war film *The Eagle Has Landed* (1976). To open his British tour he appeared at London's Victoria railway station in his persona known as the Thin White Duke. Standing in an open-topped car, Bowie performed a salute interpreted by some as a Nazi one, which caused a few of his fans to copy him. Kraftwerk had no connection with these gestures, comments and incidents. It was drawn into the discourse by celebrity osmosis. Yet the British perceptions and misunderstandings that began to surround the band's identity served to benefit its profile as much as to harm it. The rest of the chapter explores this curious state of affairs.

North-west Germany

In one way, Kraftwerk's identity is perfectly clear. It is a duo. Ralf Hütter (born 1946) and Florian Schneider-Esleben (born 1947) started making music together in 1968 and from that time on they invited drummers to work for them. This summary may seem unfair to the drummers, but it is a fact. The pair took inspiration from another duo, the provocative British performance artists Gilbert Proesch (born 1943) and George Passmore (born 1942) (Bussy, 1993, p. 83). Gilbert and George performed their epic 'living sculpture' in Düsseldorf's Kunsthalle in 1970. A tape machine played a 1930s song, 'Underneath the Arches', while they posed in bronze make-up on a table, repeating the song for hours on end. Every two years after that they held shows of their multiple photo works in the city's Konrad Fischer Gallery. Gilbert and George's characters have been described as 'rigid and hollow men, devoid of personality and entirely bereft of imagination . . . The imitation of mechanical forms and processes, the renunciation of individual creativity, the loss of sexuality and other human qualities are recurrent motifs' (Jahn, 1989). Dressed in smart suits, Gilbert and George show impeccable manners while at the same time giving rise to discomfort. Their images and gestures, done with vivid graphic clarity, confront and incite.

The patrician attitude of Gilbert and George parodies that of an English gentleman. Hütter and Schneider's version transposed this quite rationally to their homeland, where, in the late 1960s, a vibrant post-war artistic scene had started to open up issues around nationalism. There were two facets to this, and Kraftwerk dealt with both in its own way: questioning 'the silence of our fathers' about the Third Reich, and identifying what was truly German in a state politically defined, funded and half-occupied by Americans. Literary critic Andreas Huyssen wrote of the immediate post-war period:

> The country that had produced the Weimar cinema and a wealth of avant-garde art in the 1920s . . . was by and large image-dead for about twenty years: hardly any new departures in film, no painting worth talking about, a kind of enforced minimalism, ground zero of a visual amnesiac. (1995, p. 218)

Attempts in literature, film and theatre[4] persistently emerged, but it was in Kraftwerk's Düsseldorf that the most dynamic drive took place in visual and performative terms to deal with the period 1933–45. There were three artists working in the Rhine-side city who each may be said to have informed Kraftwerk's ideology and style: Joseph Beuys, Gerhard Richter and, above all, Anselm Kiefer.

Beuys (1921–86) was professor of monumental sculpture at the Staatliche Kunstakademie Düsseldorf (Academy of Art) from 1961 until his dismissal in 1972. He called himself 'an idiot under a felt hat' and stimulated debate with his enigmatic performances that often made reference to his wartime past as a young fighter pilot. He advanced the idea of performance and identity as artistic activity, which encouraged Gilbert and George (Tisdall, 1979). Richter (born 1932) fled East Germany and studied at the Academy; from 1971 he taught there. Affected by Andy Warhol's multiple portraits of everyday objects, he attempted to integrate the abstract and the figurative (Richter, 2004). Kraftwerk took this up through music, most consistently in *Radio-Activity* where tonality and electronic abstraction are contrasted and combined. The duo's image consultant between 1972 and 1982, Emil Schult, had been a student of both Richter and Beuys.

Finally, Kiefer (born 1945), also a pupil of Beuys, made huge books out of lead, and paintings infused with gold leaf, ash and straw. Their contents were architectural subjects copied from the Third Reich, as in his *Germany's Spiritual Heroes* (1973), portraying a superhuman wood-beamed hall burnished by torch flame. In a series of photographs started in 1969, Kiefer stood at places conquered by the Third Reich and gave Nazi salutes; the image is absurd – a little man dwarfed by bleak landscapes – yet, highly provocative in a society where artistic representation of Nazism was legally banned (Arasse, 2001). Kraftwerk often took the shiny, new, everyday objects of the Nazi period – its cars, the motorways, its short-range radios, the Reichsbahn network (Hildebrand, 1999), its monumentalist photography – and, like Kiefer, presented them in a utopian glow. This is not 'the normalization of the German past, the erasure of the killing of millions of people in the name of the German nation during World War II', as philosopher Jürgen Habermas put it (Habermas, 1994, p. xix). Instead the provocation is that of a society projected as though it is not yet defeated, the *unbewältigte Vergangenheit* – the past that has not been overcome.

Kraftwerk draws on Nazism, too, in its music. The spirit of Carl Orff rises from the opening glockenspiel and rattle of *Tone Float* (1968), through the treble recorder of 'Morgenspaziergang' from *Autobahn* through to what composer John White (2009) calls 'those big-boned melodic shapes' in 'Neon Lights' or the modal minimalism of 'The Robots'. Orff (1895–1982) was a German composer chiefly known for his dramatic Third Reich cantata *Carmina Burana* (1937). He produced a system of elemental music for children to sing and play in *Kindergärten*, using specially made miniature percussion instruments and recorders. Orff turned his *Schulwerk* into a lucrative industry during the Third Reich and – amazingly – after it (Kater, 2002; Goodkin, 2002). Kraftwerk's *Schulwerk*-style songs, which Tim Lyons identified above as punk-ish and folk-ish, are surely a reaction to the modernist use of what White (2009) describes as 'nervous, fidgety little building blocks' of pitches identified with the avant-garde giants such as Stockhausen and his circle in rival Cologne. In this way Kraftwerk's clusters, Doppler smears and electronic blips serve the same function as Warhol's ironic references to abstract expressionism, a teasing counterpoint to his 'what you see is what you see' figuration or photo.

Besides, there's a more personal component to Kraftwerk's ideology. Florian Schneider-Esleben's father was Paul Schneider-Esleben (1915–2005), a successful modernist architect who was acclaimed for a number of major post-war buildings in north-west Germany. Two of the most famous are the purist steel and glass Mannesmann 'skyscraper' in Düsseldorf (1954) and the Cologne-Bonn Airport Terminal of 1969 (Beckers, 1995). His style reflected 'Year Zero' sobriety in its rejection of Nazi monumental neo-classicism. In place of the recent past, post-war businesses and institutions favoured the clean modernist look of one era before, that of the 'International Style' of Germany's Bauhaus (1919–33), a 'building school' run by the architects Walter Gropius and, later, Mies van der Rohe. In post-war West Germany it was as though nothing had happened for the 12 years between 1933 and 1945. There are thus three elements at play in Kraftwerk's project. First, the pre-Nazi utopian vision of the Bauhaus period – which combined industrial crafts and fine art into a 'total work' – is projected onto the Third Reich. Second, the Third Reich's technological aspirations, such as 'motorization', are projected onto – third – the transformative modernism of West Germany's post-war *Wirtschaftswunder* ('economic miracle'). Emblemizing this post-war assertion of progressive values has been the Bavarian luxury car maker, Audi, whose slogan for many years was *Technik die begeistert* ('Technology that astonishes/enthuses'). Audi replaced this in the period of Kraftwerk's ascendancy with *Vorsprung durch Technik* ('Advance through technology'), a phrase it internationalized in order to promote the supremacy of German engineering. Ironies, contradictions and comedy spin out of Kraftwerk's triple-layered scumble. They are propelled in equal measure through the band's seductive songs and in the 'total' presentation of those songs on stage and on disc.

Who is Kraftwerk's target? It is surely those who believed that Germany as a modern country began in 1945, the *Stunde Null* (Year Zero) people. But the name of the band gives the game away: Power Station. Its work is addressed to those 'anti-progressives' – the countercultural hippies, the conservationists, the postmaterialists – for whom technological development is detrimental to the environmental quality of life (Hager, 1992; Frankland and Schoonmaker, 1992). As John Hawkins and Tim Lyons noted earlier, Kraftwerk's neat hair and smart clothes shocked the fans of the alternative scene to whom its music first appealed, and from which the band had emerged in the early 1970s. At that very time a grass-roots protest movement was evolving in West Germany (Dirke, 1997). Fearful of ecological damage, it was opposed to nuclear power and the building of *Kraftwerke*. An immense demonstration at the south-western village of Whyl in 1975, for example, led to the abandonment of a nuclear plant project there. The anti-nuclear movement itself helped to give birth in 1980 to *Die Grünen*, the national Green Party. Kraftwerk uncovers within it a regressive nostalgia for a pre-industrial, pastoral idyll, to which the Nazis were also prone (see Schama, 1995, pp. 68–72; pp. 96–109; pp. 118–20). The band does so by emphasizing the beauty and power of the industrial, underlining the allure of technological precision and sheen. But, like Gilbert and George, the message is indefinite. It is shrouded in clarity.

North West England

When in 1975 John Hawkins saw Kraftwerk in Liverpool, among the many surprising features of the concert, he noted:

> Kraftwerk got generous applause between songs from the small audience. But once the applause was over there was an empty silence as they got ready for the next number. So, the band indulged in banter between numbers – blimey! Florian or Ralf (I can't remember which) told us that they had learned their English at school, and did we know any German? Well of course we did, and they got a load of embarrassing war film clichés fired back at them: 'Achtung Englander!' and so on.

At this time the production of World War II action films was giving way to the post-Vietnam epic. Yet there were several examples, such as *Anzio* (1968) and *Battle of Britain* (1969), that were shown on Sunday afternoons on British television. They sat alongside the comedy series *Dad's Army* (1968–77), set in wartime England. Only a month after Kraftwerk's first visit, a notorious episode of the comedy series *Fawlty Towers* titled 'The Germans' was transmitted, where traumatized German guests of Basil Fawlty were treated to his impression of Hitler. In that episode Fawlty went on, 'We're all friends now, eh? All in the Market together, all differences forgotten, and no need at all to mention the war' (Cleese and Booth, 1975). This topical reference of the 'Market' alluded to the United Kingdom's entry into the European Economic Community (the 'Common Market') in January 1973. Subsequently a post-legislative national referendum was held in June 1975, where a majority of 67 per cent in a relatively high turnout (64.5 per cent) voted 'Yes' to Britain's membership of an institution first set up by West Germany and France for their mutual economic benefit (Meyer, 2005). Thus this German band, trading in nationalist sound and imagery, was evaluated through an additional layer of nationalist paradox.

There was 'the war', of course. As recently as 1999, the culture minister of unified Germany Naumann criticized Britain for being 'the only one nation in the world that has decided to make the Second World War a sort of spiritual core of its national self, understanding and pride' (cited in Beck, 2003, p. 397). Both Liverpool and Manchester were key industrial sites and ports the Luftwaffe had blitzed, most infamously at Christmas time in 1940. After the war, much of Britain's working-class hostility to Germany was symbolically channelled into professional football. England's 4–2 victory against West Germany in the 1966 World Cup continues to be celebrated even though the record from then on lay in Germany's favour.

Year	Home team		Away team		Ground
1968	West Germany	1	England	0	Hanover
1970	England	1	West Germany	3	Leon
1972	England	1	West Germany	3	London
1975	England	2	West Germany	0	London
1978	West Germany	2	England	1	Munich

Source: Beck (2003, p. 404)

By the middle 1970s there was more cause for British envy of the Germans than there was for symbolic enmity and historic bitterness. Both countries had endured the oil embargo crisis following the Arab–Israeli war of 1973. However, while Britain's domestic inflation soared sensationally in 1975 to 25 per cent, West Germany's economy was in better shape and inflation rose no higher than 6 per cent (Obstfeld, 1983). At the same time both countries were reconciled to a degree by their endurance of the unnerving and unpredictable presence of acute terrorism. It was for different sets of reasons that they shared this condition: the anti-colonial bombing campaign across England of the Provisional Irish Republican Army (PIRA), and anti-capitalist actions in West Germany of the Rote Armee Fraktion (RAF, otherwise called the Baader-Meinhof group); two armies causing chaos. The PIRA campaign was at its most intense for three years starting in March 1973, with London a persistent target. Bombs also exploded in Manchester and Liverpool, where the police uncovered a bomb factory in early 1977. But the most devastating incidents were those in Guildford (October 1974, four killed) and Birmingham (November 1974, twenty-one killed) (McGladdery, 2006, pp. 236–43). In West Germany, a 1968 arson operation by Andreas Baader led eventually to the creation of the urban guerilla RAF with its campaign of bank robberies and bomb attacks. The RAF's arrest in 1972 led to the formation of further 'cells', more civilian deaths and bombings. The eventual prison suicides of the Baader-Meinhof leaders and the murder of industrialist (and former SS officer) Hanns-Martin Schleyer in 1977 led to the period being known as the *Deutscher Herbst* [German Autumn] (Becker, 1978; Aust, 2008). So, in sum, the mid 1970s was a highly disturbing and culturally volatile period both in Britain and West Germany, against which Kraftwerk's veneer of childlike melodiousness may seem perverse.

It is in such a climate that David Bowie's neo-fascist remarks of 1976 gain transparency. He had not been alone in his thoughts. Britain's National Front, formed nine years earlier, was a political party of the extreme Right that had gained enough support by 1974 to field 54 candidates in that year's general election. With this volume of contenders it was permitted to broadcast on television and radio, where it emphasized its opposition to immigration. Nevertheless, it was a splinter group, the National Party, which first succeeded in getting two of its candidates elected as councillors at the local elections of June 1976 in Blackburn, a town north of Manchester. The coincidental stabbing that month by white racists of 18-year-old Gurdip Singh Chaggar in London secured a statement from one of the councillors, 'One down, a million to go' (Husband, 1983, p. 11). Not long after, guitarist Eric Clapton spoke from a Birmingham stage in support of racist ideologue Enoch Powell. In reaction to the comments of Bowie and Clapton, activists of the Left set up a national campaign called Rock Against Racism (see Taylor, 1982, pp. 142–4; Dowson, 2006). The Thin White Duke had quickly become a divisive political figure. Interest in fascism became enmeshed with issues of fashion. The chronological order of the various events mentioned above is listed below, with Kraftwerk's British presence added for reference.

1976

Date	Event/Place
Jan	Kraftwerk's *Radio-Activity* (English version) released UK
2 Feb	Bowie's *Station to Station* (American) tour starts in Vancouver
21 Feb	Explosion at Selfridge's store, London, injuring five people
15 Mar	Train driver shot dead by PIRA man planting a bomb, London
27 Mar	One killed, 84 injured by explosion at Ideal Home Exhibition, London
7 Apr	*Station to Station* (European) tour starts in Germany
2 May	Bowie's 'Nazi salute' at London's Victoria railway station
7 May	Two National Party councillors elected at Blackburn, Lancashire
4 Jun	Gurdip Singh Chaggar murdered in Southall, London, by white racists
5 Aug	Eric Clapton's anti-immigration remarks at Birmingham concert
9 Oct	Kraftwerk's *Radio-Activity* UK tour: Sheffield, Coventry, London
12 Dec	Rock Against Racism debut concert, Royal College of Art

Bowie's claim at this time that Kraftwerk was a 'kind of' neo-Nazi band raised concern and interest in the band's endeavours. He was able to carry over with him a large crowd of fans to Kraftwerk's cause. *NME* critic Andy Gill (1978) argued that '[t]here are now a lot of folk around who don't know why they like Kraftwerk, but are sure there must be something in them because David likes them'. Bowie lay at the heart of an aspirational 'glam' subculture, a mainly suburban phenomenon that was intrigued by transgressive portrayals of decadence, in the sense of moral degeneration. The attendant notion here, of a 'loss' of social control, was one that helped in equal measure to stimulate the rise of the extreme Right, with its appeal to order, power and discipline.

In the early 1970s, study of inter-war German culture had gained ground. It did so first as a resource for contemplating anti-fascist resistance. Satirical artwork by George Grosz, Otto Dix and John Heartfield (Helmut Herzfeld) became fashionable.[5] Most popular of all was the Hollywood version of the musical *Cabaret* (1972). Set in 1931, the cinematic narrative of *Cabaret* depicted the entertainment industry's accommodation of Nazism. In it, decadence and authority were contrasted and ultimately incorporated. The singer of the Manchester group Joy Division, Ian Curtis, saw *Cabaret* 'a dozen times' (Curtis, 1995, p. 90). The cult popularity of Liliana Cavani's film *The Night Porter* (1974), which also linked Nazism with glamorous 'depravity', shows how swiftly the exhibition of Nazi imagery was being tolerated. Furthermore, the 1973 legitimization of pornography in West Germany launched a *Sex-Welle* [sex wave] 'hard porn' German film industry that used

Nazi imagery and which built up a specialist market across Britain (Herzog, 1998).[6]

In sum, the pre-war imagery of a united Germany became a source of fascination to a post-war generation in Britain, particularly in this discourse for those in thrall of a 'decadent' scene represented in popular music by Bowie. Bowie lived on and off in West Berlin between October 1976 and late 1979. His three albums of the time, supposedly suffused with 'Cold War' character, came to be known as the 'Berlin Trilogy'. It was Kraftwerk, though, that overpoweringly represented 'Germanness' in the popular imagination, with its *Vorsprung durch Technik* style and 'rational' electronic soundworld. Kraftwerk's commanding impact is evident from the influence it had, among others, on the British post-punk scene. Yet British artists viewed the band through the crude accumulation of ideological and aesthetic layers outlined above. These strata covered over the more subtle filaments of Kraftwerk's own references and allusions. The output of Kraftwerk was superficially valued in two ways. The remainder of this chapter will attempt to show how, by examining two groups influenced by Kraftwerk: the Manchester group Joy Division (from 1980 re-named New Order) and the Merseyside duo Orchestral Manoeuvres In The Dark.

Manchester

Peter Hook, the bass guitarist of Joy Division (1978–80) and New Order (1980–93, 1998–2007), recalls how far their singer, Ian Curtis, admired Kraftwerk:

> We were introduced to Kraftwerk by Ian Curtis, who insisted we play *Trans-Europe Express* before we went on stage every time. The tape was played in the venue over the PA system, to be heard by everyone. The first time was Pips [a Manchester club well-known for its 'Bowie Room']. Ian got thrown out for kicking glass around the dance floor in time to the track. It took us ages of pleading to get him back in. Then we had a riot with all my mates from Salford fighting. Them were the days! (Hook, 2009)

To many, the link between a song about a train and a night of club violence may seem a very thin one. After all, as its lyrics make clear, 'Trans-Europe Express' is a droll response to Bowie's overheated song 'Station to Station', the train-chugging track that launches the album that Kraftwerk was invited to help promote on Bowie's 1976 tour. Bowie's 'Stations of the Cross' are dryly converted into railway stations. And there is a double layer in play: the trans-Europe network was a post-war revival of Hitler's Reichsbahn project, to which the reference to the occupied cities of Paris and Vienna alludes (Arold, 1997). For Curtis, however, kicking smashed glass in tempo across the dance floor, it was the dramatic power of the hypnotic music that mattered. In its shifts of a minor third between E-flat minor and C minor – using the Doppler effect as its terse transition – the mood is oppressive. The ascending fourths pile up and smother (they are a variant of the flute opening to the earlier 'Ruckzuck'). Being in the minor throughout and devoid of contrast to a major key, the song provides an aptly chilling overture for Joy Division, whose output was roughly six-tenths in minor modes.

In using Kraftwerk to herald Joy Division's set, Curtis was well aware that Bowie had used a recording of Kraftwerk to introduce his. Curtis was one of those, then, who came to Kraftwerk through the Thin White Duke. His wife, Deborah Curtis, has written that '[h]is fanaticism for David Bowie was taken to be a fashionable fascination', but added in a touchingly protective way:

> I think that Ian's obsession with the Nazi uniform had more to do with his interest in style and history . . . He did bring a couple of books home about Nazi Germany . . . [Also] *Photomontages of the Nazi Period* was a book of anti-Nazi posters by John Heartfield, which graphically documented the spread of Hitler's ideals . . . It struck me that all Ian's spare time was spent reading and thinking about human suffering. (Curtis, 1995, p. 90)

The band was first called Warsaw (1977), which was hardly a name free of Third Reich overtones; it was in fact a Bowie title from the 'Berlin' album *Low* (1977). When a London punk band called Warsaw Pakt attracted press attention, Curtis proposed to rename the band Joy Division, an unadulterated Nazi name for a prostitution wing (*Freudenabteilung*) of a concentration camp.[7] But it was not he who chose the notorious cover for the band's first disc. According to Deborah Curtis, 'Bernard [the guitarist] designed the sleeve, a poster folded into four of a Hitler Youth drummer, a German soldier pointing a gun at a small boy with his arms raised, and two photographs of the band members' (Curtis, 1995, p. 53). Joy Division later employed a manager, Rob Gretton, who was appalled by their Nazi allusions and positioned the band away from its past associations. Yet, in late 1978 a critic could still write, 'They still seem to lock themselves inside this Nazi-history chic, a subject that has been exploited beyond endurance over the past couple of years' (Middles, 1978a). As the band pointed out, they were not Nazis though they were not afraid to use its imagery, just as Kraftwerk and Bowie had (Middles, 1978b). Writer Mary Harron (1979) tackled them directly about the implications of Curtis's lyrics. She got a Kraftwerk-like reply: 'When I asked if the images were about Nazi Germany, they seemed quite taken aback. "That's what it suggests to you," they said'.

While Kraftwerk's musical influence on Joy Division was tentative in

effect, it is the case that the Manchester band was capable of making its own
aural choices. It moved towards minimalism and melodic clarity of its own
volition, and it did so through the kind of logic experienced by other bands
in a period when emergent digital technology was being made available
(Witts, 2009). Aided by the idiosyncratic production of Martin Hannett,
Joy Division shifted incrementally in sound from analogue to digital, most
markedly in Hannett's radical treatment of drums and voice. After the suicide
of Ian Curtis at the age of 23 in May 1980, the remaining members reformed.
It is surely at this point that Joy Division, sipping Kraftwerk since its start,
now plunged into a vat of the stuff to produce New Order. New Order's 'Blue
Monday' (1983), an electronic dance track of elemental initiative, followed
up by 'Your Silent Face' (1983),[8] would have been the closest a North West
band had come to Kraftwerk, had not Orchestral Manoeuvres In The Dark got
there first.

Liverpool

While many post-punk bands of Manchester took pithy names like the Fall
and the Smiths, those of Liverpool competed in art-school flamboyance
and majesty: Pink Military Stand Alone, the Teardrop Explodes, Echo
and the Bunnymen, Dalek I Love You, and Frankie Goes To Hollywood.
Orchestral Manoeuvres In The Dark (henceforth OMD) complied with
this Merseyside convention even though the duo came from the distinct,
middle-class enclave of the Wirral Peninsula. They can be said to be typical
of Merseyside in their embrace of new technology as it became domestically
available, and in the ingenuity of imitating well what they could not own
of it. In contrast, Kraftwerk enjoyed the financial resources to commission
and explore at leisure new devices. Andrew McCluskey and Paul Humphries
had started out in 1977 as Hitlerz Underpants, subsequently the Id, then
VCLXI, before landing on the ultra-Romantic but lumbering title that few
record-shop staff could spell. Yet, it is the penultimate name that openly
connects OMD with Kraftwerk. A VCL-Eleven is one of the valves on the
Nazi short-range radio depicted on the cover of *Radio-Activity*. OMD titled
their first album after themselves but their second album after Kraftwerk's
original name, *Organisation* (1980).

OMD was described by Robbins (1985) as 'a synthesizer duo, a pair of
chilly intellectual technocrats paying electro-pop for eggheads', a description
that is interesting in the way it assigns simplicity to the cerebral; in a period
of minimalism and conceptualism, this may seem valid. As for social class,
there is indeed a comparative fit between the middle-class context of OMD
and the *haute bourgeois* background of Kraftwerk. Humphries has been
happy to admit the early impact of the Germans, which for musical reasons
he could hardly deny:

Our musical tastes and feelings grew up in [the] mid-1970s. We hated guitar solos and big drum kits and all the clichés of rock. We'd gotten interested in German music like Kraftwerk as an alternative to what was around in '75/'76, so we'd already developed our influences before the punk explosion. (Robbins, 1985)

Here is an example of how punk sliced through a set of ongoing developments out of which evolved the broad range of music nowadays identified by the term 'post-punk'. If British punk as a genre of music is temporarily bracketed off from the corpus, then Bowie's musical value is reduced as the scuttling stylistic shifts he undertook are exposed. This leaves more consistent bands like Kraftwerk in significant positions of influence across the period. The circularity of influence and stimulus between Kraftwerk and the discotheque is well recognized, as punk does not intervene in that category. However, Kraftwerk's musical and stylistic influence on British artists – Ultravox, Tubeway Army, Depeche Mode, the Human League, British Electric Foundation, New Order, Soft Cell – is evident. Yet, it is veiled by the convoluted historicization of the era promoted by coarse journalism. In any case OMD did not imitate the Germans: it copied them.

OMD's debut hit single 'Electricity' (1979) is Kraftwerk's 'Radio-Activity' re-heated. Lyrical and musical subtleties are discarded through this process. 'Radio-Activity' swings between two keys a major third apart (A minor/ F major), a Schubertian device well used by Kraftwerk, best of all in 'Autobahn' (F major/A major). 'Electricity' converts this shift into a four-square chord sequence in A minor (where it functions as the relative minor of C major). Meanwhile the ambiguous lyric of 'Radio-Activity' is directed at an antinuclear lobby ('Radio Activity/Is in the air for you and me'). 'Electricity' turns this into an unrefined hymn to solar energy ('The alternative is only one/ The final source of energy/Solar electricity'). Of OMD's subsequent songs, 'Enola Gay' (1980) comes closest to Kraftwerk's referentialism, even if the album of 1983, *Dazzle Ships*, offers a broader war allusion. Giving name to the US airplane that dropped the atom bomb on Hiroshima in 1945, 'Enola Gay' makes clear its disapproval ('Ah-ha Enola Gay/It shouldn't ever have to end this way'). Using an up-tempo F major version of the four-square chord sequence, animated as in 'Electricity' by a stock treble motif, 'Enola Gay' sounds like a nervous, cartoon mock-up of a Kraftwerk number. Resembling much of OMD's output, the layers that elevate the Germans' songs are stripped away, leaving work that is one-dimensional and bare-boned. If Kraftwerk is a Mercedes, OMD is a Trabant.

Conclusion

Joy Division mistook the national ideology driving the project that is Kraftwerk. OMD misunderstood the musical and lyrical sophistication underlying the elegantly simple soundworld of the Germans. Nevertheless, both groups were commercially successful, due in part to the ideas and sounds that they took from Kraftwerk. Kraftwerk's contribution to popular music is significantly deeper and broader than either of these bands from North West England, but that is because, in the six years between the German duo's formation in 1968 and the full realization of Kraftwerk in 1974, they had constructed a 'total work' with a firm ideological base of the kind that many British groups seem incapable of conceiving or engaging with. This is a matter in part of education. Yet it is also a common effect of music's intimidating power, where countless minds seek refuge in its shadow. They do so by the most immediate of musical actions – they replicate and emulate. It's claimed here that Kraftwerk emulated the painter Kiefer. Kiefer's totalitarian imagery was clear as day and dark as night. Kraftwerk's use of the more 'domestic as heroic' elements of German technology veiled the allusions and softened somewhat the effect of the references to the level of postmodern meiosis. This facilitated the depth of misunderstanding that nevertheless brought a new richness to British 'post-punk' and its 'electro' and 'synthpop' derivatives.

As for the increasing British access to contemporary German culture through creative products such as Kraftwerk, it seems – according to the German culture minister of 1999 quoted above – that little has changed in Britain's xenophobic fixation with Germany. At the one time that the British and German political scenes meshed at the level of governments, led by Conservatives Thatcher and Kohl, Thatcher soundly distrusted Germans and opposed the 1990 re-unification (Nicholls, 2001, p. 6). Neither has the British comprehension of Kraftwerk improved, if comedian Bill Bailey's *Das Hokey Cokey* parody of the band is anything to go by. It is very funny, but the parody of a parody leans on British naïvety.

While Kraftwerk can now perform to huge audiences in Britain rather than to tiny ones, the gap of perception may still be as wide as that noted by John Hawkins (2009) when the Germans played at Liverpool's Empire Theatre in 1975.

> They gave us a little demonstration of some new technology that they had developed (they always had this air of scientists about them). They had a new device that allowed them to synthesize the sound of a human voice, so they said. They pushed a few buttons and a voice speaking German came out of the P.A. I think most people were bewildered by this, not very clear what was going on. However, it was a new technical

innovation and that was the main thing. The fact that I didn't really understand it made it all the more mysterious.

Years later, I worked with Zeus Held, who was a German contemporary of Kraftwerk. He told me that the voice synthesizer thing was a little joke. The voice was actually a roadie with a microphone backstage. We didn't really get it on the night. Maybe the speech itself was funny, who knows? But, as we didn't know any German, it was lost on the audience.

As we now know, this was more than a matter of language.

The author is most grateful to John Deathridge, Michael Edwards, Simon Frith and Björn Heile for their helpful comments on a draft of this essay.

Notes

1. Quoted from Johnstone, 2008.

2. According to Flür it was on this tour that the 'drum cage' was introduced, when he triggered percussion sounds inside it using arm gestures. He adds that it failed to work at Liverpool's Empire Theatre (Flür, 2000, pp. 123–4). Flür also claims that Paul McCartney's band Wings played in Liverpool on the same night (Flür, 2000, p. 120), hence the low attendance for Kraftwerk. Although the two bands were touring Britain at the same time, the 'Wings Over the World' tour came to Liverpool's Empire Theatre four nights later, on the fifteenth.

3. Presumably the slightly different accounts in English of Bowie's remark were a result of the words being translated into Swedish and then back again. See Buckley (2004), pp. 289–91; also Tremlett (1996), p. 260. For a variant, see Cann (1983), p. 152.

4. For example, in literature, Günter Grass's *Die Blechtrommel* (*The Tin Drum*, 1959); in film, Alexander Kluge's short *Brutalität im Stein* (*Brutality in Stone*, 1960); and in theatre, Rolf Hochhuth's *Der Stellvertreter* (*The Representative*, 1963).

5. Ian Curtis of Joy Division owned a book of Heartfield's work (Curtis, 1995, p. 90). Siouxsie & The Banshees' 'Metal Postcard' (1976) is inspired by Heartfield.

6. With thanks to Professor Martine Beugnet for this observation.

7. In its mixing of deviant sex and the Holocaust, this is surely one of the most provocative references that may be made to the sexualized depictions of Nazism. Curtis's source was apparently the book written by 'Ka-Tzetnik 135633': 'House of Dolls' (London, Simon & Shuster, 1955), supposedly an inmate's account of 'Joy Division' brothels. For a study of the prurient commercial exploitation of the Holocaust see Herzog (1998, pp. 394–7).

8. I am grateful to Sean Albiez for reminding me about this song.

References

Anon. (1975), News item, *Record Mirror*, 7 August, 15.

Arasse, D. (2001), *Anselm Kiefer*. London: Thames & Hudson.

Arold, S. (1997), *Die technische Entwicklung und rüstungswirtschaftliche Bedeutung des Lokomotivbaus der Deutschen Reichsbahn im Dritten Reich (1933–1945)*. Stuttgart: Franz Steiner Verlag.

Aust, S. (2008), *The Baader-Meinhof Complex*, London: Bodley Head.

Beck, P. J. (2003), 'The relevance of the irrelevant – football as a missing dimension in the study of British relations with Germany'. *International Affairs*, 79, (2), 389–411.

Becker, J. (1978), *Hitler's Chidren – the Story of the Baader-Meinhof Terrorist Gang*. London: HarperCollins.

Beckers, R. (1995), *Der Architekt Paul Schneider-Esleben*. Weimar: VDG-Verlag.

Buckley, D. (2004), *David Bowie – the Complete Guide to His Music*. London: Omnibus Press.

Bussy, P. (1993), *Kraftwerk – Man, Machine & Music*. (1st edn). London: SAF.

Cann, K. (1983), *David Bowie – a chronology*. London: Vermilion.

Cleese, J. and Booth, C. (1975), *Fawlty Towers*. Series 1, episode 6. [First transmitted BBC TV, 24 October 1975]. London: BBC.

Curtis, D. (1995), *Touching From a Distance – Ian Curtis and Joy Division*. London: Faber & Faber.

Dawson, A. (2006), 'Love music hate racism – the cultural politics of the Rock Against Racism campaigns'. *Postmodern Culture*, 16, (1). http://muse.jhu.edu/login?uri=/journals/postmodern_culture/v016/16.1dawson.html (last accessed 12 August 2010).

Del Caro, A. (1991), *Hölderlin – the Poetics of Being*. Detroit: Wayne State University Press.

Dirke, S. von (1997), *All Power to the Imagination! – the German Counterculture from the Student Movement to the Greens*. Lincoln: University of Nebraska Press.

Edmonds, B. (1976a), 'Ol' Orange Hair is back', *RAM*, March. http://www.rocksbackpages.com/article.html?ArticleID=9937 (last accessed 13 September 2009).

——— (1976b), 'Bowie meets the press: plastic man or godhead of the seventies?'. *Circus*, 27 April. http://www.rocksbackpages.com/article.html?ArticleID=8764 (last accessed 13 September 2009).

Flür, W. (2000), *Kraftwerk – I Was a Robot*. London: Sanctuary Publishing.

Frankland, E. G. and Schoonmaker, D. (1992), *Between Politics & Power – the Green Party in Germany*. Boulder: Westview Press.

Gill, A. (1978), 'Kraftwerk: The Man Machine (Capitol)'. *New Musical Express*, 29 April. http://www.rocksbackpages.com/article.html?ArticleID=10885 (last accessed 13 September 2009).

Goodkin, D. (2002), *Play, Sing & Dance: An Introduction to Orff Schulwerk*. London; Schott.

Habermas, J. (1994), *The Past as Future*. London: Polity Press.

Hager, C. G. (1992), 'Democratising technology – citizens and state in West German energy politics 1974–1990'. *Polity*, 25, (1), 45–70.

Harron, M. (1979), 'Factory records, food for thought'. *Melody Maker*, 29 September. http://www.rocksbackpages.com/article.html?ArticleID=12992 (last accessed 13 September 2009).

Hawkins, J. (2009), Correspondence with the author.

Herzog, D. (1998), 'Pleasure, sex, and politics belong together – post-Holocaust memory and the sexual revolution in West Germany'. *Critical Inquiry*, 24, (2), 393–444.

Hildebrand, K. (1999), 'Die Deutsche Reichsbahn in der nationalsozialistischen Diktatur 1933–1945', in Gall and Pohl (eds), *Die Eisenbahn in Deutschland. Von den Anfäge bis zur Gegenwart*. Munich: C.H. Beck, pp. 165–280.

Hook, P. (2009), Correspondence with the author, May 2009.

Husband, C. T. (1983), *Racial Exclusionism and the City – the Urban Support of the National Front*. London: George Allen & Unwin.

Huyssen, A. (1995), *Twilight Memories – Marking Time in a Culture of Amnesia*. London: Routledge.

Jahn, W. (1989), *The Art of Gilbert & George, or an Aesthetic of Existence*. London: Thames & Hudson.

Johnstone, R. (Exec. Prod.) (2008), *Kraftwerk and the Electronic Revolution*. [DVD]. SIDVD541. Sexy Intellectual.

Kater, M. H. (2002), *Composers of the Nazi Era – Eight Portraits*. Oxford: Oxford University Press.

Lyons, T. (2009), Correspondence with the author, June 2009.

McGladdery, G. (2006), *The Provisional IRA in England – the Bombing Campaign 1973–1997*. Dublin: Irish Academic Press.

Meyer, J. H. (2005), 'The 1975 referendum on Britain's continued membership in the EEC'. http://www.ena.lu/?lang=2&doc=21284 (last accessed 13 September 2009).

Middles, M. (1978a), 'Joy Division: band on the wall, Manchester'. *Sounds*, 16 September. http://www.rocksbackpages.com/article.html?ArticleID=10209 (last accessed 13 September 2009).

—— (1978b), 'Joy Division'. *Sounds*, 18 November. http://www.rocksbackpages.com/article.html?ArticleID=10649 (last accessed 13 September 2009).

Miles (1976), 'Krautwerk: this is what your fathers fought to save you from . . .', *New Musical Express*, 16 October. http://www.rocksbackpages.com/article.html?ArticleID=707 (last accessed 13 September 2009).

Nicholls, A. J. (2001), *Fifty Years of Anglo-German Relations – the 19th Bithell Memorial Lecture*. London: Institute of Germanic Studies, University of London.

Obstfeld, M. (1983), 'Exchange rates, inflation, and the sterilization problem: Germany, 1975–1981'. *European Economic Review*, 21, (1–2), 191–5.

Richter, G. (2004), *Editions 1965–2004, Catalogue raisonée*. Ostfildern-Ruit: Hatje Cantz Verlag.

Robbins, I. (1985), 'Orchestral Manoeuvres In The Dark: two guys and a tape deck become A'. *Musician*. http://www.rocksbackpages.com/article.html?ArticleID=1151 (last accessed 13 September 2009).

Schama, S. (1995), *Landscape & Memory*. London: HarperCollins.

Taylor, S. (1982), *The National Front in English Politics*. London: Macmillan Press.
Tisdall, C. (1979), *Joseph Beuys*. London: Thames & Hudson.
Tremlett, G. (1996), *David Bowie – Living On The Brink*. London: Century Books.
White, J. (2009), Correspondence with the author, May 2009.
Witts, R. (2009), 'A moment or two before zero and one – records and recordings in post-punk England, 1978–82', in Clark and Cook (eds), *The Cambridge Companion to Recorded Music*. Cambridge: Cambridge University Press, pp. 80–3.

9

'Dragged into the Dance' – the Role of Kraftwerk in the Development of Electro-Funk

Joseph Toltz

Once upon a time, 'the future' was something that hadn't happened yet. It lay up ahead of us somewhere in the distance, filled with an unknown potential whose features and even outlines were unguessable. But during the twentieth century, an extremely odd thing has happened. In the 1920s, science fiction writers began developing detailed scenarios of what the future would be like; and since World War II the technology for making those scenarios come true has been expanding at an unprecedented rate. By now, our sense of history as a linear progression into the future has collapsed. We're living in the future today; there's no way to escape.

(*Aikin, 1982, p. 33*)

Jim Aikin's article on Kraftwerk was written just a few months before DJ producer Arthur Baker, Afrika Bambaataa and the Soulsonic Force teamed up in New York to produce the recording 'Planet Rock'. This was a new musical concept that matched the electronic, robot-inspired music of Kraftwerk, an emerging electronic aesthetic in African-American dance music and the improvised form rap. In the US Billboard listings, the song reached #4 in the Black Singles chart, and #3 in the Dance/Disco Top 80 charts, and gave exposure to Bambaataa's vision for a new electronic rap/funk sound.

The new form that 'Planet Rock' played a large part in kick-starting would later be named 'electro funk', and paved the way for the explosive success of hip-hop in the years to come. The collision between the two distinct worlds of West German electronic music and Bronx rap can also be measured as a collision between a dominant aesthetic of creation on one hand (Kraftwerk), and a more marginal aesthetic of evocation on the other (Bambaataa and Baker). This essay will examine the three works involved in this collision:

'Trans-Europe Express' and 'Numbers' by Kraftwerk, and 'Planet Rock';
I will attempt to describe them within the framework of three critiques
(Nattiez, 1990): immanent, poietic and aesthetic. Despite key ideological
commonalities and philosophies that have developed over the years between
Bambaataa and Kraftwerk, the irreconcilable differences between their own
understanding of the compositional process mirrors a paradigm embedded
within Western aesthetic teleology – the notion of new, legitimate, innovative creation versus the imperative of evocation. Perhaps it is at this point of
aesthetic collision where exciting and unpredictable forms gain voice.

Prologue: the times and the mix

The early 1980s were heady, volatile days of cultural interaction in New York,
where the innovative DJ Afrika Bambaataa travelled out of the seven-mile
circle of the Bronx to take his music and culture into a white artsy crowd and
the punk-rock clubs of lower Manhattan. This was a philosophically driven
move that had origins as much in Bambaataa's own personal history as it did
in the politics of the day. A former Black Spade gang warlord, Bambaataa
was influenced at an early age by the break-centred style of DJ Kool Herc
and began experimenting early with eclectic mixing techniques that pointed
towards his new political philosophy of peacemaking and inclusiveness. Jeff
Chang (2005) marks the death of Bambaataa's cousin Soulski in a police
shooting in January 1975 as the turning point that cemented this philosophy and that was the motivation behind the creation of the Universal Zulu
Nation; a social justice organization dedicated to 'knowledge, wisdom,
freedom, peace, unity, love and respect' (Mitchell, 2002, RB-8). The organization recognized the futility, cyclical entrapment, oppression and racial
divisiveness spawned by gang warfare, and focused the anger and energy
into the creation and exploration of black/Latino culture through the four
elements of what would come to be known as hip-hop: dance (B-Boying),
street art (graffiti), DJing and MCing (rap).

The first commercial success of rap came from an obscure studio creation
sans DJ, in the form of the Sugarhill Gang's 'Rapper's Delight', that Chang
(2005) claims is the best-selling twelve-inch single ever pressed (p. 131). The
breakout success brought the new musical form to the attention of a world
audience, just as the street art component that had been under increasing
attack from conservative politicians was finding its way into downtown art
galleries through the Ahearn brothers and Henry Chalfant.

At the same time, a young artist called Freddy Braithwaite sought out the
more established Lee Quiñones, joined his graffiti crew and was reborn as
FAB 5 FREDDY. Within a year, FAB was in the first ever graffiti art show in
Italy, and soon he was mixing with the likes of Andy Warhol and Keith Haring
at the Mudd Club whilst at the same time checking out the rap crews and DJs

in the Bronx. FAB saw graffiti as an essential part of Bambaataa's revolutionary youth culture, as he wrote:

> I once read somewhere that for a culture to really be a complete culture, it should have a music, a dance and a visual art. And then I realized, wow, all these things are going on. You got the graffiti happening over here, you got the breakdancing, and you got the DJ and MCing thing. In my head they were all one thing. (Chang, p. 149)

Meanwhile, the Clash had recorded a rap in early 1980 for the *Sandinista!* album. They arrived in New York in summer of that year, and booked Grandmaster Flash and the Furious Five as the opening act for their show, much to the disgust and horror of many of their white punk fans. Despite this apparent cross-cultural setback, the nightclub was rapidly becoming a far more communal space; by spring 1981 Blondie had topped the charts with 'Rapture', a mainstream song referencing FAB 5 FREDDY and DJ Flash. Former Sex Pistols manager Malcolm McLaren too had arrived at the same time as the Clash to promote his newest discovery, Bow Wow Wow. McLaren booked Bambaataa and the Rock Steady Crew to open for Bow Wow Wow, but it was his associate Ruza Blue who would prove the alchemist in bringing white and black sounds together. On Thursday nights her Negril club (already providing a heady interaction between Brit-punk and reggae) was hosting Wheels of Steel nights, bringing the Bronx sound downtown. And in April 1982 a white music journalist, Tom Silverman, introduced the multi-talented Bambaataa to the DJ and fledgling producer Arthur Baker. He and Bambaataa began work together and looked to some of their favourite music including Babe Ruth, Captain Sky, Kraftwerk, Rick James, Ennio Morricone and Gary Numan. In the process a new concept in recorded music was born, teaming the electronic, robot-inspired music of Kraftwerk with rap: 'Planet Rock'.

Immanent critique

'Trans-Europe Express' is the eponymous fourth track of Kraftwerk's 1977 album. The song is based in synthesized sound, beginning with a destabilized percussive swirling rhythm (a Doppler-like sound which evokes the rhythmic pattern of a train travelling over tracks and sleepers). This is followed at [0:05] by a series of notes building up perfect-fourth intervals from E-flat resolving to an E-flat minor chord, and then the introduction of a steady, electronic rock beat (bass drum on 1 and 3, hi-hat on 2 and 4), with a new synthesizer sound for the interval-note pattern. These two sections are repeated to stabilize the pattern with additional lower harmonies, before a new section is introduced at [0:41], where a computer-modified voice speaks/whispers the words 'Trans-Europe Express' in time, four times to [0:57]. A sustained minor chord follows (the same key of the resolving note pattern previously), which after eight beats slides down a minor third to a new C minor tonality (for 8 beats), with the voice now vocalizing in that particular key (again four times from [1:16]). The sonic effect of sliding down from one key to the lower could possibly evoke the effect of hearing extraneous sounds outside a very fast train modulate when one passes them by. The four repeats of the text this time build up with harmonic notes in the fundamental minor chord.

At [1:33] we hear the first sustained melody (electronically produced) repeated followed by the beginning interval-note pattern. A 'normal' (electronically non-modified) voice, speaking dialogue in English follows at [2:00] (with a quasi-French 'Rendez-vous at Champs Élysées' as opening text), followed immediately by a sung and unmodified 'Trans-Europe Express' (sung four times, again with the harmonic notes building higher in the fundamental minor chord). An exact repetition of the sustained melody occurs at [2:26], and the fourth build-up again, followed by a different spoken dialogue at [2:52] in English (this time, locating the travel: 'In Vienna we sit in a late-night café'). At [3:02] 'Trans-Europe Express' reoccurs four times (again sung, with the harmonic notes building). This entire pattern of normal-voice sung 'Trans-Europe Express', sustained melody and fourth-interval build-ups repeats.

By [3:46] a new rapid five-beat percussive element is introduced (sonically akin to a snare drum), and this sound is played (albeit with just two beats and then three after the initial five-beat occurrence) all the way to [4:22], when we return to the fourth-interval pattern. Spoken and sung dialogue occurs as it did previously, this time evoking a meeting with the musicians Iggy Pop and David Bowie in Düsseldorf at [4:35–4:38]. At each spoken section the narrative advances, and by [5.25] the sustained melody changes to a higher register, repeating eight times, integrating the fourth-interval pattern within it. By the end the rhythm has folded into the next track, 'Metal on Metal'.

'Trans-Europe Express' works on many levels because of the combination of the repetition of simple motifs with new and interesting percussive elements and differing timbres and sonic effects. As a result of the highly repetitive nature of the rhythmic figures and electronic music structure, the spoken dialogue occupies a noticeably linear narrative in the work. It provides interest and evokes the sense of a progressive journey through continental Europe. The attraction of its simple minimalism, sparse texture and constantly repetitive figures allows a familiarity in the listener, and lends the work a potential for open-endedness.

'Numbers' is the third track from Kraftwerk's eighth album, *Computer World* (1981), and is grounded in Kraftwerk's established style of synthesized sound and vocals. It is remarkable in its distinct lack of melodic features and quirky, innovative synthesized sounds used for percussive and pseudo-melodic effect. There is a distinct contrast to the strong melodic basis of the first two tracks, 'Computer World' and 'Pocket Calculator'. It begins with a fourfold recitation of numbers in German (counting up to eight – the trope of counting numbers is recurrent throughout the work). By [0:10], the third sounding of the counting, a short, synthesized piano figure is introduced on the word 'fünf', and then a longer, lower, slower (i.e. minim) number count is introduced in a computer-modulated voice on a low B-flat pitch. At [0:24] we hear the all-important introduction of the stabilized (although slightly syncopated) rhythmic percussion section, which is maintained until the end of the work. This rhythmic section has attached to it a type of random higher-pitched semi-quaver pattern, which is more percussive than melodic, but contains pitches that continue without vocal accompaniment until [1:22] when counting appears in different languages.

As the vocals reappear, the melodic feature of the rhythmic section disappears. Each language features a different rhythmic component – the German one is a simple eight crotchets, the English one is merely two (on the second and third beats of the bar). At [1:54] the French counting (to three) appears with two minims, a minim rest and one more minim, and is later pared with the Spanish counting, which misses 'tres' in favour of the French 'trois', but adds 'cuatro' after the French 'trois'. The Italian counting (to four) occurs before the introduction of the Spanish words, and features some syncopation (between 'tres' and 'quattro'). Rhythm develops constantly throughout, and the higher-pitched semi-quaver pattern also changes. At [2:22] the vocal line disappears again, leaving the intense rhythmic pattern to feature by itself until [2:52]. Two new languages appear at this point: Japanese (counting to four, this time in a higher-pitched, androgynous voice); and Russian (counting to three in three steady, low-pitched minims). These two languages mark the end of the track, which folds directly into the following song, 'Computer World Part 2' (a contrast to the fade-outs that mark the conclusion of every other track in the *Computer World* album).

'Numbers' is a striking work, not only in the general context of Kraftwerk's output, but also because it seems so different and more experimental than the other tracks on *Computer World*. The lack of reliance on melodic drive focuses the listener towards considering rhythm as a melodic and prime interest, rather than just the driving accompaniment to the song in question. When vocals appear, they too rely more on the rhythmic sensibility than a pitch, and this rhythmic sensibility is also tied up in the language in which the numbers are being counted.

'Planet Rock' begins with Afrika Bambaataa exhorting to the crowd in a technique derived from soul singers such as James Brown, earlier DJs such as Grandmaster Flash, and not entirely different to the call-and-response patterns of early African-American music. After acknowledging important parts of the crowd (Party People, Soulsonic Force, Zulu Nation), it is only at the lyrics of 'Just Hit Me' that the beat is introduced, which is the same basic beat as that of Kraftwerk's 'Numbers', though an 808 handclap/hi-hat pattern appears sporadically that appears to be a direct rhythmic allusion to the basic beat of 'Trans-Europe Express' (most notably at [3:19]). The Soulsonic Force crew start their rap (alternating lines), and it is at 'But scream', [0:48], that the melody from 'Trans-Europe Express' is introduced, and it is repeated and treated very much as a bridge section to the next rap. This happens again at 'Be what you be, so be', [1:46]. A direct call and response occurs between crowd and rappers at 'Everybody say Rock it don't stop it', [2:36]. At [3:19] a new keyboard melody appears that was modelled on a section from Babe Ruth's 'The Mexican' (1972), which in turn was an appropriation of Ennio Morricone's main theme for *For a Few Dollars More* (1965). The synthesized melodic motifs that occur up to [4:00] are very reminiscent of the Kraftwerk style in 'Trans-Europe Express', albeit not a direct take of the fourth progressions. The 'zih zih' vocal section almost recalls the scat singing of jazz greats such as Ella Fitzgerald. The invocation of counting in Japanese is most definitely a reference to 'Numbers'. Bambaataa rejoins the dialogue from 'So hit me' down to 'now hit me', and the rap is taken up again by Soulsonic Force. The rap continues and fades out to the last two lines, repeated.

Musically and structurally, 'Planet Rock' works on layers quite different to the Kraftwerk works. Bambaataa's introduction imbues an imprimatur on the song, as he evokes group participation from the live audience (party people) to the inventive word repartee of the Soulsonic Force crew. The use of the 'Numbers' beat pattern is purely to provide a rhythmic consistency throughout the work; the further addition of the reconstructed synthesizer melody from 'Trans-Europe Express' acts first as a bridge between what is essentially the most important aspect of the song, that is, the lyrics, and later as an accompaniment under what might notionally be termed a chorus ('Rock, rock to the Planet Rock'). The lyrics provide not only a message and a philosophy, but they also add to the rhythmic and tonal complexity through the contrasting voices of Bambaataa and the Soulsonic Force crew.

Poietic critique

As suggested by Jim Aikin, Kraftwerk's philosophy is firmly implanted within the modernist (he refers to this as 'Bauhaus') agenda, 'advancing to the stage of developing a society that has a 'friendly, relaxed attitude towards working with machines . . . a complete symbiosis of organism and technology' (Aikin, p. 34). Furthermore, Kraftwerk do not lay claim to being musicians (despite the two leading members of the group having studied music formally at university); rather, they call themselves 'musical workers', conceiving themselves as 'functional parts of a music-making machine' (Aikin, p. 35). In a 1981 interview, Ralf Hütter describes Kraftwerk's music as minimalist 'to a point', where the minimal nature encourages clarity of meaning. The other two descriptive expressions he chooses are 'Industrielle Volksmusic' (industrial music of the people) and 'gerade aus' (straight ahead) (Bohn, 1981). This description hearkens back to a comment from 1977, after the release of *Trans-Europe Express*. At that time Hütter stated, 'Our music is rather minimalist. If we can convey an idea with one or two notes, it is better to do this than to play a hundred . . . there is no question of playing with a kind of virtuosity, there is all the virtuosity we need in the machines'(qtd. in Bussy, 1993, p. 87). He goes on to speak specifically about the inspiration behind 'Trans-Europe Express' and states, 'The movement [of a train] fascinates us, instead of a static or motionless situation. All the dynamism of industrial life, of modern life . . . the artistic world does not exist outside of daily life, it is not another planet' (p. 88).

In an interview at the time of the release of *Computer World*, Hütter spoke explicitly about Kraftwerk's aim to explore the emergence of computer technology and emerging fears about its use in a surveillance society. He observed that 'now that it has been penetrated by micro-electronics our whole society is computerized, and each one of us is stored into some point of information by some company or organization, all stored by numbers'. He specifically talked about the regulation of West German society (notably the transmission of passport information from border control to the Bundeskriminalamt in Wiesbaden), and of Kraftwerk's desire in this album to take computers 'out of context of those control functions and use them creatively in an area where people do not expect to find them. Like using pocket calculators to make music, for instance' (Hütter qtd in Bohn, 1981).

Six years prior to this interview, Hütter explained the creation of Kraftwerk's aesthetic in the context of the cultural crisis facing a post-Nazi Germany – an anxiety about the overwhelming presence of American music, a hesitancy and doubt about how to express German culture:

> We are the first German group to record in our own language, use our electronic background, and create a Central European identity for ourselves . . . we cannot deny we are from Germany, because the German mentality, which is more advanced, will always be part of our behaviour. We create out of the German language, the mother language, which is very mechanical, we use it as the basic structure of our music. Also the machines, from the industries of Germany. (Bangs, 1975, p. 4)

As Albiez and Lindvig indicate in this collection, Hütter's statement could be read as part of an ironic or satirical strategy to counter the stereotypical attitudes about Germany and Germans they experienced in their first tour to the US. However, these comments clearly reveal important cultural imperatives in Kraftwerk's creative process: the desire to reconstruct a

German character in music, and the necessity to configure this literally with the notion of technological skill as embedded in the German culture. In order to create, Kraftwerk seek inspiration of man-machine integration from past German industrial/mechanical/innovative triumphs of the 1920s, detached from the political implications surrounding those triumphs that were and remain refracted through Nazi ideology and atrocities. It is interesting to note that Hütter acknowledges the historical/ideological rift that his (post-Nazi) generation has had to negotiate ('we certainly represent the generation with no fathers') but also notes that in such a circumstance, 'it is also in some ways encouraging because it gives you possibilities of doing new things' (Bohn, 1981).

Afrika Bambaataa began his music-making quest a little later than Kraftwerk. The commentary that Bambaataa and his producer Arthur Baker have to make is not only a commentary on their creative process, but on the reasoning behind using Kraftwerk's material. An obsessive collector of records (especially with unusual covers), Bambaataa identified with the futuristic presentation of Kraftwerk, and integrated *Trans-Europe Express* and *Computer World* into his regular sets for progressively minded, multi-subcultural and multi-ethnic crowds. At the parties where he attracted New Wave, hip-hop and punk attendees, he indicated that '[t]hat's when you heard . . . a real cross-breed of music . . . I started digging up other electronic artists and that's when I realised that there was no black group out there doing that electronic sound' (Barr, 1988, pp. 165-6).

Arthur Baker also had an interest in Kraftwerk after buying *Autobahn* in the 1970s, and at high school had musical interests that cut across rock, pop and soul. However, he identifies that it was later as a DJ that he fully developed an interest in Kraftwerk's music, 'because it was possible to dance to it. Bambaataa loved that too: it was a quest for the perfect beat' (Bussy, 1993, p. 123). Baker has claimed that though they shared this interest, it was his idea to 'use the beat from Kraftwerk's "Numbers" and the melody from "Trans-Europe Express" and put a rap on top' (Barr, 1998, p. 166). More recently (see Buskin, 2008), he explicitly mentions the importance of call and response as a way of authenticating the 'live element' of the rap component of the work. He again claims that it was his idea to combine the beat of 'Numbers' (replicated by 'Joe'– a hired man with a drum machine recruited via a *Village Voice* advert) with the melody of 'Trans-Europe Express'. He indicates the music was completed in one session on one piece of tape, without the rappers. Baker also talks about the various 'happy accidents' that came to be accepted practices in later hip-hop recording (kick/handclaps, the orchestra hit, etc.). But by far the most revealing fact comes when he describes the rappers' initial revulsion when hearing the 'Planet Rock' backing track. Baker indicates that Soulsonic Force member MC G.L.O.B.E.

worked out that they should do the track half-time as opposed to a regular rap that would be right on the beat. The beat was so fast, it would have been difficult for them to rap right on the beat, so he created a new style which he called 'MC Popping'. (qtd. in Buskin, 2008)

Subsequently, G.L.O.B.E. wrote most of the lyrics for the song. Baker also indicates that he added the chorus himself that borrowed from a contemporary dance hit, 'Body Music' by the Strikers. In addition he notes that Bambaataa suggested using a break from Captain Sky's 'Super Sperm', which appears to have been incorporated in the rhythmic basis of his 'zih zih' scat interjection. All in all the production and composition of 'Planet Rock' was truly a collaborative process among all concerned as Baker indicates when he states that,

> [a]s it is, everything on the record played a part, as did everyone who was involved in its making, including Jay Burnett, who did a great job of engineering and whose voice is the one going 'rock rock to the planet rock, don't stop'. (qtd. in Buskin, 2008)

Aesthetic critique

The only recorded public reaction to the initial unacknowledged copyright breach by Afrika Bambaataa in 'Planet Rock' was that of resentment and anger from two former Kraftwerk musicians who were in the group at the time. Karl Bartos, co-writer of 'Numbers', has said that 'in the beginning we were very angry, because they didn't credit the authors . . . [so] we felt pissed off . . . there was nothing written down saying that its source was 'Trans-Europe Express' and 'Numbers'' (qtd. in Bussy, 1993, p. 125). Wolfgang Flür also indicates Kraftwerk's annoyance, but also that they soon resolved the situation, when stating that '[t]hey didn't even ask in the first place whether Kraftwerk was in agreement . . . the company that had released the single, Tommy Boy Records, had to fork out a lot of money after the event, but they just increased the price of the single . . . [and] recouped their fine' (Flür, 2000, p. 168).

These reactions are understandable especially when one takes into consideration Kraftwerk's insistent (and foresighted) independence, and their consequently strong negotiating position with other record companies. However, it is important to note that neither Ralf Hütter nor Florian Schneider (the two creative centres of Kraftwerk) commented in press on the creation of 'Planet Rock', probably because they had reached a financial agreement with Bambaataa as is implied by Flür.

It is also important to note that the clear appropriation of the Morricone *For a Few Dollars More* melody does not (so far) appear to have resulted in

similar controversy or litigation. Whether or not one takes into consideration
the intellectual property issue(s), 'Planet Rock' marks a turning point in the
construction of popular music. Bambaataa's contribution to the introduction
of electronic music into the commercially emerging rap/hip-hop milieu was
crucial. However, it is important to note that the electro-funk sound had
important contributions from several other artists, and that 'Planet Rock',
no matter how innovative it clearly was, did not stand in musical isolation in
the period. Early champion of electro-funk British DJ Greg Wilson suggests
that, before

> 'Planet Rock' . . . exploded on the scene in May 82, there had already
> been a handful of releases in the previous months that would help define
> this new genre. D Train's 'You're The One For Me' (Prelude), which was
> massive during late 81, would set the tone, paving the way for 'Time'
> by Stone (West End), 'Feels Good' by Electra (Emergency) and two sig-
> nificant Eric Matthew/Darryl Payne productions, Sinnamon's 'Thanks
> To You' (Becket) and, once again courtesy of Prelude, 'On A Journey
> (I Sing The Funk Electric)' by Electrik Funk (the term Electro-Funk
> originally deriving from this track, 'electric-funk' being amended to
> Electro-Funk following the arrival of Shock's 'Electrophonic Phunk' on
> the Californian Fantasy label in June [1982]).

As Wilson also indicates, in common with Baker and Bambaataa these
artists drew influences from Kraftwerk and UK electronic artists such as
the Human League and Gary Numan. Likewise Wilson suggests they also
looked back to

> a number of pioneering black musicians . . . Miles Davis, Sly Stone,
> Herbie Hancock, Stevie Wonder, legendary producer Norman Whitfield
> and, of course, George Clinton and his P Funk brigade, [who] all
> [played] their part in shaping this new sound via their innovative use
> of electronic instruments during the 70s (and as early as the late 60s in
> Miles Davis' case). (Wilson, 2003)

Noting this wider network of artists and influences, it is important to
consider why Kraftwerk proved influential for Bambaataa and others contributing to the emergence of electro-funk in this period. It can be suggested
that Kraftwerk provided electro-funk with a suitably sparse, rhythmically
regulated base, free from the teleologically thick guitar-based popular music
before them. In doing so, they gave Bambaataa and others a template, a
potential to expand musical language and bring together a new set of people
on the dance floor: those who were, at that time, disenfranchised from
the established rock industry and society as a whole (African-American/

Latino street musicians, and other minority audiences who were beginning to assert their own voices including punks, gays, etc.). In examining the success of Kraftwerk's sound, Aikin (1982) argues that the regular 4/4 time, straightforward harmonics and easy melodic lines produce a hypnotic effect, fulfilling 'our most basic subconscious expectations about how a phrase will round out; instead of being jarred by unexpected shifts, we are lulled into a receptive state'. The effect of this compositional simplicity is 'to direct the listener's attention toward the sounds in any given texture . . . and it is in these sounds themselves and their interlocking rhythmic relationships that Kraftwerk shines' (p. 38).

In relationship to 'Planet Rock', the combination of a harmonically hypnotic effect and regular beat was a highly appropriate backdrop for an improvised, narrative style of rap mixed with DJ. Though there were other important songs and artists that contributed to the development of electro-funk, there was no previous exploration or interaction of these contrasting traditions. As such Bambaataa lays claim to the teleological priority of 'innovation', a necessity for him to survive in the music industry. At the very same time, 'Planet Rock' 'evokes' musical works from various points over the preceding 17 years, and was a collaborative enterprise not solely authored by Bambaataa, Baker or MC G.L.O.B.E.

In the last decade, the phenomena of mashing, bastard pop, and Nü-Electro or electroclash (Paoletta, 2002) have brought a serious new challenge to this dynamic, where the necessity of 'innovation' has been challenged by the priority of 'evocation', rather than the reverse. From activist artists such as Danger Mouse, whose *The Grey Album* mixed instrumentation from the Beatles' 'White Album' with vocals from rapper Jay-Z's *The Black Album*, to the sexually provocative aesthetic of Peaches; from the deliberate detachment of Chicks On Speed to the twisted bastard pop of Soulwax (also known as 2ManyDJs), artists are now, more than ever, tapping into the universalist aesthetic and creative processes they perceive coming (in very different ways) from both Bambaataa and Kraftwerk. With readily available software, virtually any musician can now create newly mashed tracks; with open-source networks still in existence despite the best efforts of record companies, and with the invention of ever-smaller compressed sound files, Kembrew McLeod (2005) can comment that the '[i]nternet is the Wild West of today, sort of like Hip Hop in the late 1980s before laws and bureaucracies limited its creative potential' (pp. 83–4). At the heart of this aesthetic beats a disruptive rhythm which (in the case of 2ManyDJs) will mash the *Peter Gunn* theme together with Basement Jaxx's 'Where's Your Head At' (which in turn samples Gary Numan's 'M.E.') in a multilayered ironic interplay, perhaps not as explicitly political as Bambaataa or Kraftwerk in an old-school sense, but certainly aimed at commenting on the corporate restraint that governs musical output today. In this artistic context where the contribution of a posthuman (i.e.

electronic) sound is now celebrated, Bambaataa continues to evoke and explore; on his 2004 album, *Dark Matter Moving at the Speed of Light*, he pays homage to Gary Numan with the reinterpretation of Numan's iconic track 'Metal', collaborating with Numan himself.

'Planet Rock' endures as an iconic first-recorded representation of this aesthetic. *Plus ça change, plus çest la même chose* . . . the following is an account of Afrika Bambaataa's live set in Oakland in 1997:

> But it was Bambaataa's early morning set that really got the crowd moving. Even though the sun was nearly rising by the time he hit the stage, the bleary-eyed audience of rap and rave fans broke into break-dance circles and loopy Deadhead-style dances as Bambaataa's fat beats filled the room. In fact, when he broke into his classic 1982 track 'Planet Rock', a propulsive mix of electro-funk meltdowns, blaring shipyard sirens and Latin house, it was clear that 15 years later, Bambaataa's music is still way ahead of its time. (Kun, 1997, p. 24)

The year 1997 is also significant for Kraftwerk. As mentioned earlier, neither Schneider nor Hütter ever commented on the legal implications of Bambaataa's use of their music. However, in this year the German rap producer Moses Pelham used a two-second sample of Kraftwerk's 1977 track 'Metal on Metal' as part of a rhythm sequence in a song, 'Nur Mir', by Sabrina Setlur. Kraftwerk successfully sued Pelham in a Hamburg state court, only to have the case overturned by Germany's highest civil court in November 2008. It seems that in Germany, along with the rest of the world, outmoded notions of copyright and the new technologies are still clashing and interacting, and it is fascinating to observe the parallels here. It appears mystifying, bordering on ironic, that Kraftwerk would attempt to sue someone for sampling two seconds of their work, especially considering that the constancy of their success has been due in no small part to the absorption of their samples through a vast array of popular musical genres and artists. One can only speculate why, after so many years, Kraftwerk would choose this as a battleground – perhaps it is because they are fellow German artists that the issue strikes more personally; or perhaps this is the first time in a while that an artist has refused to pay Kraftwerk for the intended sample.

Philosophically, it may seem that Afrika Bambaataa and Kraftwerk are aeons apart. However, both were/are deeply committed to a universalist vision. Bambaataa's philosophy is geared towards social justice, communal understanding and anti-racism. Kraftwerk were imbued from the start with a modernist, quasi-futurist sensibility that sought to integrate the bionic with the organic in alternative readings, as a way of commenting on the progress of technology and society. Mark Prendergast (2000) sees the alliance of classical (music) education and progressive use of electronics with pop concepts (perfectly formed and often ironic) as Kraftwerk's 'tremendous cultural impact . . . Though often seen as over-simplistic and too mechanized in their approach, they nevertheless humanized electronic music for a mass audience' (p. 301). Perhaps the best way to read the creation of 'Planet Rock' is to see the counter-intuitive folding of a new form from an old aesthetic with an old form of the new aesthetic, into a codified recording that fulfilled the aesthetic aspirations of both – creating, evoking, integrating, reinterpreting.

References

Aikin, J. (1982), 'Kraftwerk: electronic minstrels of the global village'. *Keyboard*, March, 33–40.

Bangs, L. (1975), 'Kraftwerk feature: or how I learned to stop worrying and love the balm'. *Creem*, 7, (4). http://www.creemmagazine.com/_site/BeatGoesOn/Kraftwerk/Kraftwerkfeature001.html (last accessed 5 August 2010).

Barr, T. (1998), *Kraftwerk: From Düsseldorf to the Future (with Love)*. London: Ebury Press.

Bohn, C. (1981), 'Interview with Ralf Hütter'. *New Musical Express*. 13 June. http://kraftwerk.technopop.com.br/interview_124.php (last accessed 14 March 2010).

Buskin, R. (2008), 'Afrika Bambaataa & the Soulsonic Force: "Planet Rock"'. *Sound on Sound*, November. http://www.soundonsound.com/sos/nov08/articles/classictracks_1108.htm (last accessed 14 March 2010).

Bussy, P. (1993), *Kraftwerk: Man, Machine and Music*. (1st edn). London: SAF.

Chang, J. (2005), *Can't Stop, Won't Stop: A History of the Hip-Hop Generation*. New York: St Martin's Press.

Flür, W. (2000), *Kraftwerk: I Was a Robot*. London: Sanctuary.

Kun, J. (1997), 'Performance: Planet Rock 1997'. *Rolling Stone* 761, 29 May, 24.

McLeod, K. (2005), 'Confessions of an intellectual (property): Danger Mouse, Mickey Mouse, Sonny Bono, and my long and winding path as a copyright activist-academic'. *Popular Music and Society*, 28, (1), 79–93.

Mitchell, G. (2002), 'Founder's Awards: Afrika Bambaataa'. *Billboard*, 114, (32), RB-8.

Nattiez, J. J. (1990) *Music and Discourse: Toward a Semiology of Music*, trans C. Abbate. Princeton: Princeton University Press.

Paoletta, M. (2002), 'Nü-Electro sound emerges: DJs, new acts spark fresh dance mix in Europe and U.S'. *Billboard*, 144, (30), 1, 66–7.

Prendergast, M. J. (2000), *The Ambient Century – from Mahler to Trance: The Evolution of Sound in the Electronic Age*. London: Bloomsbury.

Wilson, G. (2003), 'Electro-funk: what did it all mean'. http://www.electrofunkroots.co.uk/articles/what.html (last accessed 14 March 2010).

10

Average White Band: Kraftwerk and the Politics of Race

Mark Duffett

For Mantronik, the history of Black Dance Music doesn't begin with James Brown, Sly Stone, George Clinton, even Van McCoy or Chic; it begins with Kraftwerk and flowers with Trevor Horn's Art of Noise. It was the krafty krauts' glistening plastic vistas and stainless girders, plus the Art of Noise's fleshless, faceless, sense-less and soul-less techno-symphonic sky's-the-limit-mastery that first made him want to make dance music.

(*Reynolds, 2007, p. 40*)

It is a staple of popular music commentary that black creativity is the main source of inspiration. Echoing the words of Martin Luther King, music journalist Nelson George (1988a) has said, 'Blacks create then move on. Whites document and recycle. In the history of popular music, these truths are self-evident' (p. 108). In the case of Kraftwerk, at first sight this truism appears to have reached its limit. Accounts of the Teutonic quartet explain that Kraftwerk's approach to sound and rhythm was adopted and adapted by a wide range of artists from the white synth bands of the New Wave to the black pioneers of electro, hip-hop and techno. In an interview with Simon Reynolds, the influential electro-funk musician Kurtis Mantronik even cited the German band as the godfathers of black electronica. In light of such assertions, it seems strange that Kraftwerk and their contribution have received so little intellectual attention. Robert Fink (2005) and Peter Shapiro (2002) begin to discuss the uptake of the 'Trans-Europe Express' melody. Sean Albiez (2005) examines the group's connections with Detroit techno. Meanwhile, Kodwo Eshun (1999) and Ian Biddle (2004) offer a more sustained discussion. These scholars are exceptions, however. Given their historic significance, the band has largely gone unnoticed in academic debate.

What follows will begin an understanding of the black interest in Kraftwerk that necessarily foregrounds both race and gender. Much more than average, Kraftwerk are a band whose race seems significant; white privilege is often said to operate by concealing whiteness and making it an invisible norm, yet references to the group's racial identity have frequently been deployed to mark out their *difference* in a cultural terrain inspired by black music. Attention will therefore be drawn to what could be called the 'whitewashing' of Kraftwerk. The chapter will then explore the value of Kraftwerkian masculinity in two pivotal cultures of black popular music: early 1980s New York electro hip-hop and Detroit techno. Hütter and Schneider's band were one among many that inspired these music scenes, but highlighting the connection shows how musicians like Afrika Bambaataa drew on their automated rhythms to challenge the established stereotypes of black masculinity. My argument, then, is that attention to race *per se* will not get us very far in understanding Kraftwerk's part in inspiring futuristic African-American dance music. Once we focus upon masculinity in the context of race, however, the group's contribution becomes explicable.

Traditional explanations of the musical influence of Kraftwerk are replete with assumptions about race and music that lack explanatory power. The first assumption is that the phenomenon is *only* an issue of race. We know that Kraftwerk, like black musicians, made music that encouraged people to dance, but to emphasize this as a common concern of both races is not to get much nearer to an explanation. Equally, the 'why Kraftwerk' question cannot be adequately handled by coming up with limited but poetic descriptions of the paradox, such as:

> 'They were so stiff they were funky,' techno pioneer Carl Craig has said of Kraftwerk. This paradox – which effectively translates as 'they were so white they were black' – is as close as anyone has got to explaining the mystery of why Kraftwerk's music . . . had such an impact on black American youth. (Reynolds, 2008, p. 3)

How can any performer be so white that they are black? While Carl Craig's paradoxical formulation seems absurd, Reynolds's description of 'Trans-Europe Express' as 'dispassionately metronomic' might offer a clearer indication of how Kraftwerk resonated with American electro-funk pioneers.

A second assumption is that the whole process of cross-racial inspiration was a mysterious miracle that should never have happened. For example, music critic John Robb (1999) has suggested, 'In one of the weirdest quirks in rock history, black kids in the ghetto started to get hip to Kraftwerk. Taking the atmospheric synth music of the German outfit, they re-invented it as a dance music of their own' (p. 236). Was the uptake of Kraftwerk's style really so weird? Kodwo Eshun is perhaps the foremost analyst of black electronic dance music as a conceptual project. Discussing interpretations like Robb's, Eshun (1999) has pointed out that white journalists' surprise over the black engagement with Kraftwerk itself borders on racism, because it assumes both that black artists are mired in a soul aesthetic (prizing uncontrolled expression over emotional control) and that they are so separatist they can never be open to sounds made by other races. Robb's commentary and those like it contain the assumption that black youth should not have been listening to Kraftwerk since the German band made such 'white' music.

At this point I wish to mention the highly politicized scholarly discussion about the concept of 'black music' as a distinct cultural formation. I am acutely aware of what funk writer Matthew Brown (1994) has called the 'colonizing hop' that white academics make when they talk about black traditions. My aim here is, nevertheless, to interrogate racist assumptions and put forward a positive, outside reading of the issue. At least one prominent scholar has used the black interest in Kraftwerk to begin deconstructing the idea of black music. Philip Tagg's famous essay locates this intransigent idea as unsatisfactory in musicological terms, because it is premised on sounds of external origin. According to Tagg (1989), '[w]e might even be considering banishing Prince and Lionel Richie [from African-American music] – not to mention all the 'b-boys' of hip-hop influenced by Kraftwerk, to the realms of the Euro-American or white' (p. 288).

Certainly there is plenty of evidence of black enjoyment of 'white' sounds, and vice versa, but all musics are a shade of grey: they come from a meandering, diasporic heritage with no singular, stable point of origin. To move beyond Tagg's argument, we need to consider why 'black music' remains a socially important category *despite* its necessary musicological impurity. One way forward is to bring in Ewan Allinson's critique of white hip-hop scholarship. It seems naïve to see black music as a path to racial integration, Allinson (1994) argues, because white audiences have so often loved the music but hated its makers. White people cannot actually 'hear' the 'true' meaning of hip-hop, because despite making up the bulk of its audience they are in effect its Other. In consequence, whites tend to romanticize black music or find other ways to accommodate it in relation to their own ideas about race, at the heart of which lie long-standing myths about black masculinity. Some of Allinson's points seem highly problematic. The notion of a privileged 'true' meaning of any cultural form is highly debatable. His siding with (projected) authorial intent devalues the range of meanings that hip-hop can facilitate, reducing its readings to racial differences in the audience. Allinson also *naïvely* assumes that rappers ignore their marketplace. Nevertheless, some of his interpretation is useful because it suggests that white writers should explore how to talk about black culture *while earning respect*. What makes this point so productive is that it contests the naïve idea that any evaluation of black music can be reduced to mistaken assumptions about racial separatism, or indeed to mistaken premises that celebrate racial or musical purity. Black music makes more sense as a mythic but useful cultural resource. In a society that keeps white supremacy in operation by marking out whiteness as a hidden norm, black culture still has a role as a vehicle for black pride. If a whole racial group is undermined by history, memory and daily life, perceived of as second-class, then it needs something of its own about which to feel proud. Following Nelson George's logic (1988a, p. 108), I therefore see black innovation in the popular arts as a conscious effort to create something distinct by staying ahead of the curve of cultural change.

Kraftwerk's reverse crossover remains intractable only because we cannot adequately discuss it using one dimension of identity alone. My argument instead begins by contesting widely held stereotypes that link race to primitivism. In particular I want to argue that pervasive assumptions about black masculinity help form the basis of established understandings of Kraftwerk's contribution. They mark out a critical silence over the cross-racial adoption of the group's music. In the wake of this silence, commentators can only speculate upon insufficient explanations based purely on race, when they should instead examine masculinity squarely within the frame of racial identity. In order to understand the exceptional black interest in the music of Kraftwerk we have to consider the group's distinct brand of masculinity and what it could have contributed to the black male popular culture of the era. Specifically, I would like to argue that before its electronic incarnation, the Achilles heel of black popular music was that it lent credence to assumptions equating blackness with primitivism; assumptions that ultimately helped to support subtle forms of white supremacism.

While their descriptions are rarely explicit, critics writing about Kraftwerk often tend to see them as the ultimate white band; a conduit between the European avant-garde and popular culture. Much is made of the founding meeting between Hütter and Schneider at the Düsseldorf Conservatory and their shared interest in the experimental music of Karlheinz Stockhausen (see Barr, 1998, p. 6; Bussy, 2005, p. 19). To Anglo-American music critics and intrigued musicians like David Bowie, Kraftwerk represented the epitome of European cool. In the wake of this cultural difference, a common story has emerged about Kraftwerk's role.

The secretive nature of its members helped to seal the myth of Kraftwerk as the singular source of origin for its music. Recalling the cultural void left after Germany's wartime failure, Hütter has explained, 'When we started it was like shock, silence. Nothing. We had no father figures, no continuous tradition of entertainment' (Savage, 1993). Such statements highlight the plight of German culture but also act to divert our attention from the group's engagement with Anglo-American forms. Furthermore, the members of Kraftwerk purposefully maintained a physical whiteness. A 1973 magazine article noted, 'Kraftwerk lie and play at night. Its musicians are pale. We could think that they are night creatures, vampires maybe' (see Bussy, 2005, p. 40). When the group was on vacation on the French Riviera, the creative core duo even told the other members to avoid suntans.

In the wake of Kraftwerk's association with bohemian Germany and physical whiteness, a very particular kind of narrative – a 'master plan' trope – has emerged. The 2007 BBC Radio 4 documentary *Kraftwerk: We Are the Robots*[1] exemplified this narrative. In the context of a collapsed post-war national psyche, the group was presented as a small collective unit of sonic scientists intent on taking over the world with their own strain of popular culture. Presenter Marc Riley summed up his understanding of the narrative:

> So, a magic formula finally reveals itself: a startlingly inventive new form of music, instigated by the aftermath of a failed war, fuelled by nationalism and executed with electronic gadgets. As the Kraftwerk story unfolds it becomes apparent that this is not merely the story of an inventive pop group with a deep love of the bicycle; it's also the story of a mind set, a philosophy, a cultural statement – a master plan.

There are several things to note about this understanding. First, by describing the growth of a new empire in a benign way it structurally mimics the rise of the Nazi state. By this I do not mean that the members of Kraftwerk had any Nazi leanings; instead, I mean they willingly became read in relation to Anglo-American *stereotypes* of the German people. When he first saw them on a record sleeve, Afrika Bambaataa said, 'They almost looked like they were some Nazi type of thing' (Ahearn, Fricke and George, 2002, p. 310). In that sense the group followed a tone set by the whole field of Krautrock, which, as Julian Cope explained on the back jacket of his book *Krautrocksampler* (1995), 'plugged into where the post-war British psyche still had the Germans pegged – as the Bogeyman Rotter of all Europe'.

There is, of course, much humour in the idea of a cell of white German master strategists meticulously planning to take over the world of popular culture. The group itself played up that role, constantly toying with its image as a cold, disinterested and soulless neo-Teutonic collective (see Albiez and Lindvig in this collection). Although the 'master plan' trope is funny, it helps to set up a view of Kraftwerk that is flawed. It falsely positions the German quartet as a point of musical origin outside of popular culture. For example, Brian Eno has categorically stated:

> They came from a more theoretical background than most English or American musicians. They're nothing to do with blues or the Afro-American tradition. Kraftwerk belong to the European avant-garde, which they turned into popular music. (Eno, 2007)

This reading ascribes a musical and racial purity to the band's music that it does not necessarily warrant. In contrast, I would like to highlight that the electronic music of Kraftwerk was not *solely* avant-garde, but was fused with rhythms derived from black American culture by the band itself.

Kraftwerk's roots were not simply in Stockhausen's avant-garde strain of culture, but also in the hybridized German art school Krautrock tradition. Wolfgang Flür had already played in several rock bands on the Düsseldorf rock scene, including the Spirits of Sound. Kraftwerk began on traditional rock instruments before deciding to go electronic, and Hütter, in particular, had been a fan of the Doors (see Cope, 1995, p. 122; Barr, 1998, p. 50). Hütter and Schneider were also influenced by acts within the critical tradition of American rock who paved the way for punk: the Velvet Underground, MC5, and Iggy and the Stooges. After going electronic Kraftwerk increasingly took their inspiration from black popular music. This was the case as early as 1973 when the LP *Ralph and Florian* contained an abstract track called 'Kristallo':

> On 'Kristallo' they juxtaposed a classically-inspired harpsichord theme against a heavily synthetic and extraordinarily funky bass line (they'd obviously been paying close attention to the bass parts played by Bootsy Collins on their favourite James Brown records) and a mechanical 4/4 rhythm. (Barr, 1998, p. 67)

The band's interest in funk was verified by former member Karl Bartos, who said that in the 1970s '[w]e were all fans of American music: soul, the whole Tamla/Motown thing, and of course, James Brown. We always tried to make an American rhythm feel, with a European approach to harmony and melody' (Sicko, 1999, p. 26). Hütter has also indicated an interest in James Brown (Barr, 1998, p. 35). The connection seems interesting because, despite their interest in black music, it is very hard to picture Kraftwerk as 'white negroes' in Norman Mailer's famous sense of the term. The group's interest in James Brown was more likely to have been about making listeners dance than locating an authentic source of essential blackness in their sound. Furthermore, they replaced the established 'white face/black voice' combination with a kind of 'white face/electronic voice/black rhythm' formation. Although he perhaps over-determines 'Trans-Europe Express' (and geographically mis-places it in Berlin), journalist Mark McCord perfectly summarizes the racial hybridity and sense of masculine mastery that may have made it appeal to rappers:

> Crowds everywhere were held absolutely captive by the robotic funk of four guys from Germany. 'Trans-Europe Express' is an eleven-minute, audio-cinema excursion through Cold War Berlin. The sound was sterile, yet dark and disciplined – almost as if machines were piloting the

track. The orchestration . . . sounded like they weren't of the twentieth century, but perhaps of some later point in time. The pounding drums suggested an acute awareness of American funk. This was the point on wax where art met electronic experimentation and skilled musicianship. (2007, p. 62)

Encouraged by the award-winning success of 'Trans-Europe Express' in the disco market, Kraftwerk recruited Leanard 'Colonel Disco' Jackson, an experienced black mixing engineer from Los Angeles, to work on their 1978 album *The Man-Machine*. Jackson had made a reputation working for Whitfield Records, owned by Motown-sound creator Norman Whitfield. Having not yet met the band, 'Colonel Disco' was convinced their tight rhythm tracks were created by black musicians (Bussy, 2005, p. 99).

Changing black masculinities

These machine/organism relationships are obsolete, unnecessary. For us, in imagination and in other practice, machines can be prosthetic devices, intimate components, friendly selves. (Harraway, 1999, p. 460)

We play the machines and sometimes they play us, it's a dialogue. Kraftwerk is the man-machine. (Ralph Hütter)[2]

For Paul Gilroy, writing in *The Black Atlantic*,

[g]ender is the mode in which race is lived. An amplified and exaggerated masculinity has become the boastful centerpiece of a culture of compensation that self-consciously salves the misery of the disempowered and subordinated. This masculinity and its rational feminine counterpart become special symbols of the difference that race makes. (1993, p. 85)

Black masculinity has long been associated with the cult of the macho, a point which some writers explain as a compensatory function emerging from the legacy of slavery (see Mercer, 1994, p. 142). Just as significant, though, is an ongoing white association of black identity with natural, unrepressed, savage sexuality:

Typically, black music was thought of by white culture as being both more primitive and more 'authentically' erotic. Infusions of black music were always seen as (and often condemned as) sexual and physical. (Dyer, 1997, p. 522)

In the middle of his 2005 film *Hustle and Flow*, director Craig Brewer raises the issue of white perceptions of black identity by letting Shelby – a white teenager who plays piano in church and has been seconded by two black musicians to help develop their sound – speak about his view of black music. Shelby enthusiastically explains his perspective while he smokes weed with three black characters:

> You see the thing is – and I believe this, man – rap is coming back home to the South. Because this, man, this is where it all began: heavy percussion, repetitive hooks, sexually suggestive lyrics, man – it's all blues, brother! Backdoor Man to 'back that ass up'. It's all about pain, and pussy, and making music, man . . . Every man – know what I'm saying? – Every man has the right, the god damn right, to contribute a verse!

Shelby's misguided lines are laughed off by Djay (a working-class rapper) and Key (an aspiring music recorder), but they clearly and concisely parody a white stereotype of black primitivism. There is the connection of rap to the blues tradition (with funk here present by its absence as the missing link); the twin emphases on sexual salaciousness and the emotive expression of human pain, and finally the collective, redemptive, communitarian context of Southern folk culture – all cemented by the perceived percussive simplicity of the sound itself.

In a recent article on listening and gender, music journalist Laura Barton put Kraftwerk into the same category as Oasis and Slayer as archetypally 'male music'. She described Kraftwerk's music as 'clinical and computerized – male heaven' (2008, p. 25). While Barton's position verges on essentialism, it is noteworthy that Kraftwerk's fan base seems predominantly male. In the radio documentary, *Kraftwerk: We Are the Robots*, for example, all the passionate reveries came from men. This is relevant because women are present only by their absence in the group's automated imaginary; they become reduced to objects of loss or longing, replaced by machines. Eshun (1999) described the group's members as 'Bachelormachines' for that reason. The quartet's sexless collective image led to comic inferences and speculations that they were gay or childlike – lost in a dreamworld of technological fusion and not 'real men' at all; a point that Flür (2003) attempted to challenge by mentioning his encounters with female fans. Instead of romantic union, however, the central element through which Kraftwerk's masculinity functions is harmony with technology. For Hütter and Schneider, mastery is a mental practice rather than a physical feat.

Kraftwerkian masculinity is calculated and rational. By replacing themselves with static, emotionless robots, and quietly laughing about it, Kraftwerk posed as a team of characterless, almost faceless, male technologists engineering a hypnotic spectacle of electronic dance music. While their automated pop seemed novel in the mid 1970s, this male practice of indirect representation through control of technology had previously been seen elsewhere; for example, in the careful composition and performance of classical music. A more recent example was when eccentric pop visionaries like Phil Spector and Andy Warhol had used musicians as their instruments (see Bannister, 2006, pp. 36–48). Reinforced by a narrative of cultural conquest characterized by careful planning, Kraftwerk lived out a conception of masculinity that was cerebral, collective, strategic and peppered with ironic, self-depreciating humour.

In what follows, I will argue that Hütter and Schneider accidentally contributed to a trajectory that disengaged black manhood from its association with primitivism and allied it instead to a different masculine trait: the calculated, rational control of advanced technology. As Eshun (2006) explains,

> Black science fiction uses . . . a possibility space which leaves behind or moves away from traditional notions of Black culture as based on the street for instance, based on traditional notions of masculinity, based on traditional notions of ethnicity. It's a boredom with those ideas. (p. 292)

Why, then, did black musicians draw upon Kraftwerk? The first pillar of a new explanation should refer to their shared context in a world of technological change. As electronic innovations were adopted in the 1960s and 1970s, they transformed the environment that gave rise to male youth culture and its collective imaginary. Specifically, the advent of manned space flight and the incursion of the microchip into the world of ordinary work and leisure had a profound impact on Western society. In this context the control of electronic technology became an increasingly significant benchmark of achievement for males of all races.

It is interesting here to think about how the Kraftwerk story parallels another great conquest of the late twentieth century: the moon landing. As NASA's Apollo 11 mission touched down in July 1969, Neil Armstrong's first steps on the moon became a historic moment recognized all over the world. In a sense, the moon landing provided an affirmation of Enlightenment faith in technological progress. Its narrative connected the (male) mastery of scientific technology, (white) planning and America's passion for patriotic spectacle in a memorable drama that shaped the imagination of musicians – both black and white – as much as any other section of society. Hardly surprising, then, that aliens, robots and space travellers became the media archetypes of the era between David Bowie's 'Space Oddity' and Michael Jackson's signature moonwalk.

Yet this spectacle was also a social diversion, a cloud of (moon) dust.

Rockets in the sky diverted attention from political chaos on the ground; countercultural turmoil, anti-war protests and the civil rights struggle. The way that scientific spectacle united the human race at this time resonated with assimilationists of both races looking for a way out of political strife. For example, the TV series *Star Trek* suggested that space, the final frontier, could be a utopian realm of racial equality, facilitating an effortless unity between black and white Americans. In parallel, emerging from the 'cosmic' imaginary of the Krautrock milieu, Hütter was moved by the Apollo mission: 'When the rocket was going to the moon, I was so emotionally excited . . . When I saw this on television, I thought it was one of the best performances I had ever seen' (Bangs, 1987, p. 159). Just over a decade later, Afrika Bambaataa's long-standing interest in science fact and fiction was part of the inspiration behind 'Planet Rock'. Its first video contained footage from the NASA space missions. Equally, as Albiez (2005) has demonstrated, the pioneers of Detroit techno who wrote songs like Cybotron's 'Cosmic Cars' had their own conception of space, which seemed to collapse the distinctions between inner and outer realms, the real and the virtual.

Just as NASA's mission inspired the dreams of the nation, so too developments in electronic technology rapidly began to change everyday life. In particular, the 1970s and 1980s saw the first significant incursion of computer-based technologies into the realm of ordinary work and leisure. In the workplace, a crisis of industrial capitalism was gradually addressed by mass automation. For those who had survived the replacement of manual labour by automated machines, breadwinning gradually came to mean using your mind to programme and operate electronic technology. With the mass adoption of the pocket calculator and digital watch, there was also palpable evidence that microchip technology was transforming consumption and everyday life. Towards the end of the 1970s, youth leisure practices were shifting rapidly with the advent of video gaming culture. Meanwhile, thanks to studio pioneers like Kraftwerk and Giorgio Moroder, the wave of transformation soon began to manifest itself in the sound of electronic dance music. More and more tracks were recorded with drum machines, vocoders, synthesizers and sequencers. According to rap historian David Toop (1991),

[t]hese [electro] records were an invitation for kids to plunge themselves Tron-like into a world of freeze-frame See Threepios [*sic*], and if adults wanted to run scared then that was their business – it was the new reality of technology that they were running from. Many of the electro musicians and producers recognize their music as the fusion that it is – street funk and hip-hop mixed with influences from British synthesizer music (Gary Numan, Human League, Thomas Dolby and Yazoo were all played on WKTU, the radio station that switched from rock to disco in 1978, and on WBLS by Frankie Crocker), Latin music,

Kraftwerk and jazz fusion, all written into the breaker, robot, pop, wave and moonwalk meltdown. The music of Miles Davis and Herbie Hancock was an important antecedent . . . [contributing to] the post – NASA – Silicone Valley – Atari – TV Break Out – Taito – Sony – Roland – Linn – Oberheim – Lucas – Spielberg groove. (p. 149)

As Toop makes clear, Kraftwerk were one source of inspiration among many for black musicians at the time. His work also shows that the mastery of new technology in spaces of both work and leisure was a crucial male aspiration. From the mid 1970s to the mid 1980s this concern guided the production of various electronic music genres.

Alongside its embrace of electronic sounds, disco signified a shift from funk to mechanized beats. If the pleasure of funk had been imagining yourself *as* James Brown – manly, dominant and in control of the band, being 'on the one' and setting the pace of the music – disco strutting was much less about being on top. In his famous 1979 essay, 'In defence of disco', Richard Dyer contrasted the head-led eroticism of traditional popular songs to the phallic stance of rock, and what he called the 'whole body eroticism' of disco. For Dyer (2002), phallic music conveyed masculinity by being thrusting, awkward and entrapping. In contrast, disco seemed less phallic and more open-ended, sinuous and releasing:

Gay men do not intrinsically have any prerogative over whole body eroticism. We are often more cock-orientated than non-gays of either sex, and it depresses me that such phallic forms of disco as Village People should be so gay identified. Nonetheless, partly because many of us have traditionally not thought of ourselves as 'real men' and partly because gay ghetto culture is also a space where alternative definitions, including of sexuality, can be developed, it seems to me that the impor- tance of disco in scene culture indicates an openness to a sexuality that is not defined in terms of cock. (p. 523)

Dyer's description rests upon a kind of problematic musical essentialism. Emphasized by the hard, heavy, grinding nature of its percussive effects, rock, for example, becomes ironically both over-determined and reduced to macho strutting. Nevertheless, Dyer's schema provides useful shorthand with which to begin thinking about those popular *interpretations* that have framed various musical genres with distinct gendered understandings. His ideas, in other words, help materialize the ideological grid through which these genres have been widely interpreted. Disco was often *seen as* dance music that enabled the whole of the dancer's body to surrender to the eroticized pleasure of the beat. By 1977, Americans perceived Kraftwerk's music as cutting-edge Eurodisco. In turn the group embraced the genre and asked disco DJ François Kevorkian to mix tracks from *Computer World* (1981).

As scientific technologies began to colonize everyday life, the era of space travel and integrated circuitry fuelled a widespread fascination with cyborgs and robots. Black popular culture had already created casual and comic variants.[3] There was James Brown's compelling imperative in 1970 to 'Stay on the scene, like a sex machine'; in 1973 Rufus Thomas urged people to 'Do the Funky Robot', and in the early part of the decade the robotic 'waack' dance (a precursor of break-dancing) appeared on *Soul Train*. It is interesting to consider George Clinton and P-Funk at this point; for some, Clinton was parodying the failure of the space race to accommodate the civil rights agenda (see Brown, 1994, p. 498). Just as significantly, his music related to earlier incarnations of funk. Clinton's wild, political party anthems retained some of the sexuality and organicism of James Brown's music, but also moved funk towards a collective, softer-edged, psychedelic, theatrical aesthetic. There was still an organic sense of 'the funk' as a sexualized black essence, but outer space became somewhere comic, somewhere humanity still got things wrong. P-Funk's hilarious, cosmic bad trip therefore retained some allegiance with traditional funk's phallocentric stance, but also portrayed the loss of rational control in a futuristic world of space-age technology.

These different approaches to robotics linked to different conceptions of masculinity. James Brown impelled listeners to become more like machines for the pleasurable purpose of procreation, but in P-Funk robots malfunctioned humorously, suggesting that masculine control had reached its limits. By pursuing their own ironic deadpan approach, however, Kraftwerk effortlessly imbued themselves, as robots, with a strong sense of indeterminacy. Although the robots and showroom dummies were emotion-free substitutes that allowed the musicians to retreat into their roles as faceless technicians, robotics was also used by the group as part of a process of social integration, suggesting equality on the dance floor, rather than macho physical dominance. Kraftwerk's comic self-labelling was therefore self-depreciating, and implied of a kind of voluntary submission. It suggested that although we control the social technology making the music, as slaves to the beat we are also controlled by it. Hence, for Hütter, '[i]t's like a robot thing, when it gets up to a certain stage. It starts playing . . . it's no longer you and I, it's It' (Bangs, 1987, p. 157).

With its whispered vocal, Kraftwerk's 'Trans-Europe Express' was a disco hit that resonated with black America. Nelson George (1988b, p. 23) discusses the seeming ubiquity of the tune when he was growing up in Brooklyn. According to Bambaataa, 'I don't think [Kraftwerk] even knew how big they were among the black masses back in '77, when they came out with 'Trans-Europe Express'' (Toop, 1991, p. 130). In fact DJ Spooky (Paul Miller) has even talked about 1970s New York as having a whole 'Afrika Bambaataa/

Kraftwerk scene' (1994, p. 36). Certainly, Grandmaster Flash would let it run on his turntables without cutting it up and others like the Cold Crush Brothers rapped over Kraftwerk's music. The vocal of 'Trans-Europe Express' suggested an alienated, pan-European sophistication – technology so efficient that it never made much noise.

The innovative adaption of part of 'Trans-Europe Express' to create 'Planet Rock' was, I think, distinctly cyborgian. It is useful here to briefly consider Donna Harraway's 1991 essay, 'A cyborg manifesto'. For Harroway, a cyborg is a hybrid product of technological change that opens up a space of conceptual potentiality, precisely because it cannot be fitted into existing understandings. As she explains, 'This essay is an argument for *pleasure* in the confusion of boundaries and for responsibility in their construction' (1999, p. 435). Cyborgs are necessarily chimeral, ironic and blasphemous, auguring new fields of contradiction wrought by technological shifts that disrupt and denaturalize the existing dualisms upon which Enlightenment identities are based. As we leave organic industrial culture and head towards a polymorphous information society, suppressive hierarchies of identity – including race – are necessarily challenged and transformed too. By irreversibly destabilizing previous ontological categories, advanced technology allows us to play with new myths of identity. 'Planet Rock' was cyborgian in bringing together a series of contradictory opposites: racial pride and assimilation, gang culture and technological control, funk and futurism, and finally elements of recorded and live music.

In helping to create hip-hop, Bronx DJ and ex–gang warlord Bambaataa's mission was to bypass disco by updating funk, a project that was neither about musical nor racial separatism, but nevertheless maintained elements of black pride; elements that became expressed in the Universal Zulu Nation. This is important because George Clinton and other artists accused disco of faking the funk. In other words, mechanized dance music was seen as a bland substitute for its more racially separatist politics and sense of emotional release. According to Bambaataa:

> I grew up in the southeast Bronx. It was an area where back in the late '60s, early '70s there was 'broken glass everywhere,' like Melle Mel said in 'The Message.' But it was also an area where there was a lot of unity and social awareness going on, at a time when people of color was coming into their own, knowin' that they were Black people, hearing records like James Brown's 'Say It Loud – I'm Black and I'm Proud,' giving us awareness. Hearing people like Sly and the Family Stone telling you to 'Stand!' 'You Can Make It If You Try,' 'Everyday People.' . . . Basically the Bronx was looking for something new . . . But after a while we got tired of hearing the Hustle and disco records – we wanted that funk. We was missing the James Brown, the Sly, the Mandrill, Earth Wind and Fire,

so we kept that funk alive with the break-beat sound. (Ahearn, Fricke and George, 2002, p. 44)

While 'Trans-Europe Express' had become a hit in New York City years before it was taken up by the Soulsonic Force, stories differ about how they actually discovered the record. Their white producer, Arthur Baker, said he heard 'Trans-Europe Express' when he visited the projects on lunch break from his work for a record distributor in Long Island City (Buskin, 2008). Bussy (2005, p. 126) suggests that Baker lent Bambaataa the record. Another version of the story is that Bambaataa discovered a Kraftwerk LP while record-shopping in Greenwich Village and got intrigued by its cover (see Ahearn, Fricke and George, 2002, p. 310). Whichever way it happened, by the time 'Planet Rock' was recorded Bambaataa had already re-racialized Kraftwerk's desexed funk in his live show by mixing 'Trans-Europe Express' with speeches from black civil rights leaders like Malcolm X and Martin Luther King (Toop, 1991, p. 130). This 'weird' German music had thus been appropriated to express black power in a multi-racial context. Now Bambaataa was extending the crossover by recording a punchy hybrid of hip-hop vocals, P-Funk imagery and futuristic melody. He had in effect inherited the iconography of P-Funk (the idea of having a wild party in space) and mixed it with Kraftwerk's sense of effortless technological mastery.

The creation of 'Planet Rock' was part of a shift in New York that supplanted potentially violent rumbles with displays of technical prowess through music or dance. Bambaataa had emerged from a macho gang culture to demonstrate his masculinity by controlling technology. While it used no sequencer, 'Planet Rock' pioneered the use of the famous Roland TR-808 drum machine and Fairlight keyboard in hip-hop (Buskin, 2008). According to Bambaataa, 'I started looking around, seeing that there was no black group that was strictly electronic. I said, "We're going to be the first band to be electronic; I'm going to call my sound the Electro-Funk sound!"' (Ahearn, Fricke and George, 2002, p. 315). Speaking of the use of drum machines and synths in 'Planet Rock', producer Arthur Baker has added, 'When we used them, we didn't try to make them sound like real instruments, whereas the likes of the Human League were trying to get a machine-oriented record such as 'Don't You Want Me Baby' to sound like a real band' (Buskin, 2008). Rather than using a macho personality to threaten violence and rule the ghetto, it was as if Bambaataa was saying that technological control was a very important (if as yet relatively undiscovered) aspect of black masculinity.

Musically too, 'Planet Rock' was at a crossroads between funk and futurist electronic music. One cyborgian element of 'Planet Rock' was its basis in hip-hop – already a funky extension of man and machine that involved the performative control of phonographic playback. One of the ways that electro hip-hop got back to the funk was that it involved the percussive use of turntable technology. In effect, it applied a funk aesthetic to the replay of recorded sound, and it is perhaps no wonder therefore that funk artists like James Brown became among the most sampled. In hip-hop, the record replaced the band. As the technology was manually controlled, the orchestration – performative control of the sound – involved cueing breaks, scratching and the other musical practices of the genre. The Soulsonic Force was an electronic ensemble, yet it included DJ Jazzy J who could manipulate the decks.

The machismo that defined funk was continued on 'Planet Rock' in the form of assertive rapping. If funk was about asserting yourself by being on the one, and P-Funk was about being hilariously off-kilter, demonstrating one's masculine prowess in hip-hop meant outwitting the beat. MC G.L.O.B.E. developed a technique specifically for 'Planet Rock' called 'MC Popping': since the 'Numbers' beat was too fast for normal rapping he did the track in half-time. Instead of quietly or mockingly announcing his status as a machine, as Kraftwerk had done, G.L.O.B.E. opened the song simply by barking 'Rock, rock to the Planet Rock. Don't stop' into a vocoder. He represents an aural vision of metallic, deadpan masculinity, shorn of emotion (and therefore primitivism) and integrated with technology: a cyborgian male.[4] In the shape of MC G.L.O.B.E., the fast, mechanized beat of 'Planet Rock' was therefore dominated by a robotic black android persona.

'Planet Rock' stood at a musical crossroads, referencing funk, P-Funk, hip-hop and Kraftwerk. While the song had some roots in funk (as one lyric put it, 'Just taste the funk and hit me'), and it was not entirely free of sexual references ('Shake it now, go ladies'), there was also a general message of exuberant dance-floor inclusivity which seemed innocent and desexed compared with some of James Brown's lyrics. Musically, the traditional funk pattern was emphasized by regular, sampled, ORCH5 stabs (Fink, 2005). The Soulsonic Force's visual iconography was clearly indebted to P-Funk. Kraftwerk's 'Numbers', meanwhile, formed the basis of an electro-disco backing; an influence that may have been contributed by various members of the outfit (see McCord, 2007, and Buskin, 2008). Finally the distinctive hip-hop vocals and melody line from 'Trans-Europe Express', re-recorded by keyboard player John Robie, added a touch of intergalactic exoticism. As Shapiro (2005) has noted, 'Planet Rock' 'lifted the most futuristic, unlocomotive element of "Trans-Europe Express"' (p. 135). Bambaataa's explanation of his adoption of the melody is notable for two phrases: he saw Kraftwerk as 'funky white boys' who made 'weird shit'. The futurist electro-disco funk of Kraftwerk – funk formed *without* the traditional sexual connotations or emotional exuberance – made them sound weird in relation to black traditions. But rather than Bambaataa trying to exoticize and alienate himself from black popular music, as Kodwo Eshun has suggested, it could instead be argued that he was *bringing in* a music that was *both* oriented to controlling the dancing body (funky) and exemplifying the weirdness of what some have called 'cold emotion'.

Around the same time, several black male musicians in the Detroit area also began to base their sound around control of new technology. The influence of Kraftwerk on Detroit's music scene was catalysed by a DJ known as the Electrifying Mojo (Charles Johnson) who mixed the group's music with Italodisco, P-Funk and other genres. Mojo was famous for his eclectic, format-busting, colour-blind playlists. When Kraftwerk released *Computer World* in 1981, he played the whole record without a break. This kind of promotion inspired the man who was later dubbed the godfather of techno, Juan Atkins. Atkins studied at Washtenaw Community College with Vietnam veteran Rik Davis; Davis encouraged Atkins to listen carefully to Kraftwerk and Tangerine Dream. The pair joined forces at the start of the 1980s under the name of Cybotron. By this time Atkins had also formed a DJ collective called Deep Space with his friend Derrick May, playing 'Numbers', 'Home Computer' and other tracks.

Kraftwerk's popularity in Detroit was affirmed when the group performed at the Nitro club. Atkins, Davis and May's suburban location and enrolment in further education located them in the lower-middle-class culture of the Detroit region. In this sense, some of the impetus behind techno came from its pioneers' *estrangement* from black, working-class masculinities, as symbolized in the productive tension on the early 1980s Detroit party scene between two contrasting, loosely class-based black youth cohorts: the Preps and the Jits (discussed by Sicko, 1999, and Albiez, 2005). With their distance from the defunct identities of the post-industrial wasteland, the socially mobile techno artists of Detroit embraced electronic technology with precisely the same aim for invisible mastery that characterized the music of Kraftwerk. It may be helpful here to see futurism simply as a new way to escape the intransigent stereotype that black men should be redundant, lagging behind in the race to use new technology, only capable of manual labour or forms of emotional release.[5] The pioneers of techno could not escape their own race, but they could unplug the association of black maleness with primitivism.

Techno drew on Eurodisco and high-energy beats, but also recruited Kraftwerk's sense of precision and 'cold emotion'. A good example of this is the 'missing link' precursor track, 'Shari Vari', by A Number of Names: a single that came out slightly ahead of 'Planet Rock' and represented Detroit's interest in European elitism. The Charivari clothing label epitomized aspirant black American interest in European chic. As a result its name was hijacked by local DJ parties and reconfigured as 'Shari Vari' (sometimes spelled 'Sharivari'). The track's vamp was adapted from a B-side by the Italodisco group Kano; its meandering keyboards and disinterested vocal were both distinctly reminiscent of Kraftwerk's 'Home Computer'. Detroit techno, like the music of Kraftwerk, then, defined itself in terms of control of technology. While its

pioneers were black and their *musical* focus had disappeared entirely into
the automated rhythms of machines, they still commented on racial issues.
Derrick May recalled:

> I think that when we first did the music, we wanted to believe that we
> were intellectual; we always wanted to tap into an intellectual level of
> the black mind. We wanted to show that black people could do some-
> thing that was high-tech, but intellectual at the same time. We wanted
> to prove that you could do something that was hi-tech that you could
> dance to, but it didn't have to be being about all being onstage and
> shuckin' and jivin' and what not. (qtd. in Huegli, 2002, p. 15)

Finally, I would like to think about the breakdown of these trajectories,
because to a degree they fought the stereotype of black primitivism in vain.
If we see black people *only* as a repository of authentic soul passion, rather
than equally able to make technological music with futurist themes, we may,
as music commentator Jon Savage (1993) has argued, be committing 'veiled
racism'. The trajectory of black masculinity that drew on Kraftwerk and
played itself out in electro-funk, hip-hop and techno has since been recolo-
nized by primitivist, race-based interpretations. In the late 1980s, 1990s and
beyond, hip-hop emphasized the macho side of the cyborg. Perhaps the first
flush of this change was the Miami Bass sound, where derivative tracks such
as MC A.D.E.'s 'Bass Rock Express' (1985) and 'Da Train' (1989) reworked
'Planet Rock' along highly egocentric lines. Meanwhile, discussions about
techno have tended to either colonize the music with primitivist assumptions or reinterpret it as a white genre – as these final, largely misguided,
commentaries demonstrate:

> The techno sound of Detroit, the most totally linear programmed music
> ever, lacking any human musicianship in its execution, reeks of sex,
> sweat and desire. The [black] creators of that music just press a few
> buttons and out comes – a million years of pain and lust. (Cauty and
> Drummond, 1988, p. 55)

> When a pyramid of synthesizer tones dissolves into a melancholy tune
> right out of 'Trans-Europe Express', it is clear that Juan Atkins, the brains
> behind Cybotron wanted to be taken as white and from Germany, and
> that 'Clear' is meant as an overt homage to the paradigmatically white
> German guys who make up Kraftwerk. (Fink, 2005, p. 353)

> A lot of people today say that techno is the white version of house, but
> that's bullshit. (DJ Laurent Garnier qtd. in James, 2003, p. 28)

Notes

1. *Kraftwerk: We Are The Robots*, BBC Radio 4, broadcast 22 November, 2007, 11.30 a.m.–12 p.m. Presenter – Marc Riley. Producer – Cecile Wright.
2. Interview with Folha de São Paulo, 1998. Available from: http://kraftwerk.technopop. com.br/interview_09.php (last accessed 14 April 2010).
3. Theo Cateforis (2004, pp. 566–8) offers a parallel discussion of robotic dance styles in black, punk and New Wave music in his article on Devo.
4. Nick Prior's article provides a wider extended discussion of 'cyborg singers' who have integrated their voices with new technologies (2009).
5. The black class divisions that shaped early Detroit techno are examined by Sean Albiez (2005, p. 135).

References

Ahearn, C., Fricke, J. and George, N. (2002), *Yes Yes Y'all: The Experience Music Project's Oral History of Hip-Hop*. New York: Da Capo.

Albiez, S. (2005), 'Post-soul futurama: African-American cultural politics and early Detroit techno'. *European Journal of American Culture*, 24, (2), 131–52.

Allinson, E. (1994), 'It's a black thing: hearing how whites can't'. *Cultural Studies*, 8, (3), 438–56.

Bangs, L. (1987), 'Kraftwerkfeature', in L. Bangs, *Psychotic Reactions and Carburetor Dung*. New York: Vintage Books, pp. 154–60.

Bannister, M. (2006), *White Boys, White Noise: Masculinities and 1980s Indie Guitar Rock*. London: Ashgate.

Barr, T. (1998), *Kraftwerk: From Düsseldorf to the Future (with Love)*. London: Ebury Press.

Barton, L. (2008), 'Lost in music'. *Guardian*, 20 February, 23–5.

Biddle, I. (2004), 'Vox electronica: nostalgia, irony and cyborgian vocalities in Kraftwerk's Radioactivitat and Autobahn'. *Twentieth Century Music*, 1, (1), 81–100.

Brewer, C. (Dir.) (2005), *Hustle and Flow*. [DVD]. Paramount Home Entertainment.

Brown, M. (1994), 'Funk music as genre: black aesthetics, apocalyptic thinking and urban protest in post-1965 African-American pop'. *Cultural Studies*, 3, (3), 484–508.

Buskin, R. (2008), 'Africa Bambaataa & the Soulsonic Force: "Planet Rock"'. *Sound on Sound*, November. http://www.soundonsound.com/sos/nov08/articles/classic tracks_1108.htm (last accessed 14 April 2010).

Bussy, P. (2005), *Kraftwerk: Man, Machine, Music*. (3rd edn). London: SAF.

Cateforis, T. (2004), 'Performing the avant-garde: Devo and whiteness in the New Wave'. *American Music*, 22, (4), 564–88.

Cauty, J. and Drummond, B. (1988), *The Manual*. London: Ellipsis.

Cope, J. (1995), *Krautrocksampler: One Head's Guide to the Great Kosmische Musik – 1968 Onwards*. London: Head Heritage.

Dyer, R. (1997), *White*. London: Routledge.

—— (2002 [1979]), 'In defence of disco', in H. Kureishi and J. Savage (eds), *The Faber Book of Pop*. London: Faber & Faber, pp. 518–27.

Eno, B. (2007), 'Kraftwerk: they are the robots'. *Q*, 256, 106.

Eshun, K. (1999), *More Brilliant Than the Sun*. London: Quartet Books.

—— (2006), 'Futurhythmachine: interview with Kodwo Eshun', in A. Bennett, B. Shank and J. Toynbee (eds), *The Popular Music Studies Reader*. London: Routledge, pp. 292–4.

Fink, R. (2005), 'The story of the ORCH5'. *Popular Music*, 23, (4), 339–56.

Flür, W. (2003), *Kraftwerk: I Was a Robot*. London: Sanctuary.

George, N. (1988a), *The Death of Rhythm and Blues*. New York: Plume.

—— (1988b), *Hip-Hop America*. Penguin: London.

Gilroy, P. (1993), *The Black Atlantic: Modernity and the Double-Consciouness*. London: Verso.

Harraway, D. (1999), 'A Cyborg manifesto: science, technology and socialist-feminism in the late twentieth century', in P. Hopkins (ed.), *Sex/Machine: Readings in Culture, Gender and Technology*. Bloomington: Indiana University Press, pp. 434–67.

Huegli, W. (ed.) (2002), *Raw Music Material: Electronic Music DJs Today*. Zurich: Scalo.

James, M. (2003), *French Connections: From Discotheque to Discovery*. London: Sanctuary.

McCord, M. (2007), 'Interstellar transmission: the birth of 'Planet Rock' and its electro repercussions'. *Wax Poetics*, 21, 60–8.

Mercer, K. (1994), *Welcome to the Jungle: New Positions in Black Cultural Studies*. London: Routledge.

Miller, P. [DJ Spooky] (1994), *Rhythm Science*. Massachusetts: MIT Press.

Prior, N. (2009), 'Software sequencers and cyborg singers: popular music in the digital hypermodern'. *New Formations*, 66, 81–9.

Reynolds, S. (2007), *Bring The Noise*. London: Faber & Faber.

—— (2008), *Energy Flash: A Journey Through Rave Music and Dance Culture*. London: Picador.

Robb, J. (1999), *The Nineties: What the F**k Was That All About?* London: Ebury.

Savage, J. (1993), 'Machine soul: a history of techno'. *Village Voice, Rock & Roll Quarterly Insert*, Summer. http://music.hyperreal.org/library/machine_soul.html (last accessed 14 April 2010).

Shapiro, P. (2002), 'Automating the beat', in R. Young (ed.), *Under-Currents: The Hidden Wiring of Modern Music*. London: Continuum.

—— (2005), *Turn the Beat Around: The Secret History of Disco*. London: Faber & Faber.

Sicko, D. (1999), *Techno Rebels: The Renegades of Electronic Funk*. New York: Billboard Books.

Tagg, P. (1989), 'Open letter about "black music", "Afro American music" and "European music"'. *Popular Music*, 8, (3), 285–98.

Toop, D. (1991), *The Rap Attack 2: African Rap to Global Hip-Hop*. London: Serpent's Tail.

Vincent, R. (1995), *Funk: Music, People and the One*. New York: St Martin's Press.

Ward, B. (1998), *Just My Soul Responding: Rhythm and Blues, Black Consciousness and Race Relations*. London: UCL Press.

Ward, E., Stokes, G., and Tucker, K. (eds) (1987), *Rock of Ages: The Rolling Stone History of Rock'n'Roll*. London: Penguin.

Weheliye, A. (2002), '"Feenin": posthuman voices in contemporary black popular music'. *Social Text*, 20, (2), 21–47.

11

Trans-Europa Express: Tracing the Trance Machine

Hillegonda Rietveld

1: Announcement

I'm on my way to Paris, where the idea emerged for Kraftwerk's electronic ode to a new connected Europe, *Trans-Europe Express* (1977). During the last century, the European avant-garde, and in particular the futurists, attempted to prepare for the new millennium by addressing the all-pervasive machine as a source of aesthetic inspiration: noise, electricity and speed were celebrated as signs of human progress (Tomlinson, 2007). And here we are, at the start of the twenty-first century: on the move, in a world filled with electronic sounds. Zooming through Kent, on its way to the tunnel in Dover to take us underneath the Channel, the Eurostar seems almost noiseless compared with the trains of Kraftwerk's 1970s. Instead, fragments of music and sound leak from passenger's mobile devices ('tsh tsh tsh tsh', imitating an imaginary machine, going on and on) providing their own propelling soundtrack to this journey. After 20 minutes of darkness, the high-speed train emerges into the daylight of Normandy, weaving its way through a flowing landscape of fields, farms and villages. Arriving in the blue cool northern light of Gare du Nord, I take an underground train to Gare de Lyon. Bathed in bright south-eastern light, the station's rail tracks seem to stretch into infinity; here, Europe seems endless. Now defunct, rail network Trans Europ Express (T.E.E.) connected the main urban areas of western Europe during the 1960s and 1970s – a symbol for the emerging European Union. *Trans-Europe Express* immortalized this in the form of minimalist pop music, inspiring a new generation of electronic music producers to make sense of a developing post-industrial techno-world based on acceleration and electronics. As Kraftwerk's Ralf Hütter explained to music writer

David Toop, train travel was about '[l]etting yourself go. Sit on the rails and ch-ch-ch-ch-ch. Just keep going. Fade in and fade out . . . In our society everything is in motion. Music is a flowing artform (1992, p. 21).

When *Trans-Europe Express* was re-mastered and released by Kling Klang, Kraftwerk's own record label, in collaboration with Mute Records in 2009, Power (2009) gave it an ecstatic welcome:

> With a ceaselessly mutable quicksilver shimmer, *Trans-Europe Express* is all at once antique, timeless, retro and contemporary. Its status as modern electronic music's birth certificate is well-earned, but its hallowed reputation should never be allowed to disguise its true value and power as a work of art.

There are certainly multiple connections to be made between *Trans-Europe Express* and other cultural and musical forms. This chapter aims to explore these – from avant-garde sonic art to electronic dance music. Throughout this intertextual analysis, the album and the title track will be referred to as *TEE*, the album, and 'TEE', the track.

Released in May 1977, when punk and disco were at their peak and the Eagles's 'Hotel California' (1976) dominated pop radio, *TEE*'s arrival was a relatively quiet affair, without a major advertising campaign. Instead, music films were produced to accompany its tracks (to be used as a backdrop during shows) and music journalists were invited on a train journey. The title track 'TEE', backed by 'Franz Schubert', was released in a 3-minute format on 7" single for at least nine national markets. Also 'Showroom Dummies/Les Mannequins', the third song on the album's A-side, enjoyed 7" and 12" single releases in the UK, US, Canada and Japan.

Various promo-only 12" disco singles appeared in French and US DJ sets. Yet, having witnessed 'TEE' emptying the dance floor of a large Parisian club, Kraftwerk's percussionist Karl Bartos regarded it as a 'flop' at the time of its release (Johnstone, 2008). In the US, and in particular in New York City, 'TEE' fared better; the dance crowd was wooed with a special 'Trans-Metal Express' promo 12" disco single of 5:25 minutes, as well as with a 13:38-minute 12" promo edition that segues 'TEE' with 'Metal to Metal' and offers the album's 9:35-minute opening track, 'Europe Endless', on the flip side. 'TEE' went down well on New York's downtown underground dance floor (Lawrence, 2003). 'TEE' peaked at #119 in the US charts (Bussy, 1993), made it to #67 in the Billboard Hot 100 and was 'disco crossover of the year' on the *Village Voice* critics' poll of 1977 (Christgau, 1978). By 1979, 'TEE' was released by Capitol in 12" format for commercial use in the US. In February 1982, the album was re-released and this time spent seven weeks in the UK music charts, peaking at #49, with the single 'Showroom Dummies' hitting #25 (Warwick, Kutner and Brown, 2004). Also that year, the melody from

TEE's title track was recycled, together with the rhythm of 'Numbers' (1981) by Afrika Bambaataa and the Soulsonic Force on their seminal electro track 'Planet Rock' (1982); this helped introduce the sound of Kraftwerk to an audience of future electro and techno DJ-producers (see Toltz and Duffett in this collection).

Although *TEE* seems to have taken time to cross over from a niche market to a wider audience, it influenced the music of a new generation of electronic musicians; these included Kraftwerk's fellow citizens from Düsseldorf, D.A.F. (Deutsch-Amerikanische Freundschaft) who had work released by Mute Records, as well as North West English bands like Section 25 and New Order who were associated with the Manchester label Factory Records. With such attention in the pioneering dance underground, *TEE*'s combination of avant-garde sound art and pop music means it is widely regarded as a key work in the canon of electronic popular music.

2: Concept album

TEE is a fine example of Kraftwerk's thematic approach to albums. On its first release, Angus McKinnon's (1977) review enthuses, 'Despite its obvious uniformity, *Trans-Europe Express* refuses to sound the same twice. It's mechanistic: it's great' (p. 36). Such 'uniformity' is better understood as conceptual consistency; each track is quite different, but together they interlink in terms of their texture, pace and reflective mood. In this sense, Kraftwerk operate within the context of Western art music. Karl Bartos has underlined this by succinctly stating, 'it is impossible to make music without a strong concept', and music writer Ingeborg Schober suggests:

> [T]he idea is like a film: you start in Paris, you go in a train and you end up in Düsseldorf . . . I think that was the concept, someone was travelling through Europe . . . the European Union, that was a new thing. (Bartos and Schober qtd. in Johnstone, 2008)

'Europe Endless' starts with the anticipation of travelling into Europe, suggesting a wide-open space that is enhanced by electronic choral harmonies on the Vako Orchestron keyboard, suggesting a cathedral (a large, seemingly timeless spiritual space), filled with hope for a future 'Promised Land'.[1] Simultaneously, the lyrics nostalgically refer to pre-war decadence and elegance. In his recent review, Power (2009) states:

> 'Europe Endless' is a utopian hymn to a Europe without borders that has its source in another of Kraftwerk's apparent daydreams: a 20th century without the scar of Nazi Germany scored into Europe's heart.

The album's opening therefore suggests a journey both into the past and the future; it manifests nostalgia for a pre-war sense of the future that seemed to have been lost.

The subsequent tracks, 'The Hall of Mirrors' and 'Showroom Dummies', are pure electro-pop, reflecting on the simulated existence of the poseur, such as performing musicians in a mediated world. The second side of the album returns to the opening theme with 'TEE' and 'Metal to Metal', this time utilizing the Vako Orchestron to create moody cello harmonies. Fink's musicological analysis (2005) demonstrates that, by this stage, the album's initial optimism seems to have gone. He interprets this as a nostalgic longing for an older, lost, classical Europe. However, both Bartos and Schober have emphasized that the European Union was much in the popular imagination during the development of the *TEE* concept (Johnstone, 2008). The actual TEE train network was the material symbol and embodiment of a new, hopeful, post-war European mobility. Therefore, I wish to argue for a different interpretation, in which 'TEE' and 'Metal on Metal' embrace the motion of the train and its materiality, enabling an immersion in the machine trip.

'TEE' is placed halfway along the album's conceptual train journey; the experience of machine-trance intensifies, further enhanced by 'Metal on Metal'. The last part of this track is entitled 'Abzug' ['Departure'] on the German version of the album – wordplay that would not work outside of the German language; it indicates the end of a long journey, a departure from the TEE, while 'zug' means 'train' in German. The words 'Trans-Europe Express' are repeated in a monotonous voice, as a trance-inducing mantra that seems to call up the 'spirit' of the TEE and everything it may signify, such as a seemingly endless journey through multifaceted Europe and, importantly, the *motorik* of the machine. The cyborgian merging of man-machine is an experience of temporary ego loss, which in some cases may create a sense of *jouissance* (Rietveld, 2004). Such a deep sense of loss is at once a liberating and a melancholic, even a nostalgic, experience. For New York, the promo disc with 'Europe Endless' on one side and 'TEE' with 'Metal on Metal' on the other was well chosen; there, the underground disco DJ would take dancers on a musical journey (Fikentscher, 2000), until they lost track of daily time and space in the trance-inducing dance groove. In an interview with Tim Lawrence (2003), Jorge La Torre remembers in 1977 experiencing a sense of spirituality at a gay club:

> The music was becoming more electronic, more beat-driven, and more tribal . . . It allowed your mind to travel. If you don't have vocals to anchor you to the dance floor it's easier for your mind to go to a different place. (p. 286)

The instrumental 'Franz Schubert' follows this epic train section. Its title refers to the nineteenth-century Viennese composer who, according to Wolfgang Flür (2005), emphasizes the album's 'German romanticism and melancholy' (p. 137). The sequence programming and meandering string melody (without the drive of the previous tracks and without percussive instruments) seems to indicate a moment of relaxation, at home after a long journey. This is completed with a 'coda' that revisits the main conceptual theme of the album: 'endless-ss-ss-ss, endlessness-ss-ss . . .' When the CD version of the album is looped, this final track merges seamlessly back into 'Europe Endless', confirming that the album was conceived as an infinite journey.

3: European connections

During 1975, Kraftwerk toured the US: in 1976 they promoted their album *Radio-Activity* with a series of concerts in France and the UK. The experience of travelling abroad made them realize that they were inherently European. This insight shaped the ideas for tracks like 'Europe Endless' and 'TEE', which were performed during their London gig in 1976 (Barr, 1998). Flür (2005) has pointed out that the actual idea and title for *Trans-Europe Express* emerged in Paris, a quintessential European capital that Ralf Hütter and Florian Schneider particularly enjoyed visiting for socializing purposes. With their French record company rep and friend, Maxime Schmitt, they met with journalist Paul Alessandrini and his wife, Marjorie, for a meal at elegant railway restaurant Le Train Bleu. In an interview with Bussy (1993), Alessandrini remembers saying:

> With the kind of music you do, which is kind of like an electronic blues, railway stations and trains are very important in your universe, you should do a song about the Trans Europe Express. (p. 86)

Did the name of the restaurant, Le Train Bleu, produce this somewhat crude and Euro-centric suggestion? The restaurant is situated on the first floor of Gare de Lyon, overlooking the platform and rail tracks, its two curving stairways cascading down, wrapping themselves around the bistro's terrace. At Le Train Bleu one could miss one's train – the atmosphere can feel as though time has stood still since the start of the twentieth century. Designed in 1900, this establishment oozes pre-war decadence. It was built when train travel seemed a luxury. It still features an opulent decorative style, including pastel and gold wall paintings, plus a formal table service that provides separate glasses for different wines to compliment each course. Here, Europe seems indeed timeless, elegant and decadent.

Karl Bartos has pointed out on several occasions that although Kraftwerk liked R&B, and incorporated its beats, their music was significantly different due to their educational and cultural background (Johnstone, 2008; Doran, 2009). The European bourgeois avant-garde have embraced the machine aesthetic since the early twentieth century, and Kraftwerk have taken important cues from this. Arthur Honegger's 1923 impressionist symphony, *Pacific 231*, is an important example: an orchestra imitates and suggests the sonic journey of a locomotive, utilizing brass, strings and drums. In an interview with John Doran (2009), Bartos explains in more detail the importance of identity in this sonic approach:

> We all felt that Germany's cultural heritage was very strong in the 1920s . . . We had the Bauhaus school before the war and then after the war we had tremendous people like Karlheinz Stockhausen and the development of the classical and the electronic classical. This . . . all happened very close to Düsseldorf in Cologne and all the great composers at that time came there . . . people like John Cage, Pierre Boulez and Pierre Schaeffer and they all had this fantastic approach to modern music and we felt it would make more sense to see Kraftwerk as part of that tradition more than anything else.

This statement explains the nostalgia for the future in Kraftwerk's music and imagery; they wished to pick up the conceptual tradition from before the devastation of World War II and work it into a sound for the future.

During his time with Kraftwerk, between 1975 and 1990, Bartos indicates that images were often used for conceptual inspiration; for this purpose, pictures were stuck around their Kling Klang studio (Johnstone, 2008). Such sensitivity to visuals also led to experimentation with film as backdrop for their performances. The accompanying film for 'TEE', emphasizes the movement of the train along its *Bundesbahn* (German railway) tracks, in dated, grainy black-and-white. Kraftwerk's four members are shown in pleasant conversation inside a six-seat train compartment, suited and groomed, the image of a comfortable (pre-war) European bourgeois elite. Günther Fröhling, the director of the film,

> built a futuristic landscape in his studio with miniature skyscrapers and other buildings, reminiscent of Fritz Lang's film *Metropolis*. Florian (Schneider) was even able to buy a functioning model of one of the streamlined, propeller-driven trains that had been developed by the Nazis from a nearby toy shop, a rarity on the toy market. (Flür, 2005, p. 135).

Metropolis (1927) is a central example of expressionism, an art movement that re-presented an encroaching machine world as an aestheticized 'other', needing to be tamed (Huyssen, 1986). The appropriation of this cinematic image allows 'TEE' to journey between contemporary and pre-war Europe. Before World War II, the art worlds of Paris and Berlin were connected by a series of avant-garde movements that shared a mix of hope and anxiety for a modernized, technologically progressive, future. This was before the trauma of the Nazi-inspired occupation of Europe. As Hütter explains to Sinker (Sinker and Barr, 1996):

> [W]hat we were very much considering was the simultaneity of past, present and future today. I think visions and memories synchronise together, and I think certain things from a little way back look more towards the future than things that are pseudo-modern today. (p. 96)

The appropriation of the past through visuals can, at the same time, be understood in the context of Warhol's pop art and situationism (which proved influential for punk progenitors such as Malcolm McLaren), in which strong iconoclastic images were constructed by recontextualizing mundane media materials. Various versions of *TEE*'s sleeve design show idealized portraits of the members of Kraftwerk, in suits and short hair, gazing beyond the horizon like performing stars from the 1940s. Inside the original sleeve of *TEE*, the band is shown in a pastoral scene, in suits and sitting stiffly upright by a little table with a red-and-white check table-cloth, dressed as bourgeois gentlemen and sporting enigmatic smiles. On first impression such imagery may seem in puzzling contradiction to the forward-thinking music the album contains, but according to Wolfgang Flür (2005) this carefully posed photograph 'was pure irony, and a counterpoint to the tousled image of the punk scene that was then emerging' (p. 133). In that sense, these photographs point to conceptual artists Gilbert and George, who in their artwork pose stiffly in traditional suits. This visual language also differentiates Kraftwerk from their German contemporaries such as Can, Tangerine Dream and Klaus Schulze; it seemed as though the hippy counterculture and the psychedelic music scene with which the band had dabbled in the past had never existed. Kraftwerk did not try to be hip – instead, they presented their faces as paradoxically faceless. As such, they created a unique image, which excited the curiosity of fans and critics and also focused attention on their brand of electronic music.

4: Train *motorik*

When 'TEE' glides seamlessly into 'Metal on Metal' the synthesized Doppler-shift of a speeding train pans through the speakers. The listener is immersed in a post-industrial fantasy of movement and acceleration. At the time of its first release, Angus McKinnon (1977) noted that 'the album's second side features an earth moving rhythm track surreptitiously similar to the one

Can pulsed through' (p. 36), comparing it with 'Halleluhwah' on Can's 1971 *Tago Mago* album. However, the more disciplined insistent *motorik* beat that is associated with Krautrock was introduced in the early 1970s by German drummer Klaus Dinger, a founding member of Düsseldorf-based rock band Neu! (and a member of Kraftwerk) (Reynolds, 2000). McKinnon (1977) also referred to David Bowie, stating about 'TEE' that it offers 'a mesmerically hypersensitive beat, a stripped down version of Bowie's 'Station to Station' *motorik*' (p. 36).

Kraftwerk had explored a similar *motorik* concept in 'Kling Klang' on *Kraftwerk 2* (1972); this features a looped electronic drum sequence with additional colouring for musical texture. A more conceptual celebration of speed, mobility and the modern machine was achieved several years later, in the track 'Autobahn' (1974), a simulated car journey along the German motorway system, which was one of Germany's pre-war achievements (see Albiez and Lindvig in this collection). *TEE* took this musical format further to celebrate the new Europe as a feeling, hypnotizing the listener with its electronic *motorik* into a mild state of immersed trance-like infinity: 'Europe endless . . . Life is timeless'. The track 'TEE' sounded somewhat different than the usual, straightforward 4/4 *motorik*. Rather than pounding on the 4/4 beat, 'TEE' offers a more subtle rhythm, inspired by the sound of train wheels hitting the connections between the rails.

Hütter places Kraftwerk's production work squarely within the context of a sonic art continuum that started with Russolo's famous 1913 futurist manifesto, 'The art of noises' (1973), by stating in an interview with Mark Sinker (Sinker and Barr, 1996) that 'music is just organised noise' (p. 98). Bartos points out to Doran (2009) that:

> by using the train motif we were following the path of someone like Pierre Schaeffer who made the first piece of musique concrète by only using the sounds of trains. That was in our mind.

Sound artist Pierre Schaeffer famously cut up tape to dislocate sounds, and to convey their concrete materiality. In 1948, when magnetic tape was a new medium, his first sound piece was an edited set of recordings of trains passing across rails, called 'Etude aux Chemins de Fer' or 'Railroad Study'. Although 'TEE' has onomatopoeic features, Bartos points out that this track is more metaphorical than literal:

> Eventually we went to train bridges and were listening to the sound the train would actually produce and by using the final rhythm it was just a little faint because a train doesn't actually sound like this! Because on a train you have two wheels and then the next wagon is starting with another two wheels and if you cross the gap on the rails it makes the

sound 'da-dum-da-dum Da-dum-da-dum' but of course you wouldn't
be able to dance to that! So we changed it slightly. (Doran, 2009)

They squeezed the rhythm of the train into a 4/4 beat. The result is a strong
propulsive groove, a *motorik* with a heartbeat-like rhythm that sounds quite
similar to an R&B soul beat. In Bartos's words, 'It's not right, but it's a damn
good beat, actually' (Johnstone, 2008).

The continuous beat of the *motorik* was part of an investigation of the
relationship between man and machine within German electronic rock.
This rhythmic approach was further enhanced by the arpeggios that could
be programmed onto the Synthanorma Sequencer. This electronic music
instrument can be heard in the recordings of Klaus Schulze and Tangerine
Dream, where an occasional involuntary pitch wobble can be noticed because
analogue electronic instruments are sensitive to temperature shifts. Kraftwerk
had one of these electronic 16-track devices customized to achieve a more
precise machine rhythm for *TEE*. Wolfgang Flür added materiality to this
machine-generated loop in 'Metal on Metal' by hammering on metal sheets
(Flür, 2005). On *Minimum–Maximum* (Hütter and Schneider, 2005) the
background film for this track shows the clashing of metal train bumpers.
As the electrified information society unfolds, such metallic clanging is the
echo of an industrial memory. Through precise repetition, an eternal sense
of now is produced, making it possible to experience the past and the future
simultaneously.

5: Electronic blues?

It may be argued that the identity of Kraftwerk was deterritorialized, (a term
taken from Albiez's [2005] study of Detroit techno). Kraftwerk's electro-
acoustic soundscapes responded to a (post-)industrial social experience that
affected societies beyond the Ruhrgebied, Germany and western Europe. In
that sense, their work engaged in a trans-Atlantic musical dialogue during
the 1970s. In this context, Alessandrini's suggestion – to create 'electronic
blues' (Bussy, 1993, p. 86) – seems to make sense; Kraftwerk's percussionist
Flür (2005) boldly subtitles a book chapter that addresses the creation of
TEE, 'The Electro Blues Starts in Paris'. Nevertheless, Fink (2005) bluntly
critiques the notion of electronic blues as 'patently silly, even offensive'
(p. 345). It would indeed seem 'silly' to think that Kraftwerk would exclu-
sively have brought electronica to blues, as this had already occurred in the
US, not least in the realm of funk, while producer Giorgio Moroder was
taking parallel steps to produce electronic disco. In the idea of 'electronic
blues', the notion of 'blues' seems to refer to a pre-war (World War II)
relationship between American popular music and the experience of the
train, while 'electronic' seems to suggest an adaptation to a contemporary,

1970s, European experience. In this, a binary opposition seems to be set up which aligns Europe with electronica and blues with acoustic instruments; a deeper reading within a post-colonial configuration of racial politics could produce a racialized interpretation that mistakenly presents 'black music' as acoustic and 'white music' as electronic. However, in this discussion, 'electro blues' indicates the relationship between the train (as trope of modern experience) and the development of electronic dance music, in the specific context of Kraftwerk's *TEE*.

Music writer Peter Shapiro (2005) observes that '[t]he rhythm of life in most of America was created by the rail road, and pre-war blues and country records were often little more than imitations of the locomotive' (p. 83). A good example is the bluegrass standard 'Orange Blossom Special', Ervin Rouse's ode to the luxury train between New York and Miami made famous by Euro-American Bill Monroe (1939). This is a virtuoso fiddle tune with a chugging, hard-driving rhythm that in its various versions has also been led by harmonica, banjo or guitar (see also Carter, 2006). In 1979, German singer Gunter Gabriel released 'Rheingold-Trans-Europa (Orange Blossom Special)' (1979), an adapted hybrid of 'the Special' with German *Schlager*-styled vocal harmonies that proudly compares the 'Rheingold' train (on the Amsterdam to Geneva TEE route) to the old East American Special. Elsewhere, another track that seems to have brought the memory of pre-war American train tunes to the European popular imagination during the 1970s is Keith Emerson's 'Honky Tonk Train Blues' (1976), which hit the charts during the same year that Kraftwerk developed their *TEE* concept and had their alleged epiphany at Le Train Bleu. Coincidentally, also in 1976, Gunter Gabriel's country-flavoured *Schlager* 'Intercity Line Nr 4' (1976) was popular on German radio.

Kraftwerk's conceptual work was in many ways far removed from these forms of locally successful popular music. However, Flür (2005) remembers that Kraftwerk enjoyed partying to R&B dance music that included tightly performed funk, such as James Brown's 'Sex Machine' (1970). Although the story of funk is complex (Ward, 1998; Lawrence, 2003) its formation was partly inspired by the work of R&B guitarist Bo Diddley. In the mid fifties Diddley introduced an influential R&B guitar rhythm in the self-named track 'Bo Diddley' (1958), of which Shapiro comments, 'Everything, including the guitar which imitated both wheels on a track and a steam engine going through a tunnel, was in the service of the beat' (2005, p. 84). Diddley's later work seems to strongly relate to repetitive machine rhythms, such as the raw flanging metallic staccato introduction to 'Bo's Bounce' (1962) that sounds, in the context of this discussion, like the fast and furious approach of a train. Diddley's rhythm guitar, occasionally enhanced by the semiquavers of maracas, may perhaps be understood as a prototype for the driving beats in rock, funk and disco. Even the title of R&B-based television series *Soul Train*, at its height of popularity in the US during the 1970s and 1980s, seems to indicate the cultural importance of the train machine groove in American dance music. Would this, partially at least, explain the positive reception of Kraftwerk's 'TEE' on New York's underground dance floor?

6: DJ culture

In April 1977, when a promo 12" of 'TEE' was distributed among a select group of disco DJs, Vince Aletti, New York's underground disco chronicler for DJ magazine *Record World*, commented

> 'Trans-Europe Express'/'Metal on Metal', two tracks that run together to form one spectacular 13:32 composition much more metallic and menacing in feeling than 'Europe Endless'. It's a stylized version of the sound of a train speeding along a track like Resonance's 'Yellow Train' fed through a computer, broken down and put together again – very relentless. Not exactly light entertainment, but quite incredible, especially on a powerful system. Highly recommended for freaky crowds, otherwise a little too off-the-wall. (2009, p. 286)

'Yellow Train' (1973), a B-side by Résonance, is based on a train line (Train Jaune) in the Pyrenees Mountains. This 2.5-minute soundscape is created from field recordings of running trains and combined with insistent drumming; the result was squeezed through a psychedelic flanging Doppler effect. By comparison, 'TEE' features the processed sound of electronic drums, suggesting the rhythm of a train running along its tracks; the looping rhythm hurls itself forward in ongoing repetition, propelling the listener forward, in a machine trance. An obscure 7" in New York, 'Yellow Train' was popular on the dance floor of Mancuso's Loft. According to Lawrence (2003) this friendly music-focused dance club hosted local gatekeepers of the cultural capital of NYC's underground disco world, such as DJs and club promoters, who gathered to relax and catch up after their evening shifts in other local dance clubs. Importantly, Mancuso organized one of the early disco record pools that sent promotional records out to specific DJs, who in turn shaped the musical context for dancers. From this, we may conclude that New York's disco underground has been instrumental in putting 'TEE' on the dance cultural map.

'TEE' was received with enthusiasm by the New York clubbing in-crowd, where leading dance DJs (re)contextualized the 'TEE' rhythm with the funk groove of R&B disco selections. Some underground DJs would take their dancers on a spiritual journey, which required lengthy musical workouts with repetitive beats. 'Europe Endless', 'TEE' and 'Metal on Metal' would have suited such tranced-out disco dance experiences. The only possible restraint was the length of the 12" vinyl record, but with a reliable constant beat, two copies could be mixed by the DJ. Ralf Hütter spoke of his surprise when

> somebody took me to a club . . . when *Trans-Europe Express* was out. It was some loft club in New York – after hours – just as DJ culture was beginning; when DJ's began making their own records, their own grooves. They took sections from 'Metal to Metal' . . . and when I went in it was going 'boom-crash-boom-crash', so I thought 'oh, they're playing the new album'. But it went on for ten minutes! And I thought 'what's happening?' That track is only something like two or three minutes. And later I went to ask the DJ, and he had two copies of the record and he was mixing the two. . . . This was real development, because in those days you fixed a certain time on the record (under twenty minutes a side) in order to the print into vinyl. It was a technological decision to say how long the song would last. We always used to play different timings live, but there we were in this after-hours club, and it was ten minutes, twenty minutes of the recording, because the vibe was there. (Sinker and Barr, 1996, p. 101)

In this way, the DJ could maintain and enhance a specific feeling that a component of a recording may contain. This is where the practice of break mixing stems from: DJs could take the instrumental break of a record and repeat it, in principle, endlessly. The arrival of affordable drum machines in the 1980s, such as the Roland TR-808, eventually made this creative practice even easier, as a rhythm break could be programmed into the machine and extracts of recordings would be played on top of this. Such creative DJ practices eventually gave rise to genres such as electro in New York and house music in Chicago.

'TEE' also gained popularity beyond the exclusive downtown clubs of Manhattan. As Afrika Bambaataa told David Toop,

> Kraftwerk – I don't think they even knew how big they were among the black masses in '77 when they came out with 'Trans-Europe Express'. When that came out I thought that was one of the weirdest records I ever heard in my life. (Toop, 1984, p. 130)

'Weird' meant that 'TEE' offered a refreshing new musical direction in terms of sound and structure. According to Brewster and Broughton (2006), Bambaataa overlaid 'TEE'/'Metal on Metal' with Malcolm X speeches, while his DJ peer Grandmaster Flash put on the 13-minute track 'when he needed a toilet break' (p. 264). Producer Arthur Baker remembers that, in the early 1980s, 'I'd sit in the park and there'd be guys with a big beat-box break dancing to it. I used to hear it all over' (p. 265). In February 1982,

'TEE' was re-released; later in that same year, Afrika Bambaataa & the Soulsonic Force and Arthur Baker created the seminal electro rap release 'Planet Rock' (1982). The distinctive melody of 'TEE' was recreated by John Robie on top of the drum pattern of 'Numbers' (1981). Created several years after 'TEE', its rhythm seems even funkier than the one in 'TEE', especially when it is heard as part of 'Planet Rock' in which the Roland TR-808 drum machine boosts the bass. According to Fink (2005), distinctive orchestral samples, minor-key ORCH5, rhythmically stabbed on a Fairlight computer synthesizer, added to the ghostly memory trace of European classical music invoked by the melody line from 'TEE'. The result is a science-fiction themed breakdance electro-funk, a black futurist *Star Wars* fantasy in which, as Fink (2005) argues, 'it is European art music that is cast, consciously or not, in the role of ancient, alien power source' (p. 352). On a more pragmatic note, according to Brewster and Broughton (2006), for Bambaataa this cultural mix was a way to 'grab the black market and the punk rock market' (p. 265), a mixed demographic that, at the time, gathered in New York's Roxy club, a huge roller disco that doubled as a dance club. Similar to 'TEE', 'Planet Rock' was not a major chart success outside specialist dance charts at the time. However, it is now widely regarded as a key moment in the development of electro, from which followed new electronic genres, such as electro-funk, Latino freestyle and Miami Bass (see Toltz and Duffett in this collection).

7: 'Abzug'

There are further electronic dance music outcomes from the meeting point between new-world 'Planet Rock' and old-world 'TEE', beyond the frequent sampling of these two tracks by rap and R&B artists (for example, Emanon's 'Lady L Meets Emanon' [1986]; 113's 'Ouais Gros' [1999]). In Detroit, Cybotron created 'Clear' (1983), a proto-techno track that adapts sequences and string harmonies from 'TEE'. The programming of the Roland TR-808 drum machine offers a variation of 'Planet Rock', creating a funky ongoing dance groove. Its monotone vocal dryly states the computer instruction 'clear', sounding as humanly distant and abstract as the repeated words in Kraftwerk's 'TEE' and 'Abzug'. Juan Atkins, its co-creator, combined in this track his interest in New York's electro-funk and Kraftwerk; he was further inspired by British electro-pop and especially by funk, in particular the electronic funk of Detroit's Parliament/Funkadelic. He subsequently became an important creative force in the formation of Detroit techno (Savage, 1996; Trask, 1996; Sicko, 1999). Detroit techno took additional influences from the electronic disco beat of Chicago house music. The latter dance scene, in turn, was familiar with 'TEE' as musical connections were made with New York's underground dance scene, via DJ Frankie Knuckles (Collin, 1997;

Rietveld, 1998; Reynolds, 2000; Bidder, 2001). Juan Atkins, as well as his techno colleague Kevin Saunderson, made trips to the underground dance scene in New York (Garratt, 1998). Saunderson also organized some dance parties in Chicago during the 1980s with his friend, Derrick May. In turn, May, released 'Strings of Life' under the pseudonym 'Rhythim Is Rhythim (1987), an electronic dance track that bases its rhythm programming on house music of its time while, as musicologist Fink (2005) argues, its string sections seem to refer to the European melancholy of 'TEE'. In 1995, Carl Craig's 'Mind of a Machine' recreates the mood of 'TEE' suggesting a train rhythm with snare-like white noise and a string-pad-generated monophonic melody line. Of interest here is that although Detroit techno is certainly given a sense of place, like Kraftwerk's self-conscious location in Düsseldorf, the music itself seems deterritorialized through the complex processes of cross-Atlantic musical dialogue (Albiez, 2005).

At the start of the twenty-first century the electro-clash scene made reference to electro's punk connections through a revival of 1980s electronic pop that is indebted to the influence of *TEE*, the album. For many of those electronic musicians in the British post-punk generation, Kraftwerk's sound was a major influence. Listening to bands on Mute Records, such as Depeche Mode or Fad Gadget, one hears links with 'The Hall of Mirrors' and 'Showroom Dummies', in terms of texture, pace and structure, as well as their sense of cynicism.[2] In 1983, Arthur Baker produced the track 'Confusion' by the British band New Order, who had embraced electronic instruments as soon as they became reasonably affordable. Notably, New Order's Bernard Sumner produced 'Looking from a Hilltop' by Section 25 (1984); with its repetitive sequences, string harmonies in epic melancholic tonality (Fink, 2005) and sound effects[3] this seems the rightful British post-punk follow up of 'TEE', wrapped in a warped, spacey electro coating.

Back in Germany, electronic post-punk had superseded cosmic Krautrock, as well as the electronic Eurodisco of Giorgio Moroder. In Frankfurt, Talla 2XL coined the term 'Techno' in the early eighties in the record shop where he worked, to file the new electronic sound as 'music created technologically', such as 'New Order, Depeche Mode, Kraftwerk, Heaven 17, then later Front 242' (Sextro and Wick, 2008). In 1984, Talla and Alex Azary opened the Techno Club, which hosted the electronic music of the post-punk generation for a devoted, mostly male, techno-punk crowd. A stripped-down electronic version of the *motorik* can be heard in the 1980s sound of the Neue Deutsche Welle (groups such as Nitzer Ebb and D.A.F.) and industrial electronic body music (such as Belgian Front 242). Eventually, the Techno Club moved to Dorian Gray. In this Frankfurt-based music scene, DJ Dag and DJ Sven Väth matured, eventually combining hard-hitting electronic *motorik* with Chicago acid house and Detroit techno to produce hard house and, by 1991, the trance aesthetic. Like a relentless digital machine, averaging a speed of 145 bpm, trance moves along a 4/4 kick drum and regular semiquaver electronic sequences.

Trance tends to take dancers on a trip to nowhere in particular. In the words of Reynolds (1998), 'Trance is trippy, in both the LSD and motorik senses of the word, evoking frictionless trajectories of video-games, virtual reality . . . hurtling through cyber space' (p. 184). Alongside 'Metal on Metal' and 'Europe Endless', 'TEE' hurtles the dancer into an accelerated machine journey. The self-defining trance compilation, *Trance Europe Express* (1993), recognizes this link in its very title, introducing the electronic production work of techno artists such as Orbital, Moby, Total Eclipse and CB Bolland. These artists share a disco-punk machine aesthetic that the sardonic editorial in the accompanying booklet calls 'tuneless efforts – which, to be frank, it is hard to imagine the milkman whistling' (Mead, 1993, p. 9). By comparison the machine-driven minimalism of 'TEE' is succinctly melodic and even wistfully Romantic, with a memorable melody line that, in fact, makes it an excellent pop dance record. In 2004, Dutch DJ Tiësto famously DJ-ed a trance set at the opening ceremony of the 2004 Olympics in Athens, in which trance functioned as an energized soundtrack to a transnational 'non-place' (Augé, 1995), offering a sonic space rather than a specific recognizable sense of place. Although the *motorik* and post-industrial sentiments of 'TEE' can be related to as abstracted trance-entities, it is exactly this melody that returns it to a sense of place, to Europe, and even back to Germany, where the ghost of Franz Schubert awaits the wary traveller.

8: Endless endless

Throughout the late twentieth and early twenty-first centuries, the complexity of musical connections has intensified through global cultural networks that link electronic dance music activities across nodes of cosmopolitan activity. 'TEE' has become part of the gene pool of electronic dance music, a musical memory trace of an immersive electronic journey through the landscape of a 'brave new world'. Yet, as music histories are narrated and re-narrated, *TEE* and its title track in particular have gained a hallowed status in the canon of electronic (dance) music, due to a combination of factors. First, its considered conceptual approach to an electronic journey has led to a reformatting of music; as a result, it has gained a loyal following. Second, although *TEE* sounds treacherously minimalist in its execution, its thoughtful use of a wide range of influences, from avant-garde sound art and Romantic music to pop songs and front-line funk, have given it a huge crossover potential among a variety of pioneering music scenes. In this way, Kraftwerk reached art school punks, streetwise electro DJs, Krautrock fans and Detroit techno producers. Third, 'TEE's popularity with the gatekeepers of New York underground disco has planted it firmly within the chronicles of dance music – of *electronic* dance music, that is.

Notes

1. The Old Testament theme of the 'Promised Land' is referenced in African-American gospel songs, and finds its way into secular music through soul and house, to express the hope for freedom from slavery. Here it is adapted to signify hope for a new Europe, free from border restrictions.

2. As a critical cultural theorist, I refrain from a technical, musicologically correct, analysis in support of this assertion.

3. Roland Barthes (1977) has eloquently argued that language to effectively describe the affective qualities of sonic performances is reputedly slippery.

References

Albiez, S. (2005), 'Post soul futurama: African American cultural politics and early Detroit techno'. *European Journal of American Culture*, 24, (2), 131–52.

Aletti, V. (2009), *The Disco Files 1973–78: New York's Underground, Week by Week. The Records, the Charts, the Stories*. London: DJhistory.com.

Augé, M. (1995), *Non-Places: Introduction to an Anthropology of Supermodernity*. London: Verso.

Barr, T. (1998), *Kraftwerk: From Düsseldorf to the Future (with Love)*. London: Ebury Press.

Barthes, R. (1977), 'The grain of the voice', in *Image, Music, Text*. London: Fontana.

Bidder, S. (2001), *Pump Up the Volume*. London: Channel 4 Books/Macmillan.

Brewster, B. and Broughton, F. (2006), *Last Night a DJ Saved My Life: The History of the Disc Jockey*. London: Headline.

Bussy, P (1993), *Kraftwerk: Man Machine and Music*. (1st edn). London: SAF.

Carter, B. (2006), *The Orange Blossom Special*. New York: Dell.

Christgau, R. (1978), 'Pazz & joppers dig Pistols – what else is new? The fourth (or fifth) annual pazz & jop critics' poll'. *Village Voice*, 23 January. http://www.robertchristgau.com/xg/pnj/pj77.php (last accessed 23 February 2010).

Collin, M. (1997), *Altered State: The Story of Ecstasy Culture and Acid House*. London: Serpent's Tail.

Doran, J. (2009), 'Karl Bartos interview: Kraftwerk and the birth of the modern'. *The Quietus*, 11 March. http://thequietus.com/articles/01282-karl-bartos-interviewed-kraftwerk-and-the-birth-of-the-modern (last accessed 20 February 2010).

Fink, R. (2005), 'The story of ORCH5, or, the classical ghost in the hip-hop machine'. *Popular Music*, 24, (3), 339–56.

Fikentscher, K. (2000), *"You Better Work": Underground Dance Music in New York City*. Hanover and London: Wesleyan University Press.

Flür, W. (2005), *Kraftwerk: I Was a Robot*. London: Sanctuary.

Garratt, S. (1998), *Adventures in Wonderland: A Decade of Club Culture*. London: Headline Book Publishing.

Hütter, R. and Schneider, F. (Prods/Dirs) (2005), *Kraftwerk: Minimum–Maximum*. [DVD]. 336 2949. Kling Klang/EMI.

Huyssen, A. (1986), 'The vamp and the machine', in *After The Great Divide: Modernism, Mass Culture and Postmodernism*. Basingstoke and London: Macmillan Press.

Johnstone, R. (Exec. Prod.) (2008), *Kraftwerk and the Electronic Revolution*. [DVD]. SIDVD541. Sexy Intellectual.

Lang, F. (Dir. 1927/2003), *Metropolis*. EKA40061. Eureka! Entertainment.

Lawrence, T. (2003), *Loves Saves the Day: A History of American Dance Music Culture 1970–1979*. Durham and London: Duke University Press.

McKinnon, A. (1977), 'Review, TEE'. *New Musical Express*, 28 May, 36.

Mead, H. (1993), 'Editorial'. *Trance Europe Express*, TEEX CD1, p. 9.

Power, C. (2009) 'Trans-Europe Express'. *Drowned in Sound*, 13 October. http://drownedinsound.com/releases/14730/reviews/4138106 (last accessed 14 April 2010).

Reynolds, S. (1998), *Energy Flash: A Journey Through Rave Music and Dance Culture*. London: Macmillan.

—— (2000), 'Kosmik dance: krautrock and its legacy' in P. Shapiro (ed.) *Modulations: a History of Electronic Music: Throbbing Words on Sound*. New York: Distributed Art Publishers/Caiprinha Productions.

Rietveld, H. C. (1998), *This Is Our House: House Music, Technologies and Cultural Spaces*. Aldershot: Ashgate.

—— (2004), 'Ephemeral spirit: sacrificial cyborg and communal soul', in G. St John (ed.), *Rave and Religion*. New York: Routledge.

Russolo, L. (1973), 'The art of noises (1913)' in U. Apollonio (ed.), *Futurist Manifestos*. London: Thames & Hudson.

Savage, J. (1996), 'Machine soul: a history of techno', in *Time Travel: From The Sex Pistols to Nirvana: Pop, Media and Sexuality, 1977–96*. London: Chatto & Windsus.

Sextro, M. and Wick, H. (Dir. 2008), *We Call It Techno: A Documentary About Germany's Early Techno Scene and Culture*. [DVD]. SES-DVD-002. Sense Music & Media, Media Atelier. Germany.

Shapiro, P. (2005), *Turn the Beat Around: The Secret History of Disco*. London: Faber & Faber.

Sicko, D. (1999), *Techno Rebels: The Renegades of Electronic Funk*, New York: Billboard.

Sinker, M. and Barr, T. (1996), 'Electro kinetik' in C. Kempster (ed.), *History of House*. London: Sanctuary.

Tomlinson, J. (2007), *The Culture of Speed: The Coming of Immediacy*. London: Sage.

Toop, D. (1984), *The Rap Attack: African Jive to New York Hip Hop*. London: Pluto Records.

—— (1992), 'Throbbery with intent'. *The Wire*, no. 98, April, London, pp. 20–5.

Trask, S. (1996), 'Future shock', in C. Kempster (ed.), *History of House*. London: Sanctuary.

Ward, B. (1998), *Just My Soul Responding: Rhythm and Blues, Black Consciousness and Race Relations*. London: UCL Press.

Warwick, N., Kutner, J. and Brown, T. (2004), *The Complete Book of the British Charts: Singles and Albums*. London: Omnibus Press.

Discography

The following list features Hütter and Schneider's/Kraftwerk's major releases between 1970 and 2009 (the original release date is followed by details of current releases – there are no official re-releases of *Kraftwerk, Kraftwerk 2* and *Ralf and Florian*).

Organisation (1970). Tone Float. SF8111. RCA Victor. UK.
1. Tone Float / 2. Milk Rock / 3. Silver Forest / 4. Rhythm Salad / 5. Noitasinagro

Kraftwerk (1970). 6305 058. Philips.
1. Ruckzuck / 2. Stratovarius / 3. Megaherz / 4. Von Himmel Hoch

Kraftwerk 2 (1971). 6305 117. Philips.
1. Klingklang / 2. Atem / 3. Strom / 4. Spule 4 / 5. Wellenlänge / 6. Harmonika

Ralf and Florian (1973). 6305 197. Philips.
1. Elektrisches Roulette / 2. Tongebirge / 3. Kristallo / 4. Heimatklänge / 5. Tanzmusik /
    6. Ananas Symphonie

Autobahn (1974/2009). 50999 6 99586 1 8. Mute / Kling Klang.
1. Autobahn / 2. Kometenmelodie 1 / 3. Kometenmelodie 2 / 4. Mitternacht /
    5. Morgenspaziergang

Radio-Activity (1975/2009). 50999 9 66019 2 1. Mute / Kling Klang.
1. Geiger Counter / 2. Radioactivity / 3. Radioland / 4. Airwaves / 5. Intermission /
    6. News / 7. The Voice of Energy / 8. Antenna / 9. Radio Stars / 10. Uranium /
    11. Transistor / 12. Ohm Sweet Ohm

Trans-Europe Express (1977/2009). 50999 9 66020 2 7. Mute / Kling Klang.
1. Europe Endless / 2. The Hall of Mirrors / 3. Showroom Dummies / 4. Trans-Europe
    Express / 5. Metal on Metal / 6. Franz Schubert / 7. Endless Endless

The Man-Machine (1978/2009). 50999 9 66022 2 5. Mute / Klingklang.

1. The Robots / 2. Spacelab / 3. Metropolis / 4. The Model / 5. Neon Lights / 6. The Man-Machine

Computer World (1981/2009). 50999 9 66023 2 4. Mute / Kling Klang.
1. Computer World / 2. Pocket Calculator / 3. Numbers / 4. Computer World 2 /
   5. Computer Love / 6. Home Computer / 7. It's More Fun to Compute

'Tour de France' (1983) [Single]. 12EMI 5413. EMI.
1. Tour de France (Long Version) / 2. Tour de France / 3. Tour de France (Version)

Electric Café [*Techno Pop*] (1986/2009). 50999 9 66050 2 8. Mute / Kling Klang.
1. Boing Boom Tschak / 2. Technopop / 3. Musique Non-Stop / 4. The Telephone Call /
   5. Sex Object / 6. Electric Café [extra track 'House Phone' on *Techno Pop*]

The Mix (1991/2009). 50999 9 66052 2 6. Mute / Kling Klang.
1. The Robots / 2. Computer Love / 3. Pocket Calculator / 4. Dentaku / 5. Autobahn /
   6. Radio-Activity / 7. Trans-Europe Express / 8. Abzug / 9. Metal on Metal / 10. Home
   Computer / 11. Music Non-Stop

'Expo 2000' (2000) [Single]. 7243 8 88333 0 1. EMI / Kling Klang.
1. Expo 2000 Radio Mix / 2. Expo 2000 Kling Klang Mix 2000 / 3. Expo 2000 Kling Klang
   Mix 2002 / 4. Expo 2000 Kling Klang Mix 2001

Tour de France Soundtracks (2003/2009). 50999 9 66109 2 3. Mute / Kling Klang.
1. Prologue / 2. Tour de France (Étape 1) / 3. Tour de France (Étape 2) / 4. Tour de France
   (Étape 3) / 5. Chrono / 6. Vitamin / 7. Aéro Dynamik / 8. Titanium / 9. Elektro
   Kardiogramm / 10. La Forme / 11. Régéneration / 12. Tour de France

Minimum–Maximum (2005). 7243 5 60611 2 5. EMI.
[CD1] 1. The Man-Machine – Warszawa, Sala Kongresowa / 2. Planet Of The Visions –
   Ljubljana, Krizanke / 3. Tour de France Étape 1 – Riga, Olimpiska Hall / 4. Chrono
   – Riga, Olimpiska Hall / 5. Tour de France Étape 2 – Riga, Olimpiska Hall / 6. Vitamin
   – Moskwa, Lushniki / 7. Tour de France – Paris, Le Grand Rex / 8. Autobahn – Berlin,
   Tempodrom / 9. The Model – London, Brixton Academy / 10. Neon Lights – London,
   Royal Festival Hall

[CD2] 1. Radioactivity – Warszawa, Sala Kongresowa / 2. Trans-Europe Express –
   Budapest, Sportarena / 3. Metal On Metal – Budapest, Sportarena / 4. Numbers
   – San Francisco, The Warfield / 5. Computer World – Moskwa, Lushniki / 6. Home
   Computer – Warszawa, Sala Kongresowa / 7. Pocket Calculator – Moskwa, Lushniki
   / 8. Dentaku – Tokyo, Shibuya Ax / 9. The Robots – Moskwa, Lushniki / 10. Elektro
   Kardiogramm – Tallinn, Exhibition Hall / 11. Aéro Dynamik – Riga, Olimpiska Hall /
   12. Music Non-Stop – Moskwa, Lushnik

The Catalogue [Box Set] (2009). 50999 9 67506 2 9. Mute / Kling Klang.
Remastered versions of *Autobahn, Radio-Activity, Trans-Europe Express, The Man-Machine, Computer World, Electric Café* [retitled *Techno Pop*], *The Mix, Tour de France Soundtracks* [retitled *Tour de France*].

Other discographical references

113 (1999). 'Ouais Gros'. Les Princes De La Ville. SMA 496286-1. Small.

A Number of Names (1981). 'Sharevari'. P-928. Capriccio Records.

Anderson, Laurie (1982/2007). 'O Superman (For Massenet)'. *Big Science*. 130428. Nonesuch.

Ashra (1977). *New Age of Earth*. 28 958 XOT. Virgin Records.

Avraamov, Arseny (1922). 'Symphony of Sirens'. On: Various Artists (2009). *Baku: Symphony Of Sirens. Sound Experiments In The Russian Avant Garde*. ReR RAG 1&2. ReR Megacorp.

Babe Ruth (1972/1995). 'The Mexican'. *First Base*. REP 4554-WP. Repertoire Records.

Bambaataa, Afrika (2004). *Dark Matter Moving at the Speed of Light*. TB 1601-2. Tommy Boy Entertainment.

Bambaataa, Afrika & the Soulsonic Force (1982). 'Planet Rock'. TB B23. Tommy Boy Music.

Basement Jaxx (2001). 'Where's Your Head At'. XLS 140 CD. XL Recordings.

Beach Boys, The (1964/2001), 'Fun, Fun, Fun'. *Surfer Girl / Shut Down Volume 2*. 7243 5 31515 2 2. Capitol Records.

—— (1965/2001), 'Barbara Ann'. *Beach Boys' Party! / Stack-O-Tracks*. 7243 5 31641 2 6. Capitol Records.

—— (1967/2001), 'Heroes and Villains'; 'Good Vibrations'. *Smiley Smile / Wild Honey*. 7243 5 31862 2 7. Capitol Records.

—— (1976/2001), 'Just Once in My Life'. *15 Big Ones / Love You*. 7243 5 27945 2 2. Capitol Records.

Blondie (1980/2001). 'Rapture'. *AutoAmerican*. 72435-33595-2-2. Capitol Records.

Bowie, David (1969/1999). 'Space Oddity'. *Space Oddity*. 7243 5 21898 0 9. EMI.

—— (1976/1999). *Station to Station*. 7243 521906 0 7. EMI.

—— (1977/1999). *Low*. 7243 5 21907 06. EMI.

—— (1977/1999). *"Heroes"*. 7243 5 21908 05. EMI.

—— (1979/1999). *Lodger*. 7243 5 21909 04. EMI.

Brown, James (1970/2002). 'Get Up I Feel Like Being a Sex Machine'. *The Godfather – James Brown – the very best of . . .* 589 841-2. Universal Music.

Can (1973/2009). *Future Days*. CDSPOON9. Spoon Records.

Captain Sky (1978). 'Super Sperm'. On: Various Artists (2009). *Super Breaks. Return to the Old School*. BGP2 204. BGP Records.

Clash, The (1980/1999). *Sandinista!* 495348 2. Columbia.

Cluster (1971/2006) *Cluster 71*. Water 160. Water.

—— (1972/2004). *Cluster II*. SPV 49492 CD. SPV GmbH.

—— (1974/2004). *Zuckerzeit.* 07314 527565-2. Brain.

—— (1976/2006). *Sowiesoso.* Water 186. Water.

Cluster & Eno (1977/2009). *Cluster & Eno.* BB029. Bureau B.

Craig, Carl (1995). 'Mind of a Machine'. *Landcruising.* 4509-99865-2. Blanco y Negro.

Cybotron (1982/1990). 'Cosmic Cars'. *Clear.* FCD-4537-2. Fantasy.

—— (1983/1990). 'Clear'. *Clear.* FCD-4537-2. Fantasy.

"D" Train (1981). 'You're the One for Me'. PRL D 621. Prelude Records.

Danger Mouse (2004). *The Grey Album.* DM-001. Unofficial White Label Release.

Diddley, Bo (1962). 'Bo Diddley'. *Bo Diddley.* LP 1431. Chess.

—— (1962). 'Bo's Bounce'. *Bo Diddley.* LP 2984. Checker.

Eagles, The (1976). 'Hotel California / Pretty Maids in a Row'. E-45386. Asylum Records.

Electra (1982). 'Feels Good'. EMDS 6527. Emergency Records.

Electric Funk (1982). 'On a Journey (I Sing the Funk Electric)'. PRLD 622. Prelude Records.

Emanon feat. Lady L (1986). 'Lady L Meets Emanon'. *The Baby Beat Box* EP. PW 7403. Pow Wow Records.

Emerson, Keith (1976). 'Honky Tonk Train Blues'. MAN 5406. Manticore Records.

Eno, Brian (1975/2009). *Another Green World.* 50999 6 84527 2 8. Virgin.

—— (1977/2009). *Before and After Science.* 50999 6 84528 2 7. Virgin.

—— (1978/2009). *Ambient 1: Music for Airports.* 50999 6 84523 2 2. Virgin.

Eno/Moebius/Roedelius (1978/2009). *After the Heat.* BB 030. Bureau B.

Foxx, John (1980/2007). *Metamatic.* EDSD 2013. Edsel Records.

Froese, Edgar (1975/1990). *Epsilon in Malaysian Pale.* CDV 2040. Virgin.

Gabriel, Gunter (1976). ,'Intercity Linie Nr 4'. 17 002 AT. Hansa.

—— (1979). 'Rheingold-Trans-Europa'. *Rastlose Cowboys und ehrbare Mädchen.* 2371 982. Polydor.

Harmonia (1974/2004). *Musik von Harmonia.* 06024 981 298-3. Motor Music.

—— (1975/2004). *De Luxe.* 0731 4 527566-2. Brain.

Harmonia & Eno '76 (2009). *Tracks & Traces.* CDGRON102. Grönland.

Herman, Woody (1954/2005). 'Autobahn Blues'. *The Woody Herman Band.* B002ZJEUCS. Documents / Membran Music.

Joy Division (1979/2007). *Unknown Pleasures.* 2564 69778 9. London Records 90.

King Crimson (1997). *The Night Watch.* DGM9707 2. Discipline Global Mobile.

La Düsseldorf (1976/2008). *La Düsseldorf.* water227. Water.

—— (1978/2008). *Viva.* 6.23626. water228. Water.

—— (1980/2005). *Individuellos.* ARC-7114. Arcàngelo.

MC A.D.E. (1985). 'Bass Rock Express'. 3-85-FS-9. 4 Sight Records.

—— (1989). 'Da' Train'. FS-5634. 4 Sight Records.

Monroe, Bill (1939/2010), 'Orange Blossom Special'. *Orange Blossom Special.* MD Music Company.

Moroder, Giorgio (1977/1999). 'From Here to Eternity'. *From Here to Eternity.* REP 4759-WG. Repertoire Records.

Morricone, Ennio (1967/2004). 'For a Few Dollars More (Main Theme)'. *For a Few Dollars More*. 828765 89972. BMG Records.

Neu! (1972/2001). *Neu!* 7243 5 30782 25. Grönland.

—— (1974/2001). *Neu!2*. 7243 5 30781 26. Grönland.

—— (1975/2001). *Neu!75*. 7243 5 30782 25. Grönland.

New Order (1983). 'Blue Monday'. Fac 73. Factory Records.

—— (1983/2008). 'Your Silent Face'. *Power, Corruption and Lies*. 2564693698. London Records 90.

—— (1983). 'Confusion'. Fac 93. Factory Records.

Numan, Gary (1979/2009). *The Pleasure Principle*. BBQCD 2063. Beggars Banquet.

—— (1980/1998). *Telekon*. BBL 19 CD. Beggars Banquet.

—— (1981/1999). *Dance*. BBL 28 CD. Beggars Banquet.

Orchestral Manoeuvres In The Dark (1980/2003). 'Electricity'. Fac 6. Factory Records.

—— (1980/2003). 'Enola Gay'. *Organisation*. DIDCDRF6. Virgin.

—— (1980/2003). *Organisation*. DIDCDRF6. Virgin.

—— (1981/2007). 'Architecture and Morality'. *Architecture and Morality*. 0946 3 89075 2 7. Virgin.

—— (1983/2008). *Dazzle Ships*. CDVR 2261. Virgin.

Pink Floyd (1971/2008). *Meddle*. 50999 511105 2 9. EMI.

—— (1973/2003). *Dark Side of the Moon*. 7243 5 82136 1. Harvest.

Pop, Iggy (1977/1990). *The Idiot*. CDOVD 277. Virgin.

—— (1977/1990). *Lust for Life*. 2-91343. Virgin.

Résonance (1973). 'OK Chicago / Yellow Train'. 48003. Sirocco.

Rhythim Is Rhythim (1987). 'Strings of Life'. MS. Transmat.

Rother, Michael (1977/2000). *Flammende Herzen*. 398.6580.2. Random Records.

—— (1978/2000). *Sterntaler*. 398.6581.2. Random Records.

—— (1979/2000). *Katzenmusik*. 398.6582.2. Random Records.

Rush (1976/1997). *2112*. 534 626-2. Mercury.

—— (1981/1997). 'Red Barchetta'. *Moving Pictures*. 534 631-2. Mercury.

Schaeffer, Pierre (1948/2000). 'Etude aux Chemins de Fer' (Railroad Study). *L' Oeuvre Musicale*. B00005Y972. EMF Media.

Schulze, Klaus (1973). *Cyborg*. SPV 305252. Revisited Records.

Setlur, Sabrina (1997). *Nur Mir EP*. 3P6649352. Pelham Power Productions.

Shock (1982). 'Electrophonic Funk'. D-207. Fantasy.

Simple Minds (1980/2003). *Empires and Dance*. 7243 8 13012 2 7. Virgin.

—— (1981/2003). *Sons & Fascination / Sister Feelings Call*. 7243 813169 24. Virgin.

Sinnamon (1982). 'Thanks to You'. BKD 508. Becket Records.

Stone (1981). 'Time'. WES 22139. West End Records.

Strikers, The (1981/1993). 'Body Music'. *Inch by Inch / Body Music*. SP5-1256. Unidisc.

Sugarhill Gang (1979/1999). 'Rapper's Delight'. *Back to the Old School – Rapper's Delights*. NEE CD 306. Sequel Records.

Summer, Donna (1977). 'I Feel Love' (single-sided). NBD 20104. Casablanca Records.

Thomas, Rufus (1973/2004). 'Do the Funky Robot'. On: Various Artists (2004). *Everything I Do Gonna Be Funky*. BSR 1006-2. Brown Sugar Records.

Tubeway Army (1979/2008) *Replicas*. BBQCD 2057. Beggars Banquet.

Ultravox (1976/2006). *Ultravox!* IMCD 324. Island Records.

—— (1978/2006). *Systems of Romance*. IMCD 326. Island Records.

—— (1980/2008). *Vienna*. 5099923436527. Chrysalis.

—— (1981/2008). *Rage in Eden*. 5099923437029. Chrysalis.

Various Artists (1993). *Trance Europe Express*. 1VCD1.Volume.

Velvet Underground & Nico, The (1967/2002). *The Velvet Underground & Nico*. 0731458958826. Polydor.

Visage (1981). 'Frequency 7 (Dance Mix)'. *Mind of a Toy* [12" Single]. POSPX 236. Polydor.

Yes (1972/2003). *Close to the Edge*. 8122-73790-2. Elektra.

—— (1983/2004). *90125*. 8122-73796-2. Elektra.

Index

Note: music titles in *italics* denote albums; titles in single quote marks denote individual tracks.